Palgrave Studies in Education Research Methods

Series Editors

Patrick Danaher
University of Southern Queensland
Toowoomba, Queensland, Australia

Fred Dervin
The University of Helsinki
Helsinki, Finland

Caroline Dyer
School of Politics and International Studies
University of Leeds
Leeds, United Kingdom

Máirín Kenny
Wexford, Ireland

Bobby Harreveld
School of Education and the Arts
Central Queensland University
Rockhampton, Australia

Michael Singh
University of Western Sydney
Penrith, New South Wales, Australia

Bobby Harreveld • Mike Danaher • Celeste Lawson
Bruce Allen Knight • Gillian Busch
Editors

Constructing Methodology for Qualitative Research

Researching Education and Social Practices

palgrave
macmillan

Editors
Bobby Harreveld
School of Education and the Arts
Central Queensland University
Rockhampton, Australia

Mike Danaher
School of Education and the Arts
Central Queensland University
Rockhampton, Queensland, Australia

Celeste Lawson
North Rockhampton Campus
Central Queensland University
North Rockhampton, Queensland,
Australia

Bruce Allen Knight
Central Queensland University
Townsville, Queensland, Australia

Gillian Busch
Central Queensland University
Rockhampton North, Queensland,
Australia

Palgrave Studies in Education Research Methods
ISBN 978-1-137-59942-1   ISBN 978-1-137-59943-8   (eBook)
DOI 10.1057/978-1-137-59943-8

Library of Congress Control Number: 2016941616

Cover illustration: © Jennifer Borton / Getty Images

Printed on acid-free paper

This Palgrave Macmillan imprint is published by Springer Nature
The registered company is Macmillan Publishers Ltd. London

ACKNOWLEDGEMENTS

The editors and authors are very grateful to the following individuals, without whom this book would not have been published.

- Mr Andrew James and Ms Eleanor Christie and their colleagues at Palgrave Macmillan for the warm, professionally considerate and efficient manner in which our proposal was considered as well as the continued courteous efficiency with which the production process has been managed.
- The anonymous reviewer of the book proposal who provided such insightful feedback to us via Palgrave Macmillan.
- The Office of Research and the School of Education and the Arts at Central Queensland University provided the funding support for the research symposium from which this edited collection has been constructed.
- Ms Jodie Gunders has provided truly exemplary project management at all stages of the book's production. Her knowledge, skills and commitment have been integral to bringing this collaboration to fruition.
- The scholars who provided double-blind peer reviews of one or more submitted chapters in this book:

  - Dr Lindy-Anne Abawi, University of Southern Queensland, Toowoomba, Australia
  - Dr Amy Antonio, University of Southern Queensland, Springfield, Australia

- Professor Josie Arnold, Swinburne University of Technology, Melbourne, Australia
- Associate Professor Jon Austin, University of Southern Queensland, Toowoomba, Australia
- Dr Wendi Beamish, Griffith University, Brisbane, Australia
- Dr Jane Bone, Monash University, Frankston, Australia
- Mrs Phyllida Coombes, independent scholar, Bundaberg, Australia
- Dr Geoff Danaher, independent scholar, Yeppoon, Australia
- Dr Christina Davidson, Charles Sturt University, Wagga Wagga, Australia
- Dr Mark Dawson, University of Southern Queensland, Toowoomba, Australia
- Dr Sue Elliot, University of New England, Armidale, Australia
- Ms Yvonne Findlay, University of Southern Queensland, Toowoomba, Australia
- Dr Nicole Green, University of Southern Queensland, Toowoomba, Australia
- Dr Hanna Guttorm, University of Helsinki, Helsinki, Finland
- Dr Barbara Harmes, University of Southern Queensland, Toowoomba, Australia
- Dr Marcus Harmes, University of Southern Queensland, Toowoomba, Australia
- Dr Linda Henderson, Australian Catholic University, Melbourne, Australia
- Dr Henk Huijser, Xi'an Jiaotong-Liverpool University, Suzhou, People's Republic of China
- Dr Candace Kuby, University of Missouri, Columbia, USA
- Associate Professor Jennifer Lock, University of Calgary, Calgary, Canada
- Associate Professor Nana Osei-Kofi, Oregon State University, Corvallis, USA
- Dr Rebecca Scollen, University of Southern Queensland, Toowoomba, Australia
- Dr Sarah Shear, Pennsylvania State University, Altoona, USA
- Ms Lyn Sherrington, Griffith University, Brisbane, Australia
- Professor Margaret Sims, University of New England, Armidale, Australia
- Dr Jill Smith, University of Auckland, Auckland, New Zealand

- Dr Maryanne Theobold, Queensland University of Technology, Brisbane, Australia
- Dr Beth Thomas, State University of New York, New Paltz, USA
- Dr Donna M. Velliaris, Eynesbury Institute of Business and Technology, Adelaide, Australia
- Associate Professor Susan Walsh, Mount Saint Vincent University, Halifax, Canada
- Ms Amber Ward, University of Missouri, Columbia, USA

Contents

CONTRIBUTORS FOR EDITORS

Gillian Busch is Senior Lecturer in Education at Central Queensland University, (CQU). Her research interests include children's talk-in-interaction in disputes and family mealtimes and children's interactions with grandparents using SKYPE or Facetime. Gillian has methodological expertise in qualitative approaches including ethnomethodology and conversation analysis. Gillian's PhD (The Social Orders of Family Mealtime) was awarded the Early Childhood Australia Doctoral Thesis Award (2012). Gillian is currently involved in a research project examining young children and celebrations. Email: g.busch@cqu.edu.au

Mike Danaher is a Senior Lecturer in the Humanities at Central Queensland University. He has published in the fields of environmental and geographical education. Mike has more than 45 publications. His published research books include *Researching Education with Marginalized Communities* (co-authored with Janet Cook, Geoff Danaher, Phyllida Coombes and Patrick Danaher) and *Strategic Uncertainties: Ethics, Politics and Risk in Contemporary Educational Research* (co-authored with Phyllida Coombes and Patrick Danaher). Email: m.danaher@cqu.edu.au

Bobby Harreveld is Professor of Education in the School of Education & the Arts, Deputy Dean (Research) and Deputy Director of the Learning, Equity, Access & Participation (LEAP) Centre at Central Queensland University Australia. She is co-author of *Deschooling L'earning: Young Adults and the New Spirit of Capitalism* (2014) with Michael Singh; and the co-editor of *Work-integrated learning in engineering, built environment and technology: Diversity of Practice in Practice* (2011) with Michael Keleher and Arun Patel. Her research interests include capability development for research education, learning and earning, the brokering of knowledge co-production and the creation of education pathways and workplace transitions. She is also a recipient of the Vice-Chancellor's Award for Excellence in Research Supervision. Email: b.harreveld@cqu.edu.au

Bruce Allen Knight is Professor of Education at Central Queensland University. He has extensive teaching experience in primary and special education and University settings. His research interests are in learning design and pedagogy. He has more than 200 publications and worked on large research projects worth more than AUD$5 million from such granting bodies as the Australian Research Council. In 2006 he was honoured with a Fellowship of the International Academy of Research in Learning Disabilities. Email: b.knight@cqu.edu.au

Celeste Lawson is a Lecturer and Head of the Professional Communication Program at Central Queensland University. After a successful career as a police officer, Celeste moved into academia, completing her PhD in 2013. Her research interests include policing, police culture, organisational communication and social media in an organisational context. Celeste is prepared to push methodological boundaries, particularly in the use of qualitative research in traditionally quantitative environments. She is currently exploring the use of social media as a tool for professional development in geographically and professionally diverse occupational environments. Email: c.lawson@cqu.edu.au

LIST OF FIGURES

LIST OF TABLES

CHAPTER 1

Introduction

Bobby Harreveld, Mike Danaher, Celeste Lawson,
Bruce Allen Knight, and Gillian Busch

When researching education and social practices, methodological considerations are no longer—if indeed they ever were—linear, seamless, or even consistently coherent. Increasingly, the markers of difference among research methodologies in the social sciences are challenged, ambushed even, as fit-for-purpose methodological relationships are constructed. This edited collection echoes such developmental trajectories from the oppositional stances of quantitative, qualitative, and mixed-methods to the emerging nimble, fluid, recursive, and iterative paradigms evocative of the messiness characterising the web of independent problems that emerge as research progresses (Ackoff, 1979; Law, 2004; Hester & Adams, 2014).

Through an eclectic mix of research cases where methodological approaches are manoeuvred to fit the research context, this book engages with the confusion and difficulties faced by doctoral candidates and early career researchers. The authors reject the positivism–interpretivism binary

B. Harreveld (✉) • M. Danaher • C. Lawson • G. Busch
School of Education and the Arts, CQUniversity Australia,
Rockhampton, QLD, Australia

B.A. Knight
School of Education and the Arts, CQUniversity Australia,
Townsville, QLD, Australia

© The Author(s) 2016
B. Harreveld et al. (eds.), *Constructing Methodology for*
Qualitative Research, DOI 10.1057/978-1-137-59943-8_1

when constructing the appropriate methodological framework for the project. They have realised the constraints that some research methods imply—the binary of quantitative versus qualitative enquiry. Conceptually, they provide a differentiation from previous work in the area of postgraduate and early career research education for capacity building (Denholm & Evans, 2009; Midgley, Tyler, Danaher, & Mander, 2011; Danaher et al., 2014). Yet at the same time, they acknowledge an intellectual debt to these works while incorporating its unique conceptual meshing of research work in tension with a virtual plethora of orientations towards designing and undertaking research.

Qualitative research is a broad church encompassing a bewildering profusion of similarity with elusive differences often requiring years of immersion to understanding its scholarship. Those seeking this understanding, bring with them ways of knowing their worlds that both challenge and are challenged by the fundamental tenets of qualitative research. In this process, non-linearity is foregrounded and situated in the interdisciplinary spaces of qualitative research. Most significantly, it highlights researchers' experiences manoeuvring through the '-ologies' of a qualitative research paradigm, namely, its ontology (nature of its reality), epistemology (the relationship between the researcher and what can be known about that reality), axiology (values underpinning the ethical stance of the research process), and its methodology (how to go about investigating what can/could be known) (Punch, 2014). This focus on methodological manoeuvring is fundamental to the construction of a qualitatively framed research worldview or paradigm that engages with the 'why' behind the methods of data collection and analysis to encapsulate the actuality of experiences.

When constructing methodology for qualitative research, an initial challenge for novice qualitative researchers and experienced research-supervisors in education, creative and performing arts, the humanities, and social sciences more broadly is to assimilate these high-end philosophical notions of ontology, epistemology, and axiology. This challenge may be met by negotiating methodological allegiances while developing research expertise investigating and interpreting critically the contextualised social practices of various projects (Wray & Wallace, 2011). Yet too often, such work invariably begins from the standpoint of naïve novices uncontaminated by previous knowledge of and experience with singular or multiple research methodological frameworks. This collection challenges such a fallacy. It demonstrates that those disciplines espousing singularly quantitative approaches may have not had cause to question the philosophical basis for the methods employed to construct knowledge until engaging in educational and other social world problems where researchers reflexively engage with 'the baggage you take in, the biases and interests and areas of ignorance' (Richards, 2005, p. 42) as they are entrenched in data analysis, (re)interpretation, and elucidation of data.

Constructing a research design requires deliberation of qualitative versus quantitative approaches and the ubiquitous mixed-methods frameworks for investigations in both the social sciences and professional fields in which applied research is practised (Marshall & Rossman, 2011; Creswell, 2012; Denzin & Lincoln, 2013; Anfara & Mertz, 2015). However, it is often when ethical considerations are encountered and subsequently challenge social scientists at all stages of their research careers, that the messiness of methodology is encountered. The latest fourth edition of Ranjit Kumar's (2014) *Research Methodology: A Step-by-Step Guide for Beginners* is an example of such thinking. Nevertheless, as Marshall and Rossman (2011) illustrate in their work on *Designing Qualitative Research*, research processes are more likely to be frustratingly fluid and intriguingly iterative, as well as recursively rigorous.

CONSTRUCTING QUALITATIVE RESEARCHERS

Over the last decade, there has been considerable concern over the fate of social science research workforce development in the context of commodified national and international higher education policy agenda (Edwards, 2010; Sursock & Smidt, 2010; Bexley, James, & Arkoudis, 2011). At the same time, people are coming into the research field seeking ways of investigating seemingly insurmountable social issues, illogical politically induced changes impacting decision-making in local/global policy, professional practices, and people's everyday lives (Flick, 2011). Career trajectories reflect this process as novice researchers bring to their investigations a rich diversity of ages, dispositions, cultures, linguistic capabilities, and lived experiences.

Thus, this book gives voice to these twenty-first-century researchers who choose to engage with societal, political, legal, and economic tentacles of power inscribed in everyday life; and with forces that name and control what counts as research and the work of researchers (Lee, Goodyear, Seddon, & Renshaw, 2011). This is necessary because reconceptualising the logic and effect of qualitative research work undertaken by novice and experienced researchers is as much a political project as it is an educational project. As an exercise of power in a democratic society, it is anything but self-evident and more than worthy of considerable analytical critique (Lee et al., 2011; Seddon et al., 2013).

Constructing methodology for qualitative research is a process of strategic risk taking for researchers (Harreveld, 2004). Articulating the messiness of methodology requires the bricoleur qualitative researcher to articulate through explicit engagements with assumptions about investigative worlds, the topics worthy of consideration and the tactics of enquiry into the topics from within those worlds (Denzin & Lincoln, 2013; Zipf, Chap. 5). 'Bricoleurs allow for dynamics and contexts to dictate which questions get asked, which methods to employ and which interpretive perspectives to use' (Rogers, 2012, p. 6). Accordingly, the collection has been guided by a grand tour question (Leech, 2002): How do qualitative researchers manoeuvre through the maze of methodology to make meaning for their research projects?

Educators and social scientists engage with a range of methodological allegiances and contestations when being and becoming researchers. Our approach is qualitative in its methodological orientation and ethnographic in its execution (Fetterman, 2010; Marshall & Rossman, 2011). The text has been developed iteratively through a research symposium followed by a series of writing workshops with inbuilt cycles of reflective collegial critique complemented with a double blind peer-review process for each chapter and the text as a whole.

The possibilities of methodological choice explored in this collection are ontologically audacious yet epistemologically cautious. While epistemology may require an explicit phenomenon of enquiry from within a particular societal framing, ontological perspectives are more wide-ranging in their theoretical construction. This process engenders confidence in the bricolage approach (Rogers, 2012) when seeking synergies between the investigative technique/s and the construction of ontological facets of the research context.

CONSTRUCTING METHODOLOGY

The book flows structurally through two iterative processes when constructing methodology for qualitative research. First, there is the positioning of the researcher within the process; and second, that of manoeuvring self within the practices of qualitative research across necessarily selective social science disciplines in education, arts, and humanities. Constructing self methodologically investigates the individuals in qualitative research as they bring their worldviews to the project that may be challenged and/or confirmed through consideration of its ontological, epistemological, and axiological dimensions that influence and are influenced by methodological allegiances and alliances. These chapters reflect those challenges, their contestations, and resolutions. The practices of manoeuvring are concerned with the ways in which qualitative researchers construct methodological frameworks that mesh with and respond to their work as practitioner-researchers.

Gemma Mann (Chap. 2) presents an autobiographical account of her journey from experienced quantitative to novice qualitative researcher. When moving into the qualitative realm of education research, Gemma found that she could not leave behind totally her quantitative background constructed during PhD studies in physics. She is both an expert and a novice researcher, utilising knowledge of quantitative methods while constructing a qualitative framework for her project investigating quantitative literacy. Further, Gemma is both student and teacher as the non-binary, non-linear nature and complex maze of her journey unfolds—a journey in which seemingly incongruent ideas and experiences overlap. Her chapter illustrates the skills of that previous methodological experience brought into—translated into—her current work as an education researcher.

Research in medical imaging, particularly diagnostic radiography, has traditionally been quantitative, reflecting its clinical scientific focus. This is the world in which Cynthia Cowling is undertaking an ethnographic study of the sociological practice of radiography, including a comparison of its workplace practices in a number of different countries. In terms of the radiography profession, the authors of Chap. 3 represent both insider (Cynthia) and outsider status (Celeste Lawson). Methodologically, Celeste is the experienced qualitative researcher as Cynthia reprises previous knowledge and experiences with qualitative research from earlier studies in anthropology while coming to terms with the challenges of manoeuvring through both occupational and cultural differences in the construction of radiography work. This chapter provides a voice to the validity of ethnography for research in a discipline usually yoked to the quantitative framing of what counts as knowledge and its construction.

Michael Cowling is a researcher in the field of information and communication technology (ICT), who comes from a background steeped in experimentation and is making a methodological shift to contribute to qualitative research discussions in learning and teaching. Building on the work of Chinn, Buckland, and Samarapungavan (2011), who argue that epistemological perceptions must be broadened to help with cognition, his chapter (Chap. 4) fractures the epistemology learned as an academic in this field. He seeks to explain this positivist epistemology as encountered when completing PhD research in ICT, a discipline in which the 'scientific method' was espoused. The process through which Michael came from technology research to navigate an epistemological shift for learning and teaching research whilst still being involved with the ICT discipline forms the core of this chapter.

Taking a bricoleur approach to navigating self through the methodological maze enables Reyna Zipf to take a nebulous concept, creativity, and research it in a complex setting, secondary school science lessons (Chap. 5). She interrogates her novice researchers' methodological journey to arrive at a methodological approach underpinned by a *bricoleur* stance. This is presented through four milestones: entering the maze; inside the maze; emerging from the maze; and arriving at your methodological destination. Reyna positions 'entering the methodological maze' as risky business that involves overcoming fear of failure. Inside the maze requires methodological navigation skills, and emerging from the maze necessitates negotiation with self. Arriving at a methodological destination was facilitated by a researcher-as-*bricoleur* stance. Such a stance enabled manoeuvring between and through pathways in the methodological maze; it was the tool by which holes in the maze hedge were made allowing hitherto separate pathways to be joined.

Teaching research methodologies is both a joy and a challenge for Teresa Moore (Chap. 6). She has found that big words such as epistemology, ontology, axiology, and methodology can paralyse the novice researcher who just wants to do the project, run some numbers and see their findings change the world. Introducing students to the conceptual and abstract nature of qualitative methodologies broadens the landscape for both novice and experienced researchers to think differently and become intimately part of their research project. Doctoral students are not an empty vessel requiring facts, procedures, and methods, but rather bring with them personal experiences, history, skills, and knowledge. In this chapter, Teresa explores how manoeuvring Research Higher Degree students through the maze of methodology in a specific research methodology course offers students the opportunity to expand their own conceptualisation of meaning and negotiation of methodology when designing and interpreting doctoral research, along with examining her continuing growth as a researcher, supervisor, and educator.

In Chap. 7, Rickie Fisher proposes a methodology for a fusionist ontology within a grounded theory study to understand the reasons for people's career changes to become secondary school teachers. For the career change participants in his study, similar to himself as a novice researcher, becoming secondary school teachers could be explained in terms related to whatever they had previously been; that is, their previous career engagements, experiences, and prior states. The fusion between what may have been and what may become is dynamic. As Zaborskis (2011) explains, 'becoming implies growth and change… we are always "becoming", what the self was is lost, but that self is now something new that it was not before' (p. 1). Like the career change participants, the novice researcher manoeuvres through the maze of methodology in their journey to define their past and present social realities. The fusionist ontology provides a purposeful basis for his interpretive constructivist grounded theory—becoming—that encapsulates the Janus-like past and future contiguity of career change; and also that of becoming a researcher.

Ali Black and Sarah Loch are two academics who cannot do their work as qualitative researchers without being who they are (Chap. 8). Through the use of photography and poetry, they share their vulnerability as qualitative researchers struggling with ways to speak their lives in the academy. Ali and Sarah attend to the place of the personal in researching qualitatively. Many academics feel significant pressure to produce research, receiving dogged messages about what counts as research, the impact of research, and preferred audiences and outcomes. Their chapter explores the manoeuvring we do, the manoeuvring upon us to be producers of research, but also their deliberate and conscious appreciation that they cannot do this work without being who they are. Moreover, who they are cannot be separated from how they are being produced as researchers through their methodologies, or from the methodological choices they make. This chapter's honest and frank approach encourages others to consider the potency for 'making meaning' with research.

Leanne Dodd's chapter explores the challenge encountered when transitioning from the role of creative practitioner to that of practice-led researcher of creative practice. She invokes the lessons of stylish academic writing espoused by Sword (2012, p. 99): 'show, don't tell'. A key challenge for the practitioner engaged in this progression, whose aim is often to enrich their creative work through research, is that the language of theory is at odds with creative production. This is a dichotomy that Chap. 9 sets out to resolve. Professional training equips the creative writing practitioner such as Leanne with the skill to compose narrative based on the premise of 'Show, don't Tell'; however, a conflicting academic writing style, where the main purpose is to 'tell', is mandated for the exegetical component of her creative writing thesis. Through an evidence-based case study of strategic risk taking, Leanne establishes a 'Show and Tell' methodology approach for creative writing practitioners and for the academy. She offers a methodology to produce synergised research outcomes for practice-led researchers where the importance of the embedded new knowledge in the creative component is reflected in the exegetical component.

Writers of historical fiction may not be academics, yet research is an important task they undertake to build an authentic and credible portrait of an imagined past. Alison Owens is writing a historical novel and in Chap. 10, she articulates the role that narrative inquiry plays as her research methodology. Alison notes that the 'bricoleur as bower-bird' (Webb & Brien, 2011) or 'magpie' (Pullinger, 2008) approach to research are perhaps apt metaphors for her work that utilises a variety of data in the crafting of her story. In seeking to describe, explain, and justify the research framework for historical novelists such as herself, she argues the efficacy of narrative inquiry as a qualitative approach for storytellers such as herself who are exploring the creative writing process itself in the exegesis accompanying a creative writing artefact. She concludes that framing historical fiction writing as creative practice-led research deploying narrative inquiry is a methodological choice enhancing understanding of how the past informs the present and the future while also enabling the creativity through with writers engage fact to generate fiction.

Margaret Jamieson is writing a historical romance novel as part of her PhD. Both she and her supervisor, Mike Danaher, are crafting a practice-led methodology for the accompanying exegesis. In Chap. 11, they analyse the specific stages of this practice-led methodology (visioning, planning, journeying, reflecting, and evaluating). Central to this chapter is the relationship between the novice researcher doctoral candidate and the supervisor who is both novice (to the methodology) and expert (in supervision). Their insights disrupt the binaries of novice-expert, student-supervisor. Both are learning the intricacies of practice-led research methodologically. Both are teaching—Margaret is teaching Mike about her historical romance writing process; and Mike is teaching Margaret to become a researcher. The power of the reflective journal in this process emerges as pivotal to practice-led research, linking the creative writing artefact to the exegesis.

In Chap. 12, Donna Brien and Margaret McAllister explore what happens when two joint research projects progress from a multi-disciplinary to an interdisciplinary approach to qualitative research. Working together across nursing and creative writing disciplines revealed methodological choices to be made at all stages of the research process including data collection, interpretation, and eventual dissemination. The methodological challenges and opportunities of moving from single disciplinary to multi- to eventual interdisciplinary research form the core of this chapter. Donna and Margaret are finding that this research approach is opening up wider opportunities than may have perhaps been possible if each had stayed researching within her own disciplinary tribe. Their findings suggest a significant contribution to twenty-first-century doctoral education and early career researcher education.

Steven Pace establishes a dialogue between two contested concepts in qualitative research methods, grounded theory, and autoethnography (Chap. 13). He engages with one specific everyday consideration of early career and novice researchers: adopting a research method, especially when it is alternative, contested, and highly and critically negotiated. Steven concisely describes and analyses the negotiations around and development of grounded theory. The negotiations around autoethnography, especially its ontology, epistemology, and axiology, are challenging indeed. Through this debate, we learn that there is no easily won clarity and confidence in making methodological choices. Misconceptions abound. Well-meaning supervisors with understanding limited to their own experience may caution against such exploration, such as other readings of theory, ontology, and epistemology, in favour of their own known methodology as a 'safer' option.

When researching qualitatively the borderlands of transition from trade-qualified workers to secondary school teachers, methodological options abound. In Chap. 14, Bill Blayney and Bobby Harreveld explore three interrelated discourses of methodological manoeuvring: conceptual, methodological, and analytical. Discourses of transition constitute the conceptual manoeuvre as the study is framed in terms of the discourses of research participants who have lived in-between the different worlds of trade work, university study, and teaching work. Pragmatically and strategically, case study is proposed as both methodology and method because of its ontological and epistemological perspectives consistent with the study's aim and research questions and congruent with their values and beliefs as to what counts as research, how it is conducted and reported. Analytically, four phases of case construction are deployed: establishing the case data set; creating emergent themes through linguistic features identified in interview transcripts; then composing a narrative representation of participants' lived experiences through career transition; and finally undertaking a cross-case analysis that developed the themes into borderland discourses that explain the tensions and contradictions through which participants develop new identities as teachers.

Researching 'with' children is a critical topic. Ali Black and Gillian Busch explore the methodological minefields, motivations, and ethical concerns encountered in this process (Chap. 15). From the rich literature published on researching with children, Ali and Gillian consider how researcher values and ethical commitments position children, determine their visibility, and influence wider cultures of listening to children. They use narratively assembled research encounters and dilemmas related to research infrastructures (e.g. university ethics committees) to explore the challenges of attending to and negotiating ethical territories and relations of power including their own positionality and partiality as researchers. Their chapter engages readers in a dialogue in which not only scholarly sources, but also their verbal and visual depictions of reflexivity are crafted into the narrative. For Ali and Gillian, knowledge production is a joint venture with children, adult participants, and themselves as researchers.

Delving further into the context of researching the everyday worlds of children and families, Gillian Busch and Susan Danby explore the use of ethnomethodology and conversation analysis in Chap. 16. As with Chap. 4, the supervisor–student, or advisor–advisee, relationship is foregrounded as Gillian meets many challenges as a (then) fledgling researcher grappling with ethnomethodology per se, and subsequently when grappling with the intricacies of analysis of digitally recorded videos of family meal times. This reflective text highlights these challenges through a storytelling device whereby each author presents her reflective account of a series of manoeuvres encountered throughout the doctoral journey. Here the conventional guidance from the experienced supervisor (Susan) is unpacked in terms of the methodology of ethnomethodology and its suitability for Gillian's proposed study. Encountering transcription as central to analysis of conversations is both an interpretative and representational process that constituted yet further complex challenges, especially when it involved wider sharing of data with others in a postgraduate student research community, conferences, and intensive workshops. From trepidation about this public sharing, Gillian finds instead solace and support. Susan's storytelling throughout their relationship is a tool for building technical competency and engendering confidence throughout the ebbs and flows of the research journey.

In our capstone chapter, Patrick Danaher responds to the dilemmas, principles, and strategies proposed when constructing methodology for qualitative research. He does so through reimaging two logically distinct but interrelated and inter-reliant phenomena that he terms the rooms for methodological manoeuvres. First, qualitative researchers inhabit and embody prospective spaces (rooms) for constructing and assembling theoretical and methodological resources for designing and enacting their projects. Second, there is also a retrospective space through which and in which researchers may reflect, regroup, and even change direction as their project proceeds. This retrospective space is the room to manoeuvre methodologically and theoretically. These spaces are creatively constructed through contemporary and emerging methodologies as well as the lived experiences of novice and experienced researchers deploying such methodologies.

A Coda

This book is the product of inductive analysis. It unpacks the seeming certainties of methodological decision-making in qualitative research to expose webs of vulnerability that illustrate the deceptive strength of reflexive social researchers' fragility. Such vulnerability takes courage and confidence to articulate. In so doing, it provides a meta-narrative of these researchers' transitional learning journeys. The chapters that follow will resonate with readers differentially as they empathise with some more than others. Yet we hope that you will be able to read yourselves in to the tensions and tangles of qualitative research when confronted with the difficulty of establishing facets of educational and social 'truth' while achieving a best-fit methodological choice to suit your studies' ontological contexts.

It is timely perhaps to revivify the pioneering spirit of qualitative research, its sense of mission, and its innovativeness (Ackoff, 1979). In our book, the seeming clarity and precision in the discourses of methodology are questioned. You will find in the chapters that follow deliberate engagements with the messiness of methodology and the methods chosen to enact it. As John Law (2004) has argued, methodological imagination, intuition, and innovation is still needed because the politics of undertaking qualitative research is still precariously positioned in messiness once cleanliness, definitiveness, and singularity are challenged. Preissle (2011, p. 685) reminds us that 'scholars and academics awake each day to make their worlds – to teach, study, and write with the confidence that what they are creating from the past and the present will contribute to scholarship in the coming years'. For readers whose specialisms are not overtly discussed in this book, there should be an elegant sufficiency to transfer and enlighten your particular education contexts and social practices when constructing methodology for qualitative research.

REFERENCES

Ackoff, R. L. (1979). The future of operational research is past. *Journal of the Operational Research Society, 30*(3), 189–199.

Anfara, V. A., & Mertz, N. T. (Eds.) (2015). *Theoretical frameworks in qualitative research* (2nd ed.). Los Angeles: Sage.

Bexley, E., James, R., & Arkoudis, S. (2011, September). *The Australian academic profession in transition: Addressing the challenge of reconceptualising academic work and regenerating the academic workforce.* Commissioned report prepared for the Department of Education, Employment and Workplace Relations. University of Melbourne: Centre for the Study of Higher Education. Retrieved 11 November 2011 from http://www.cshe.unimelb.edu.au

Chinn, C. A., Buckland, L. A., & Samarapungavan, A. L. A. (2011). Expanding the dimensions of epistemic cognition: Arguments from philosophy and psychology. *Educational Psychologist, 46*(3), 141–167.

Creswell, J. W. (2012). *Educational research: Planning, conducting, and evaluating quantitative and qualitative research* (4th ed.). Boston, MA: Pearson Education.

Danaher, P. A., Davies, A., De George-Walker, L., Jones, J. K., Matthews, K. J., Midgley, W., et al. (Eds.) (2014). *Contemporary capacity-building in educational contexts.* Basingstoke, UK: Palgrave Macmillan/Palgrave Pivot.

Denholm, C., & Evans, T. D. (Eds.) (2009). *Beyond doctorates downunder: Maximising the impact of your doctorate from Australia and New Zealand.* Camberwell, VIC: ACER Press.

Denzin, N. K., & Lincoln, Y. S. (Eds.) (2013). *Collecting and interpreting qualitative materials.* Thousand Oaks, CA: Sage.

Edwards, D. (2010). The future of the research workforce: Estimating demand for PhDs in Australia. *Journal of Higher Education Policy Management, 32*(2), 199–210.

Fetterman, D. M. (2010). *Ethnography step-by-step* (3rd ed.). Thousand Oaks: Sage.

Flick, U. (2011). *Introducing research methodology: A beginner's guide to doing a research project*. London: Sage.

Harreveld, R. E. (2004). Ethical and political dimensions of strategic risk-taking in research. In P. N. Coombes, M. J. M. Danaher, & P. A. Danaher (Eds.), *Strategic uncertainties: Ethics, politics and risk in contemporary educational research* (pp. 39–51). Flaxton, QLD: Post Pressed.

Hester, P. T., & Adams, K. (2014). *Systemic thinking: Fundamentals for understanding problems and messes*. Dordrecht: Springer.

Kumar, R. (2014). *Research methodology: A step-by-step guide for beginners* (2nd ed.). Los Angeles: Sage.

Law, J. (2004). *After method: Mess in social science research*. New York: Routledge.

Lee, A., Goodyear, P. Seddon, T. & Renshaw, P. (2011). Position paper submitted to AARE and ACDE executives. September.

Leech, B. (2002). Asking questions: A technique for semi-structured interviews. *Political Science and Politics, 35,* 665–668.

Marshall, C., & Rossman, G. B. (2011). *Designing qualitative research*. Sage: Los Angeles.

Midgley, W., Tyler, M. A., Danaher, P. A., & Mander, A. (Eds.) (2011). *Beyond binaries in education research*. New York: Routledge.

Preissle, J. (2011). Qualitative futures: Where we might go from where we've been. In N. Denzin & Y. Lincoln (Eds.), *The SAGE handbook of qualitative research* (pp. 685–698). Thousand Oaks, CA: Sage.

Pullinger, K. (2008, 20 September). How to write fiction: Research. *The Guardian*. Retrieved from: http://www.theguardian.com/books/2008/sep/20/kate-pullinger.writing.fiction2

Punch, K. (2014). *Introduction to social research: Quantitative & qualitative approaches* (3rd ed.). Thousand Oaks, CA: Sage.

Richards, L. (2005). *Handling qualitative data: A practical guide*. Los Angeles: Sage.

Rogers, M. (2012). Contextualising theories and practices of bricolage research. *The Qualitative Report, 17*(7), 1–17.

Seddon T., Bennett, D., Bennett, S., Bobis, J., Chan, P., Harrison, N. & Shore, S. (2013). Education research Australia: A changing ecology of knowledge and practice. Published online 12 July 2013, Springer.

Sursock, A., & Smidt, H. (2010). *Trends 2010: A decade of change in European higher education*. Brussels: European University Association. Retrieved 7 November 2011 from http://www.eua.be

Sword, H. (2012). *Stylish academic writing*. Cambridge, MA: Harvard University Press.

Webb, J., & Brien, D. (2011). Addressing the "ancient quarrel": creative writing as research. In M. Biggs & H. Karlsson (Eds.), *The Routledge companion to research in the arts*. pp. 186-203. London: Routledge.

Wray, A., & Wallace, M. (2011). Accelerating the development of expertise: A step-change in social science research capacity building. *British Journal of Educational Studies, 59*(3), 241–264.

Zaborskis, M. (2011, August 4). *How becoming of you* [Web log post]. Flexner Book Club Blog. Retrieved September 9, 2011, from http://flexner.blogs.brynmawr.edu/

A Non-binary Methodological Manoeuvre: Expert Quantitative and Novice Qualitative Researcher

Gemma Mann

Introduction to My Manoeuvres and Where That Might Lead

It has been said that researchers always have to consider their epistemology, theoretical framework, and methodology when embarking on qualitative research (Crotty, 1998). This does not take into account the individual nature of research, the experiences of the researcher, and the undefined, complex world that we are doing research in where there are competing or changing views. This chapter explores not so much a leap from quantitative to qualitative research, but a merging, or strategic manoeuvring between the two. It shows how lessons learnt from experience can be transferred to a new methodology, and form a bridge between capabilities in quantitative frameworks and the application of those skills to qualitative

G. Mann (✉)
School of Education and the Arts, CQUniversity Australia,
Rockhampton, QLD, Australia

© The Author(s) 2016
B. Harreveld et al. (eds.), *Constructing Methodology for Qualitative Research*, DOI 10.1057/978-1-137-59943-8_2

15

frameworks. This has implications for beginners in any type of research, or experienced researchers changing frameworks, supervising students, working in a multi-disciplinary team, or wanting to consider their outlook on research.

The autoethnographic style of this chapter brings the experiences of the author to the fore (Sparkes, 2000) and is written in a personalised style (Wall, 2006). This autoethnographic reflection provides insights into understanding the transfer from quantitative to qualitative methodologies, and the merging of the two (Bullough & Pinnegar, 2001). The overarching framework is that researchers do not need to be *either* quantitative or qualitative and can utilise skills and experience to see the world in a non-binary way. This will allow researchers to partake in any research, manoeuvre their way through their research career, not feel limited by what they have done before and feel 'expert' in, and to transfer the skills to give them an advantage in areas where they feel they are 'novice'.

Family Life, Early Research, and Quantitative Methods

Education in life begins with parents (Bicknell, 2014). I had an upbringing that most would consider academic. My parents were teachers, and I saw them both study university degrees. Even so, they were completely different influences on my life. From the beginning, I was manoeuvring my way through various understandings and different 'world views' as my mother would say. The famous Physicist, Richard Feynman (2011), attributes much of his early learning of maths and science to his parents, but also highlights how different his parents were.

My mother was a humanities teacher, and one of her favourite subjects was 'Integrated Studies': a mixture of all humanities subjects. It was the epitome of everything qualitative. My father, on the other hand, was technical and practical as a Manual Arts and Graphics teacher. He taught me everything about numbers, measurements, calculating, drawing, and building. This was the epitome of everything quantitative.

One conceptualisation, however, that my mother and 'Integrated Studies' taught me was to have a holistic world view. I was never taught that the social 'way of seeing' and mathematical 'way of seeing' would be anything other than congruous, so I grew up totally immersed in everything. Even in senior school, I did science subjects and Modern History just for interest. I was quite the 'geek' and also read *The Turning Point* by Fritjof Capra (1983) and its impact is significant to this day. I was not like either of my parents, but rather like both of my parents, a non-binary, holistic mix.

When I was in high school, my mother was finishing her Master of Education and when I was studying for my Bachelor of Science, she completed her PhD in Medical Education. By this stage, I was totally engrossed in my Science degree, and deeply passionate about all things physics, and so when she suggested I read her thesis, I said I would one day.

My undergraduate programme was in a very quantitative environment. I had to complete experiments to prove theories, and later was given a set of equipment and an idea and then form a hypothesis, design the experiment, collect the data, and hence prove the theory. My Honours thesis required me to prove experimentally that solid state phase transformation in microscopic stones trapped in window glass could crack a 2 x 2 metre window and bring it down on pedestrians from high-rise buildings (Barry & Ford, 2001).

Despite all of that, however, it is very interesting how non-specific physics actually is (Hoffman, 2013; Solov'ev, 2012) especially the human understanding of it (Smith & Vul, 2013). It really does help to have a world view that is not strictly positivistic, or needing to define everything precisely quantitatively. I was very comfortable with this, thanks to the holistic influences of my parents.

A particular extreme paradox of this ambiguity that physicists accept is the famous thought experiment of Schrödinger's cat (Gribbin, 1991). Put a cat in a box with a radioactive substance and a bottle of poison. The radioactive substance has a 50 % chance of decaying at any time in one hour. If it decays, this releases the poison which kills the cat. The most interesting thing about this experiment is that underlying physics says that in a radioactive atom, if it is not observed, or looked at, then the atom has BOTH decayed and not decayed at the *same time*. There is even a mathematical formula for this effect. If the atom is both decayed AND not decayed, then the cat is both alive AND dead. It is only when the box is opened and the situation observed that the wave equation collapses to a singularity and we find whether the cat is indeed alive or dead, but for one hour, the cat is both alive AND dead.

Ultimately my PhD from 2002 to 2006 was the epitome of quantitative research with an extremely deep, technical focus to extensively 'prove' just one single, major theory, with valid, reliable, and statistically significant results. Overall, I had approximately ten years being immersed in 'hardcore' quantitative research methods.

THE SHIFT TO QUALITATIVE RESEARCH

When I was first 'officially' introduced to qualitative research, I was not interested, and I did not need it on the path that I was following. I was reminded of my mother's research degrees where she talked about qualitative research, and had so many journal articles around the house and it all just seemed too much reading and all too wordy.

During my PhD, however, I began to have a lot to do with an Engineering Education research centre that was multi-disciplinary. This had a subtle influence on my thinking. Many of these people also had an Engineering background, but talking to anthropologists, sociologists, and educationalists, made me realise that this 'human' side of research was also important. In the end, are we not engineering technology for human use?

Going to Purdue University and undertaking post-doctoral research in Engineering Education for a year in 2007 helped me to begin to explore 'non-quantitative' research. I was alerted to the need for a theoretical framework by Karl Smith (Redish & Smith, 2008), when I attempted to submit a paper to the Journal of Engineering Education, but had no idea where to begin. I heard of such things as Grounded Theory Methodology (Strauss & Corbin, 1998), Vygotsky's Zone of Proximal Development (Doolittle, 1995), and Kolb's Experiential Learning Cycle Model (Kolb, 1976). We did interviews and what we called coding and categorisation. How it all worked, however, was never consolidated in my mind. Besides, I was going home and did not think I would continue with that.

MAJOR SHIFT TO QUALITATIVE RESEARCH IN MASTER OF EDUCATION

Here I am, six years later and a year into my Master of Education, grappling with qualitative research. I have an edge, however, over novices who are trying to come to terms with research as a completely new experience because I am an experienced researcher, even though it was in quantitative research. New researchers have to learn how to do research, the basics, the philosophy, the process, how to reconcile theoretical underpinnings with the experimental process, and so forth (Krassen Covan, 2010).

While the research design process is extremely different between quantitative and qualitative research (Marshall & Rossman, 2011), bringing research experience with me and already having a deep appreciation of academia does bring a level of confidence to my qualitative research

(McAlpine & Amundsen, 2009). As such the manoeuvre from quantitative to qualitative research is not particularly risky from my point of view (Harreveld, 2004). I see it less as a contradictory dichotomy (Creswell, 2008) and rather more as a non-binary state. I am both a quantitative AND qualitative researcher, both an experienced AND a novice researcher.

The construction 'Binary', although not necessarily named as such, is also often applied to many areas of life. Mathematics and computing base entire logic systems on the fact that things are either on (1) or off (0) giving the binary numeric system (Price, 1969). Biology classifies living things into species where one organism must exist only as one species (Reece et al., 2014), or gender as male or female (Lorber, 1996). The binary is also seen in the social world where people are expected to see things one way or all the other: being pro-gun or anti-gun, pro-life or pro-choice. It is reasonable that this binary has been seen in the research world where a researcher is described as either quantitative or qualitative, but is not always accurate. How can one person be both expert and novice?

It is an awkward situation, but one that offers opportunity by taking my skills into consideration. I find myself adept at finding journal articles, if only I know what terms to use for the search. I know how to formulate an argument and use literature to support it, but I do not know quite enough words yet to make a story. I feel like I need a lot of advice, but only to get started and then I can run with that.

TRANSFERABLE SKILLS: THINGS I FOUND EASY

Being in a non-binary state of expert and novice, mean there are skills that are transferable (Cargill, 2004). There are challenges, but being open to more than one point of view is where I feel I have an advantage in overcoming those challenges (Snyder & Snyder, 2008).

The main element I learnt when beginning qualitative research after being immersed in quantitative research is that taking the binary blinkers off allowed me to see that I did not need to forget who I was as a quantitative researcher in order to become a qualitative researcher. In fact, many people were telling me the skills I needed to know in order to do qualitative research—implying that they would not be things that I needed in quantitative research—and I found that I already knew these. I just had not recognised that my skills would overlap. From practical to analytical, and in particular methodological perspectives, it surprised both my supervisors and me to find the following five transferable skills.

1. Time Commitment

When I commenced my Master's, I was prepared for it to take a fair amount of time. I had always been good at making time for study and knew it needed concentration and cognitive application. Ever since I was at school, I would spend hours studying and deliberating over challenging concepts until they consolidated in my mind. The PhD also required a lot of time at each step of the process. Predominantly, something often not seen as particularly true of quantitative research was the long and arduous literature review. This meant long hours reading and writing and effort in comprehension.

I was enrolled in the PhD full-time, and had an office at the university, so this made it easy to learn routine and what suited me in terms of the length of time I could put in before I needed a break. Now I realise that I do not need to be in an office at work, but I can also set myself up in a similar manner at home, without any distractions, and I find I am disciplined enough to put in the hours necessary on any given day.

Any research methodology will take time for it to be thorough, comprehensive, and rigorous, and as such this is something that is not specific to either quantitative or qualitative research.

2. Long-Term Commitment

The PhD also prepared me for the long-term nature of the commitment; that research is a drawn out process, and it is impossible to see the whole picture from the beginning. Luckily, I am slightly more of a sequential thinker, not a global thinker. This helps at times when the big picture is difficult to see. I am not blocked by this, and can take the next step, whether it be read another paper, look over data in a different way, or do something practical such as another experiment or transcribe an interview. No matter if it is quantitative or qualitative research, having this flexibility can keep motivation through such a long journey.

The long-term nature also means that at times the trajectory will change. Whether in the quantitative field or qualitative realm, I find that I write down some research questions, and then over time as I read and collect data I expect that the focus will change. This is normal, and acceptable (Silverman, 1993). Despite the changes, however, what I have learnt is to keep going, stay committed, and that it is all part of a productive process.

I have conversations with my supervisors about the chapters that my thesis will need to cover and I realise how much I have to do. I am less daunted, however, having been through this process before. I know that it will all come together in the end. Whether in a quantitative, number-driven environment, or in a qualitative, conceptual environment I have learnt that concentrating on one thing at a time is key for me to get through.

3. Taking Notes

Throughout my PhD, I was always reading and interpreting journal articles and papers. It was not enough to simply read something and put that away in a filing cabinet. I had to read for meaning (Roberts & Roberts, 2008) and extract the information for my current study. I had to write ideas down along with the connotations, limitations, and implications. While this is what note-taking, or note-making is all about, and is a skill required for all study (Coman & Heavers, 1991), it is different with the volumes required for such a large project and is something in which I have become proficient.

It is the same with the articles I am reading at the moment. I cannot simply read them and think that I have digested the knowledge. I still need to understand the relevance for the current study, extract the meaningful information, and physically write it down in my own words (Fisk & Hurst, 2003). The higher-order interpretation and consolidation skills required for research means that note-making is taken to a new level—one required in both quantitative and qualitative study.

4. Critical Review and Context

In reading and distilling meaning from documents, I developed the ability to critically review information. In contrast to some anecdotal beliefs, I have heard about quantitative research, I had to look at the context of the study, who the researchers were, why they were doing the research, and what their backgrounds were. Similarly, I need to do this as a qualitative researcher now to see how what I am reading fits with everything else. Reading critically is especially essential where there are conflicting viewpoints. Even in quantitative studies there can be a huge variety of outcomes depending on all of the variables, and it takes just as much effort to interpret these results in the context of the literature as qualitative outcomes.

In quantitative, positivistic, scientific world, it is 'expected' that results will be valid and reliable, repeatable, and mathematically or statistically 'provable', (Karsai & Kampis, 2010) and so to come up with completely different results requires intensive critical analysis and argument. Quite often in a scientific study, there is not such an emphasis on critiquing the actual methods of previous researchers as in qualitative research, and it is more about confirming or disputing the results.

In my PhD work, researchers from different industries expected certain ways of doing things. Just because there is a mathematical relationship between certain experimental outcomes, does not mean I did not have to investigate the premises that the mathematical relationship was built on. I had to go back to first principles and definitions for that particular field. Now I have to go back to definitions but ones related to qualitative research.

5. The Importance of the Right Method

In my earlier quantitative research, I had to carefully investigate the method in all of the studies that I read about. In science, there are different ways of doing the same experiment and that can give different results meaning that an expected 'theory' may not be achieved. The exact way of measuring the strength in magnesium has to be very different from the industry standard used in steel because the metals have drastically different deformation mechanisms. My work on magnesium required a whole different method, and the argument about this was taken all the way to Standards Australia to have the AS 1391–2007 updated (from the 1991 to the 2005 edition).

The method was the critical point as to the acceptance of the end results, rather than the results on their own. This kind of evaluation is usually considered the domain of qualitative research where the methodology is the arguable variable, and so long as the methodology is accepted, then the results are accepted. Usually in quantitative research, the method is set and the results should match everything that has been before and ever will be again.

I have come to see that I was one of the lucky ones in my quantitative experience. Quite often in a scientific study, there is not such an emphasis on critiquing the methods and theoretical foundations of previous researchers. This, I would have to say, is the most significant and advantageous skill that being an expert researcher has brought to my new-found manoeuvring towards, and immersion in qualitative research.

Challenges: Things I Found Hard and How Being Non-binary Helped

Despite many similarities, there were also a few challenges. Two of the major ones are as follows:

1. The Words and Sentences

Although I had touched on some of the elements of Grounded Theory and coding in my Postdoctoral position, I did not have to come to terms with reading articles on these methods. I was not formally inducted to the theory. I was in a research group that had been doing this study for a year, and I was told to code data. Now to read the words and even comprehend one sentence is a major challenge. The first paper I read for this Master's I needed to read each sentence many times over, sit back and think about it, and then re-read the sentence. This was a familiar situation to me, from my quantitative study, including my PhD. There were always words I did not know and I knew that eventually it would be easier. It is just an extremely different way of writing from the fact-based style of quantitative articles.

2. Digesting the Content

Understanding the content also required much effort. I found myself falling very short on the meanings of the technical terms. For example, even the relatively simple 'methodological framework' along with more complex notions such as 'epistemology', 'ontology', 'ethnomethodology', and 'pragmatist philosophy' were all alien concepts.

My PhD research taught me to go with the flow, follow-up, and trust that eventually it would make sense. I had to deal with some complex concepts in the physical world too, including the energy functions of atoms. I accept that these are concepts that I will learn, so write them down and as I read, I slowly develop a deeper understanding. Even issues that I should have been familiar with from quantitative research, like 'validity', 'reliability' (Malterud, 2001), and evidence (Xu & Storr, 2012) suddenly became new concepts that had completely different connotations. Other concepts that I thought I had a hold of like 'induction' and 'deduction' suddenly became obscure, plus the completely new 'abduction' (Bryant & Charmaz, 2010)!

Learning about the methodologies was complicated but in the end rewarding (Cooper, Fleischer, & Cotton, 2012). I needed to learn the subtle nuances of a particular methodology and that required a considerable effort. I knew, however, that I could accept these and wade through the arguments around any particular methodology and be discerning in my reading as I had been through that sort of process in quantitative research.

In the end, I found myself in a sort of blurred state, and I make the link with being in a non-binary state. For each challenge, it was a case of remembering the experience and how I dealt with it, rather than panic because this is something new and difficult. I had to lose focus on the purely qualitative research thought process and blend it with the world of quantitative thought processes and be in both head spaces at the same time. I needed to ignore the stereotypes of each methodology and exist in the unstable state until it all worked out. Unbeknownst to me, this state of mind and immersion in the blurriness would later become useful in the analysis stage of using grounded theory methodology with the memo making and categorisation (Lempert, 2010). Physics had even taught me to blur the lines as my first assignment in my first ever university course was to investigate Bose–Einstein condensation (Collins, 1995) where atoms at incredibly low temperatures will become indistinguishable from each other. This time around I can accept that both quantitative and qualitative can exist in the same frame of reference.

BRINGING IT ALL TOGETHER

As a result of my research journey, the concepts of labels have become important. Many people do not like labels as it defines them too much into being a single thing—obviously, against the non-binary, multiplistic idea that I am trying to emphasise here. While much work has been done with labels in the fields of disability, sexuality, and gender, I have certainly found it can also apply to being a researcher. For a while I have had a problem with both labels and the *lack* of labels. I know that labels can be seen as limiting, and as always, it is not just black or white. Big, small, gay, straight, male, female, up, down, fat, thin, and so on, there are always examples of people or things that do not fit just into one end of the category. So do we do away with labels altogether? Should there be no label 'male' and no label 'female' because some people feel they are not either of these and others feel that they are both of these at the same time? What then happens to people who want to identify as male or female? I know this seems like a linguistic argument, but really the underpinnings of this are that labels are necessary. Without labels we cannot associate things and we cannot find similarities. We do not need to rule out *other* labels or characteristics that maybe typically would be seen as incongruent with that particular label.

I have read many articles where the authors have defined themselves either explicitly or implicitly through their research arguments as *either* a quantitative researcher, or qualitative researcher, or as either positivist or constructivist. Does that mean that we have to assume that in everything they do they are that way inclined? Or that they will remain that way over time? Or even that they are not indeed both at the same time? We see but a small snippet of their work where they label themselves, or we can apply the label, quantitative or qualitative, constructivist or positivist. We need the label to understand what they are doing at that point in time, or in that particular study, so we can identify what we already know about that facet and they do not need to describe it again (or papers would become unnecessarily lengthy).

In grounded theory methodology, the concept of categorisation is immensely impacted by this discussion around labels, and binary or non-binary models. Dey gives a very good analysis of this (Dey, 2010), and relates it to biology and the classification of plants and other organisms. His work also discusses people, concepts, ideas, actions, and words not fitting into mutually exclusive categories, and that there are many different ways we can 'label' and hence categorise things.

It does not have to be one way or the other. I am not just talking about mixed methods either. This is deep seated, epistemological views of the world, and part of oneself as a researcher (Werner & Rogers, 2013). Can a researcher have different epistemologies? If a researcher is human, then yes, different epistemological view points, and indeed different methodologies can be used in different settings (Candy, 1991). It is possible to not only be two things, but hundreds all at once (Beckham, 2014).

It is not even a spectrum. We are multidimensional humans. If it was just on a spectrum and nothing else, there is no duality, no non-binary, there is simply in the middle. There is simply half one way and half the other way, rather than ALL of BOTH. The problem with the spectrum and potentially being in the middle is that it implies that you have to lose some of one end to gain some of the other end. To be in the middle means a bit like you sit on the fence, or are undecided, and my argument is that this does not need to be the case.

There is a physics phenomenon that also illustrates how something can be two things at once. It is called 'wave-particle duality' (Hendry, 1980). We know waves can be made in any pool of liquid. Particles, on the other hand, are like billiard balls on a table, bouncing very predictably. So they seem very different. Elementary, subatomic particles, however, are BOTH waves and particles at the same time. They travel like waves as if they were one continuous fluid, but also bounce off one another as if they were individual solid balls. It was not difficult for physicists to accept they are both waves and particles, because they regularly deal with infinity, time speeding up and slowing down, and other concepts.

CONCLUSION: WHERE TO FROM HERE

My story has illustrated that it is possible to go from being a quantitative researcher to being a qualitative researcher. It has also shown that being an experienced researcher even in an extremely different field can make the journey easier if one is open to transferring the skills and knowledge, and using past experiences to overcome challenges.

It is intriguing to see that it is not limited to the realm of the qualitative world and constructed knowledge or socially meaningful labels that we find uncertainty, blurred lines, and the non-binary nature of life, but also in the traditionally positivistic world of the physical sciences. Perhaps quantitative and qualitative research are not so different after all, and that people in each field cannot assume certain characteristics of the other methodology without first taking the plunge and doing a bit of methodological manoeuvring themselves.

There is no linear journey; no binary scale in becoming or being a researcher, epistemologically or methodologically speaking. It is really up to the individual to utilise their expertise, understand their own skills and embrace their own non-binary, non-specific, blurry situation, and be open-minded about the possibilities, no matter what black hole or time-warp it may take you through.

REFERENCES

Barry, J. C., & Ford, S. (2001). An electron microscopic study of nickel sulfide inclusions in toughened glass. *Journal of Materials Science, 36*(15), 3721.

Beckham, A. (2014). *Owning your duality. TEDx Talks.* Boulder, CO: YouTube.

Bicknell, B. (2014). Parental roles in the education of mathematically gifted and talented children. *Gifted Child Today, 37*(2), 83–93.

Bryant, A., & Charmaz, K. (2010). Grounded theory in historical perspective: An epistemological account. In A. Bryant & K. Charmaz (Eds.), *The SAGE handbook of grounded theory* (pp. 31–57). Thousand Oaks, CA: Sage.

Bullough, R. V., & Pinnegar, S. (2001). Guidelines for quality in autobiographical forms of self-study research. *Educational Researcher, 30*(3), 13–21. doi:10.310 2/0013189x030003013.

Candy, P. C. (1991). *Self-direction for lifelong learning: A comprehensive guide to theory and practice.* San Francisco: Jossey-Bass, c1991.

Capra, F. (1983). *The turning point: Science, society, and the rising culture.* London: Fontana Paperbacks.

Cargill, M. (2004). Transferable skills within research degrees: A collaborative genre-based approach to developing publication skills and its implications for research education. *Teaching in Higher Education, 9*(1), 83–98.

Collins, G. P. (1995). Gaseous Bose-Einstein condensate finally observed. *Physics Today, 48*(8), 17.

Coman, M. J., & Heavers, K. L. (1991). *What you need to know about developing study skills, taking notes & tests, using dictionaries & libraries.* Lincolnwood, IL: National Textbook Company, c1991.

Cooper, R., Fleischer, A., & Cotton, F. A. (2012). Building connections: An interpretative phenomenological analysis of qualitative research students' learning experiences. *Qualitative Report, 17.*

Creswell, J. W. (2008). *Educational research: Planning, conducting, and evaluating quantitative and qualitative research* (3rd ed.). Upper Saddle River, NJ: Pearson/Merrill Prentice Hall, c2008.

Crotty, M. (1998). *The foundations of social research: Meaning and perspective in the research process.* St Leonards, NSW: Allen & Unwin.

Dey, I. (2010). Grounding categories. In A. Bryant & K. Charmaz (Eds.), *The SAGE handbook of grounded theory* (pp. 167–190). Thousand Oaks, CA: Sage.

Doolittle, P. E. (1995). *Understanding cooperative learning through Vygotsky's zone of proximal development.* Paper presented at the Lilly National Conference on Excellence in College Teaching (Columbia, SC, June 2–4, 1995).

Feynman, R. (2011). What is science? *Resonance: Journal of Science Education, 16*(9), 860–873. doi:10.1007/s12045-011-0104-2.

Fisk, C., & Hurst, B. (2003). Paraphrasing for comprehension. *Reading Teacher, 57*(2), 182–185.

Gribbin, J. R. (1991). *In search of Schrödinger's cat.* London: Black Swan, c1984.

Harreveld, R. E. (2004). *Ethical and political dimensions of strategic risk taking in research* [electronic resource]. Flaxton, QLD: Post Pressed.

Hendry, J. (1980). The development of attitudes to the wave-particle duality of light and quantum theory, 1900–1920. *Annals of Science, 37*(1), 59.

Hoffman, B. (2013). A logical treatment of special relativity, with and without faster-than-light observers. BA Thesis, Lewis and Clark College, Oregon.

Karsai, I., & Kampis, G. (2010). The crossroads between biology and mathematics: The scientific method as the basics of scientific literacy. *BioScience, 60*(8), 632. doi:10.1525/bio.2010.60.8.9.

Kolb, D. A. (1976). Management and the learning process. *California Management Review, 18*(3), 21–31.

Krassen Covan, E. (2010). The discovery of grounded theory in practice: The legacy of multiple mentors. In A. Bryant & K. Charmaz (Eds.), *The SAGE handbook of grounded theory* (pp. 58–74). Thousand Oaks, CA: Sage.

Lempert, L. B. (2010). Asking questions of the data: Memo writing in the grounded theory tradition. In A. Bryant & K. Charmaz (Eds.), *The SAGE handbook of grounded theory* (pp. 245–264). Thousand Oaks, CA: Sage.

Lorber, J. (1996). Beyond the binaries: Depolarizing the categories of sex, sexuality, and gender. *Sociological Inquiry, 66*(2), 143.

Malterud, K. (2001). Qualitative research: Standards, challenges, and guidelines. *Lancet, 358*(9280), 483–488.

Marshall, C., & Rossman, G. B. (2011). *Designing qualitative research*. Los Angeles: Sage.

McAlpine, L., & Amundsen, C. (2009). Identity and agency: Pleasures and collegiality among the challenges of the doctoral journey. *Studies in Continuing Education, 31*(2), 109–125. doi:10.1080/01580370902927378.

Price, C. E. (1969). Representing characters to computers. *American Documentation, 20*(1), 50–60.

Redish, E. F., & Smith, K. A. (2008). Looking beyond content: Skill development for engineers. *Journal of Engineering Education, 97*(3), 295–307.

Reece, J. B., Meyers, N., Urry, L. A., Cain, M. L., Wasserman, S. A., Minorsky, P. V., et al. (2014). *Campbell biology*. Frenchs Forest, NSW: Pearson.

Roberts, J. C., & Roberts, K. A. (2008). Deep reading, cost/benefit, and the construction of meaning: Enhancing reading comprehension and deep learning in sociology courses. *Teaching Sociology, 36*(2), 125–140.

Silverman, D. (1993). *Interpreting qualitative data: Methods for analysing talk, text and interaction*. London: Sage.

Smith, K. A., & Vul, E. (2013). Sources of uncertainty in intuitive physics. *Topics in Cognitive Science, 5*(1), 185–199. doi:10.1111/tops.12009.

Snyder, L. G., & Snyder, M. J. (2008). Teaching critical thinking and problem solving skills. *Delta Pi Epsilon Journal, 50*(2), 90–99.

Solov'ev, E. A. (2012). On the foundations of quantum physics. *Physics Essays, 25*(1), 27–33. doi:10.4006/0836-1398-25.1.27.

Sparkes, A. C. (2000). Autoethnography and narratives of self: Reflections on criteria in action. *Sociology of Sport Journal, 17*(1), 21–43.

Strauss, A. L., & Corbin, J. M. (1998). *Basics of qualitative research: Techniques and procedures for developing grounded theory*. Thousand Oaks: Sage.

Wall, S. (2006). An autoethnography on learning about autoethnography. *International Journal of Qualitative Methods, 5*(2), 1–12.

Werner, T. P., & Rogers, K. S. (2013). Scholar-craftsmanship: Question-type, epistemology, culture of inquiry, and personality-type in dissertation research design. *Adult Learning, 24*(4), 159. doi:10.1177/1045159513499549.

Xu, M. A., & Storr, G. B. (2012). Learning the concept of researcher as instrument in qualitative research. *Qualitative Report, 17*(21), 1–18.

CHAPTER 3

Dipping Qualitative Toes into a Quantitative Worldview: Methodological Manoeuvres in a Multicultural Context

Cynthia Cowling and Celeste Lawson

INTRODUCTION

I am a novice researcher situated in a health profession (radiography) with a small research footprint and a strong preference for quantitative clinical studies. Only 5 % of articles published in peer reviewed journals, devoted to radiography, are qualitative (Bolderston, 2014). I wanted to investigate the sociological aspects of radiographic practice from a global comparative perspective. The study was not seeking a clinical focus, although one could argue that results of a qualitative study could well impact the clinical managements of patients. An ethnographic methodology seemed a natural choice. The rationale and manoeuvres needed to satisfy not only

C. Cowling (✉)
School of Education and the Arts, CQUniversity Australia/Monash University, Melbourne, VIC, Australia

C. Lawson
School of Education and the Arts, CQUniversity Australia, Rockhampton, QLD, Australia

© The Author(s) 2016
B. Harreveld et al. (eds.), *Constructing Methodology for Qualitative Research*, DOI 10.1057/978-1-137-59943-8_3

31

the radiographic community but communities situated in varied cultures proved challenging. This chapter provides an overview of the journey to choose my methodology and the rationale needed to rigorously justify my approach. The benefits of an ethnographic approach in health care research were considered, and the use of ethnography as a methodology by radiography researchers was identified. Problems and issues of qualitative research were considered, and how they were resolved. My own journey was then traced, including the issues and pitfalls encountered in the development, design, and implementation of an ethnographic qualitative study.

My PhD research involved a comparison of sociological radiographic practice in eight countries from a variety of socioeconomic and cultural environments—Australia, India, Taiwan, Trinidad and Tobago, United Arab Emirates (UAE), USA, UK, and Finland. This complex data collection required rigorous manoeuvring to satisfy the groups being studied as well as my need for robust data. In the first instance, a convincing case for a qualitative study was required. Once established, each country site had to support and approve their involvement in the study. The differences in perceptions, policies, social, and economic circumstances, the macro country culture and well as the micro workplace culture all influenced my ability to achieve the aims of the study.

CHOOSING A METHODOLOGY—ETHNOGRAPHY

Western Medicine has long prided itself on its observance of the scientific method and the need to work within evidence-based environments. An emphasis on explicit knowledge downplayed research into the social, organisational, and interrelational contexts of health care provision (Gabbay & le May, 2004). The reliance on scientific enquiry within a positivist paradigm, and where a hypothesis/deductive approach was used, ignored the insights, intuitions, and social fabric integral to the practice of any health profession. Quantitative researchers removed such factors from the inquiry, so as not to falsify the results (Denzin & Lincoln, 2003; Wieman, 2014).

Modern approaches acknowledge that even within this rigorous predictive methodology, research could be messy as scientists determine complex variables (Wieman, 2014). Contextual influences cannot be avoided and the differences between the two schools of research have narrowed. Descriptive observations have their place and are recognised as a valuable component to research design whether qualitative or quantitative. This tacit acceptance of the importance of qualitative elements to research has led health care researchers to more frequently adopt the approach.

Qualitative research seeks to describe and explain social phenomena. It involves the careful collection and analysis of comprehensive data of the day-to-day activities, problems, and issues that may occur and which provide meaning to individuals (Denzin & Lincoln, 2013; Hammersley & Atkinson, 2007). Historically, detractors of the qualitative paradigm argued that such an approach was unscientific, exploratory, and subjective (Huber, 1995). They contested that interpretations of data collected were too influenced by external cultural and political factors and provided only a humanistic soft science commentary. Their adherence to the positivist, quantitative approach was driven by the need for principles that encompassed objectivity, determinism, and a deductive design. Critics of the quantitative approach pointed out that reality is not objective but interpreted social action (Sarantakos, 2005), that objectivity should not always be relied upon, and that the subjectivity of the perceptions and interpretations that the researcher brings, has its advantages (Reeves, Kuper, & Hodges, 2008).

A qualitative methodology, however, within radiography was not well represented and provided my first hurdle. Research within radiography was traditionally quantitative, seeking to legitimatise its clinical and scientific focus. Bolderston (2014) suggested that it was easier, relatively speaking, to be part of a medically driven clinical team than to be involved in a qualitative initiative. She also argued that radiography research had little sociological content and even less anthropological background. Bolderston agreed that rigour needed to drive qualitative design and analysis; however, external limitations could impede the most rigorous study in the general stream of research. I had experienced firsthand having a journal paper rejected on the grounds that there were no statistics or graphs.

The chosen research area, diagnostic radiography, had limited research (both quantitative and qualitative) from which to draw for this study. Sim and Radloff cited a number of reasons for the lack of research in radiography, including poor understanding within the industry of the significance of research; employers not providing time and facilities to support research; and a general lack of confidence of radiographers in their ability to carry out research. Some within the radiography industry did not wish to move beyond the comfort zone where others were ultimately responsible and accountable (Yielder & Davis, 2009). The radiography workplace culture relied on adherence to protocols and a rigid formulaic approach to work, where compliance and a resistance to promote research was synonymous with obedience, submission, traditionalism, conventionality, and acquiescence (Levitt-Jones & Lathlean, 2009; Yielder & Davis, 2009). Nixon (2001) suggested that radiographers could realistically only call themselves semi-professional because of this reality and felt that until there was better sharing and participation with other professions and an increased value in research, this situation would not change. Adams and Smith (2003) and Campeau (1999) noted a lack of qualitative research in particular, and argued that there was a real need for research to help define the role of radiographers and how they performed that role. Decker and Ipholen (2005) identified gaps in research and specifically suggested the use of ethnography to better understand the everyday workings of the radiographer. Strudwick, an ethnographic radiographer, noted the paucity of qualitative research in her PhD study into the culture of a diagnostic radiography department (2011).

My PhD study was suited to a qualitative approach. The focus of the research pertained to global sociological practice within an interpretative paradigm and was best served by an ethnographic methodology particularly because of its cross-cultural component. However, the justification of ethnography as a methodology was challenging, particularly when contrasted with explicit clinical research as was expected in my field. Hammersley and Atkinson (2007) claimed that while ethnography was difficult to define, at its core it was a method of understanding and interpreting everyday lives in a way that examined specific actions in order to produce research. Recent academic debate encouraged the use of ethnography in health care. The subjectivity and interpretative nature of such research has value within medicine and, provided rigour and substantive analysis is demonstrated, research findings from descriptive observations reveal insight into the practice of medicine and radiography (2007). Ethnography is an approach suited to the health professions, since it is a legitimate way to study the behaviours, relationships, and interactions that occur between individuals and teams within the health care community (Pope, Ziebland, & Mays, 2000).

Ethnography is a deceptively simple research methodology (Reeves et al., 2008), yet there are many complexities. There are several sub-genres of ethnography that have emerged including performance, realist, and critical ethnography. Although my study looked at relationships of power, it was never my intention to have a politically biased agenda (as is usual in critical ethnography [Hammersley & Atkinson, 2007]). This would have made the job of entering a variety of workplaces across the multiple countries even more difficult and would have compounded the challenge to get approval. The design was therefore based on classical or conventional ethnographic methodology. The study was a broad-based comparison across cultural and socioeconomic boundaries. The cross-cultural design required a sensitivity to the diversity of cultures being observed so that data analysis could cut across these wide disparities to allow common themes to emerge (Madison, 2012). Ethnography enabled me to see how the radiographers were affected by their world in a variety of locations (Chandratilrake, McAleer, & Gibson, 2012; Hall, 1976; Hofstede, 2010).

The Issues: Site Selection, Research Methods, Approvals

Once the methodology of ethnography was decided upon, the methodological manoeuvring was just beginning. There were a number of issues to navigate: selecting the sites for data collection; insider status of the researcher; choosing research methods for the sites; and getting appropriate approvals.

Site Selection

Selecting the sites where the study would be conducted was influenced by a number of factors. In a qualitative study, the research question drives the sample size and type. It is acceptable to investigate a small number of sites. The quality of the data gathered was more important to the study, rather than the volume. The choice of countries was both pragmatic and pragmalinguistic (Bowe, Martin, & Manns, 2014). Countries were selected on the basis of diversity of socioeconomic levels and country culture, and where English was a first language or where it was well understood. Using English-speaking environments would enable participants to speak and function in their own culture without fear of the negative impact of misinterpretation (Hamilton & Woodward-Kron, 2010). Countries were also selected on the basis of my familiarity with the radiography practice and the culture of that country.

One hospital site was chosen in each country. Sites had to comply with some common principles deliberately designed to reduce the number of variables across the sites to ensure consistency for the data analysis stage.

The hospital had to be publically funded and be regional rather than an intensive metropolitan centre. Observation needed to take place in an environment not used to having research students. This would help avoid the perception of burn out from staff overburdened with being studied. The hospital needed to be large enough to support approximately 20–30 fulltime equivalent radiographers on staff. This would provide sufficient variety of experiences amongst the radiographers being interviewed.

Insider Status

The role of the researcher in ethnography has been much debated. An outsider researcher, on the one hand, provides neutrality and objectivity (Yates, 2004). The insider, on the other hand, brings tacit knowledge critical to the understanding of the situation or experience (Merton, 1972). As a radiographer, I was an insider able to add epistemological rigour to textual material gathered (Kerstetter, 2012). I was also an outsider as an academic from the University sector, which could be perceived as bringing with it a privileged and powerful status. In some countries, I was also an outsider because I came from another country. For both insider and outsider, trust had to be earned (Baird, 1998). Baird (1998) used her insider knowledge to select the sites she studied, based on her knowledge of practices and personnel. My research followed a similar vein. Knowledge of the working conditions in each location was necessary in order to establish consistency between sites. It was not practical to conduct a pre-visit to determine suitability of sites in multiple countries, so personal knowledge of the country and relationships with the people in those countries became critical. This proved valuable as access to sites became relatively problem-free, and who to contact to get site-specific approvals was already known. Trust was easy to establish as I was recognised as a senior executive member of an international voluntary radiographic organisation. Within the radiographic community this was held in higher regard than the fact that I was a member of a privileged academic group within a university.

During the data gathering, being an insider could be a disadvantage. It was important not to be intrusive or judgemental. (Denzin & Lincoln, 2013) believes a researcher could start as a non-participant observer and end up as a non-observing participant (Whyte, 1984). Baird (1998) addressed this through the use of a reflective journal. She critically analysed her actions and thoughts separately to the observations. These concerns were addressed by being open with responses to any questions asked about my presence, and by dressing appropriately during the observation sessions (like wearing a lab coat in the hospital). Observation sessions were scheduled for locations where the radiographer would not feel as though they were being examined on their operational technique. For example, there was no observation conducted in X-ray rooms or when radiographers were clinically interacting with patients.

Choosing the Research Methods

The research methods were selected carefully to be consistent with a qualitative ethnographic methodology. Ethnography captures the sights and sounds of the workplace environment and the thoughts of the people inhabiting it. Three methods were selected to provide a triangulation of the data: (1) participant observation; (2) semi-structured interviews; and (3) document analysis of relevant policies or health ministry directives. Further, a reflective journal would also be kept. Baird (1998) recommends a journal to record the thoughts and actions of the researcher, while Ember and Ember (2009) feel a journal minimises errors in cross-cultural ethnographic studies by including awareness of cultural biases and a judgemental attitude.

In relation to observation, it seemed realistic and manageable to spend a week at each site, and while more time would have been preferred (1998), there were time and financial constraints. My insider status with the countries and radiographers served to counter the shortness of time. Observation periods were arranged in the morning and afternoon in such areas as staff rooms and waiting rooms.

Five radiographers at each site were selected for an interview. Interview questions were carefully structured to enable open responses and additional probing in order to elicit rich, thick descriptive responses (Jorgensen, 1989). The analysis of documents provided context for the culture and the working environment within which the radiographer operated (Geertz, 1973). A variety of documents were gathered including brochures, reports, position descriptions, and operational directives.

Approvals

The ethics submission for this study was considered low risk because the purpose was to study the everyday working life of the radiographer and their interactions and interrelationships with stakeholders rather than patients and/or clinical actions. The submission considered informed consent, privacy, harm, and exploitation. Ethical approval was obtained on the proviso that a letter of approval be obtained from each hospital site indicating their willingness to participate in the study. Obtaining the letters of approval seemed an easy step because verbal support had already been received, however this step proved challenging on a number of levels. Policies and procedures relating to research approval varied from country to country. Different steps were required depending on the country, and the approval was required from different levels of hierarchy. Further, some countries misunderstood the purpose of the study, assuming it was quantitative or that it involved patient contact, when neither was the case.

Approvals from England and Finland were straightforward. They were countries familiar with radiographic research, including qualitative studies. In India the request passed over many desks over a six-month period before the written approval was finally received. The UAE requested a full ethics submission, which was approved after three revisions. Taiwan, an Asian country well known for its demanding scientific radiographic education, could not fully comprehend the intent or method of a qualitative study. However when the study was explained as interviews with a few radiographers and the researcher wandering around the department, but not in the X-ray rooms, the approval was swift and comprehensive. Interestingly, during the interviews in Taiwan, participants were not able to comprehend that I could be a sociologist and a medical science academic at the same time. In Trinidad and Tobago, the approval process followed "island time", where the relaxed culture meant steps took much longer to complete than anticipated.

LESSONS FROM DATA GATHERING

The strength of the data collection methods was that it enabled a level of flexibility without compromising the integrity of the study. A lot of effort had gone into the planning of the study, however once the actual data collection was underway it became apparent that the plans would not always work as expected. Observation techniques needed to be adapted to the local conditions. There were variations in countries' cultures and workplace conditions, meaning that some scheduled data collection sessions did not eventuate. For example, in Trinidad and Tobago, the workday started at 7.00 am and ended by about 2.30 pm. It was pointless scheduling observation sessions after this time. Further, different departments had moments of furious activity followed by complete abandonment of the area. Observation had been scheduled for the staff room, but once I arrived at the site it became apparent the staff room was not used by staff so observation sessions were moved to other locations. The exception was when the soccer world cup semi-finals were on the television and everybody it seemed descended upon the staff room.

In relation to the interviews, having a semi-structured approach allowed flexibility in how the questions were phrased and asked. Yet, the carefully constructed open-ended questions occasionally seemed stilted in the field and were rephrased or contextualised to be appropriate for the site or for the individual. In different sites some words were interpreted in a manner unexpected, perhaps due to language use. For example, the term "critical" was used in a question to refer to important daily job activities of the radiographer. One radiographer interpreted the word as meaning the condition of the patient, with their response being "doing dead patients". The disparity in culture with regard to communication styles as identified by Ember and Ember (2009), Hofstede (2010), and more recently Hall (1976) were carefully considered. Familiarity with each country culture enhanced my ability to rephrase in a manner appropriate to that culture.

In Trinidad and Tobago, the radiographers were happy to be interviewed, but they were reluctant to have the interviews recorded. Nuances in responses and valuable contextual data were lost because of this. Recording the interviews served an additional purpose beyond recording the words of the radiographer. It also enabled a critique of the interviewing style. *Were the probing questions open-ended enough, or did it seem that a certain response was expected? Did I talk too much? Was I truly objective?* I also realised the importance of observing before I interviewed because it meant I could contextualise better the responses of the radiographers and offer probes that were relevant Meyer (2014).

In relation to site locations, the variety and quality of information, and the differences in workplace environments of each site required flexibility on the part of the researcher. From an ethnographic perspective, the working conditions were so different from site to site that the same recording device could not be used. For example, in Taiwan, workers had set tasks that were performed. These tasks could be interpreted within the context of the various job descriptions and hospital policies. The hospital was clean and clinical, and the presence of an iPad to record notes was not out of place. In India daily tasks were much more fluid. One position was that of "dark room assistant", a title based in history when X-rays were developed on film, but there was no longer any dark room in the hospital. His tasks were never completely revealed during the study. The hospital was less organised and less technologically advanced in comparison to Taiwan, and notes were more appropriately recorded using a clipboard and pencil in order to "fit in".

In diagnostic radiography, a breach of conduct or practice can result in improper or unnecessary use of ionising radiation and any code of practice requires a radiographer to identify this. However, it was difficult to intervene without risking the element of trust. Johnson called this *intervention dilemma* (Rubin & Rubin, 1995). Strudwick (Johnson, 2004) felt it important to be directed by her professional code of conduct and in her observations made it known that she would intervene only if this code was specifically breached. She suggested that strategies of complete openness show the researcher has nothing to hide. I followed this suggestion by addressing obvious breaches and misuse of radiation to individuals in a private confidential manner. This, as well as being previously known at the site ensured the continuance of trustworthiness and in fact elevated the level of respect the site had for me.

It had been expected that similar documents could be obtained from each site, yet this was not the case. At some sites documents, like policies or procedural manuals, were readily obtained. At others, the documents existed but were ignored in practice. And at other sites, no operational documents were evident. Any relevant documents were obtained, be they brochures for patients, hospital directives or position descriptions. The final collection of documents for analysis was unexpectedly eclectic.

Lessons from Data Analysis

Radiographic researchers Murphy and Yielder (2009) have highlighted the fact that rigour was important in all qualitative studies particularly when doing research in an environment far more comfortable with a quantitative approach. Dependability required a clear audit trail of activities underpinned by knowledge and documentation; and confirmability required cross-checking and results assessed by others (Strudwick, 2011). Therefore, this analysis needed to ensure rigour, validity, and reproducibility to satisfy any methodological criticism. It is needed to be systematic, inclusive, and inductive. The data was analysed using a thematic approach to explore common emerging themes and concepts. Codes needed to be developed on two levels, one as an audit trail and one as a mechanism to demonstrate materialising themes.

A significant lesson was that the research data were analysed in relation to individual sites, beginning with Trinidad and Tobago. Individually analysing each site provided useful context for me as a researcher. It was initially imagined data would be gathered from all sites and then analysed once, at the same time. Had this approach been adopted, important contextual analysis revealed at individual sites would have been missed, and the same mistakes realised in Trinidad and Tobago would have been repeated at the other sites. In this way, Trinidad and Tobago became a pilot for the other sites. As a result of completing the fieldwork and analysis in Trinidad and Tobago, the research methods were refined in preparation for the other sites. This slight refinement did not affect the validity of the method (Murphy & Yielder, 2009); it ensured better preparation in terms of flexibility, data gathering, and keeping an open mind. It also enabled a draft translation of the fieldwork into coding and themes to be ultimately presented in linguistic form as a research study.

Qualitative research is an iterative process. The very act of coding ultimately improved the fieldwork activities. The analysis of data in the minute detail required of a rigorous ethnographic study was challenging. Previous research experience involved the big picture and end results. The thoroughness and minute attention to every detail, conversation, verbal and non-verbal communications was initially overwhelming. Whilst the process was challenging and frustrating, it was ultimately rewarding as the themes emerged from quantifiable and detailed examination, rather than thought bubbles. The analysis also provided valid documentation to share with colleagues familiar with radiography, but not with this particular study, who could consider codes and themes which could then be compared and discussed, thus adding additional validity and rigour to the study (Burnard, 1991).

Once the coding had taken place, there was a strong desire to return to the sites, particularly Trinidad and Tobago where the pilot study had taken place. At the time of conducting the fieldwork in Trinidad and Tobago, none of the themes were yet identified, and the data gathering methods were not refined. There were data collection mistakes, and a second visit could reveal additional information. Burnard (1991) recognised that returning to a site after the analysis process could be a further validating exercise. By returning to Trinidad and Tobago, the views of the radiographers could be discussed against the important themes that emerged from the initial site visit. Fortunately a return visit to Trinidad and Tobago was possible, but this was not possible for all sites.

CONCLUSION

The methodological manoeuvres of this chapter refer to the flexibility needed to achieve successful data collection, analysis and ultimately a PhD when working qualitatively in a quantitative environment. It demonstrates that ethnography can be seen from literature to function well as the methodology of choice for this study. The "real" world of clinical diagnostic radiography was slower to embrace this, and the added complexity of studying sociological practice in a number of different countries means that the processes need to be adaptive and sensitive to the contextualisation of the data collected. This chapter has not been about moving from one research style to another, but rather describes an exciting journey of discovery into a qualitative world long neglected in the quantitative environment in which this research takes place. One interviewee asked me why I was doing my study. I asked her in her 30 years of practice whether anybody had asked her about her life as a radiographer and she said "No". I said "that is why".

REFERENCES

Adams, J., & Smith, T. (2003). Qualitative methods in radiography research: A proposed framework. *Radiography, 9,* 193–199.

Baird, M. A. (1998). *The preparation for practise as a radiographer. The relationship between the practicum and the profession.* (PhD), La Trobe, Melbourne.

Bolderston, A. (2014). Five percent is not enough. Why we need more qualitative research in the medical radiation sciences. *Journal of Medical Imaging and Radiation Sciences, 45,* 201–203.

Bowe, H., Martin, K., & Manns, H. (2014). *Communication across cultures: Mutual understanding in a global world.* Cambridge: Cambridge University Press.

Burnard, P. (1991). A method of analysing interview transcripts in qualitative research. *Nurse Education Today, 11,* 461–466.

Campeau, F. E. (1999). *Radiography: Technology, environment, professionalism.* Philadelphia, PA: Lippincott Williams and Wilkins.

Chandratilrake, M., McAleer, S., & Gibson, J. (2012). Cultural similarities and differences in medical professionalism: A multi-region study. *Medical Education, 46*(3), 257–266.

Decker, S., & Ipholen, R. (2005). Developing the profession of radiography. *Making use of oral history. Radiography, 11,* 262–271.

Denzin, N., & Lincoln, Y. (2003). *The landscape of qualitative research: Theories and issues* (2nd ed.). Thousand Oaks, CA: Sage.

Denzin, N., & Lincoln, Y. (2013). *Strategies of qualitative inquiry* (4th ed.). Los Angeles: Sage.

Ember, C. R., & Ember, M. (2009). *Cross cultural research methods* (2nd ed.). Lanham, MD: AltaMira.

Gabbay, J., & le May, A. (2004). Evidence based guidelines or collectively constructed mindlines? Ethnographic study of knowledge management in primary care. *British Medical Journal, 329*(7473), 1013.

Geertz, C. (1973). *Interpretation of cultures; Selected essays.* New York: Basic Books.

Hall, E. (1976). *Beyond culture.* Garden City, NY: Anchor Books.

Hamilton, J., & Woodward-Kron, R. (2010). Developing cultural awareness and intercultural communication through multi-media: A case study from medicine and the health sciences. *System, 38*, 560–568.

Hammersley, M., & Atkinson, P. (2007). *Ethnography. Principles in practice* (3rd ed.). London: Routledge.

Hofstede, G. J. (2010). *Cultures and organizations: Software of the mind: Intercultural cooperation and its importance for survival* (3rd. ed.). New York: McGraw-Hill.

Huber, J. (1995). Centennial essay: Institutional perspectives on sociology. *American Journal of Sociology, 101*, 194–216.

Johnson, M. (2004). Real world ethics and nursing research. *Nursing Times Research, 9*, 251–261.

Jorgensen, D. L. (1989). *Participant observation, a methodology for human studies.* Thousand Oaks: Sage.

Kerstetter, K. (2012). Insider, outsider or somewhere in between: The impact of researachers' identities on the community based research process. *Journal of Rural Social Sciences, 27*(2), 99–117.

Levitt-Jones, T., & Lathlean, J. (2009). "Don't rock the boat": Nursing students' experiences of conformity and compliance. *Nurse Education Today, 29*(3), 612–616.

Madison, D. S. (2012). *Critical ethnography: Method, ethics and performance.* Thousand Oaks: Sage.

Merton, R. (1972). Insiders and outsiders: A chapter in the sociology of knowledge. *American Journal of Sociology, 78*, 9–47.

Meyer, E. (2014). *The culture map: Breaking through the invisible boundaries of global business.* New York: PublicAffairs.

Murphy, F. J., & Yielder, J. (2009). Establishing rigour in qualitative radiography. *Radiography, 16*, 62–67.

Nixon, S. (2001). Professionalism in radiography. *Radiography, 7*(1), 31–35.

Pope, C., Ziebland, S., & Mays, N. (2000). Qualitative research in health care: Analyzing qualitative data. *British Medical Journal, 320*(7227), 114–116.

Reeves, S., Kuper, A., & Hodges, B. (2008). Qualitative research methodologies: Ethnography. *British Medical Journal, 337*, a1020.

Rubin, H., & Rubin, I. (1995). *Qualitative interviewing: The art of hearing data*. Thousand Oaks: Sage.

Sarantakos, S. (2005). *Social research* (3rd ed.). Basingstoke, UK: Palgrave.

Strudwick, R. (2011). *An ethnographic study of the culture in a diagnostic imaging department*. (DProf Health and Social Care), University of Salford, Salford.

Whyte, W. (1984). *Learning from the field*. Beverley Hills: Sage.

Wieman, C. (2014). The similarities between research in education and research in the hard sciences. *Educational Researcher, 43*(1), 12–14.

Yates, L. (2004). The secret rules of language: Tackling pragmatics in the classroom. *Prospect, 19*(1), 3–21.

Yielder, J., & Davis, M. (2009). Where radiographers fear to tread: Resistance and apathy in radiography practice. *Radiography, 15*, 345–350.

CHAPTER 4

Navigating the Path Between Positivism and Interpretivism for the Technology Academic Completing Education Research

Michael A. Cowling

INTRODUCTION

Research is a complex endeavour. Whether we are talking about scientific work with chemicals, technology work with computers or education work with students, the parameters of a research design are a complicated set of variables that must be uniquely set for each research project. Whilst it could be argued that the purpose of all research is the same in its quest for knowledge and answers to unanswered questions, the variations in these questions can be quite wide, leading towards significantly different research design depending on the discipline (Bryman, 2012).

Many universities seek to address this by teaching students about the more popular research methodologies within their discipline but, by its very nature, this leads to a discipline-focused understanding of research design by a particular researcher. In short, whilst this research has the same

M.A. Cowling (✉)
School of Education and the Arts, CQUniversity Australia,
Brisbane, QLD, Australia

© The Author(s) 2016
B. Harreveld et al. (eds.), *Constructing Methodology for Qualitative Research*, DOI 10.1057/978-1-137-59943-8_4

process, the experience of that process by each individual researcher will be different, with their resulting understanding of research design influenced by their discipline background.

Against this context of differing discipline-focused research design we have the situation of a researcher looking to change their research focus. The movement of researchers from a traditional quantitative model to a qualitative model would suggest a much broader focus on research design. In particular, in my case, as a technology researcher looking to the field of education, I find myself confronting challenges to a taken-for-granted mindset regarding epistemology, leading to a change in the other facets of their research design. How best can I deal with this change when my existing mindset regarding research design is so discipline focused and quantitative in nature?

This chapter will discuss my own experience as a researcher in the field of information and communication technology, a field typically steeped in experimentation, working through the methodological manoeuvring required to contribute to qualitative research in learning and teaching. Building on the work of Chinn, Buckland and Samarapungavan (2011), who argue that epistemological perceptions must be broadened to help with cognition, this chapter will break apart my original epistemology as a technology academic, explaining the components of this positivist epistemology. This will include how it was communicated to researchers completing research in technology during the author's PhD, focusing in particular on how epistemology in this discipline was downplayed in favour of discussion of methods and taken-for-granted methodology.

A bridge will then be established between this common epistemology of technology researchers and the epistemology of qualitative learning and teaching researchers. This presents a contrast to the work of Sinatra and Chinn (2012), who looked at the enhancement of scientific reasoning in students as a form of conceptual change, instead looking at how technology researchers could implement social science concepts. Specifically, the use of positivist epistemology in learning and teaching research will be explored using my own work as a case study, along with methods for researchers to interpret other paradigms such as interpretivism. Finally, using work such as that by Hofer and Bendixen (2012) on "personal epistemology", the position of different epistemologies and their relationships to research questions will be discussed, with strategies identified to allow researchers coming from technology research to navigate an epistemological shift for learning and teaching research and discussion on why this might be required.

The purpose of this chapter is to serve as a mechanism to allow interrogation of the methodologies and epistemologies used in these disciplines and to show how methodological manoeuvring might be conceptualised and completed by technology researchers endeavouring to complete research into learning and teaching, using the research journey of the author as a case study. As a case study of one, examples from my own journey as the author will be discussed, particularly focusing on the specifics of how I completed a transformative learning journey, allowing me to view the world through a different lens. Through this, others are encouraged to assess their own epistemology and how it fits with the research, they do.

THINKING: HOW WE INTERPRET THE WORLD

There are many different ways to think about research design. This book provides examples of those different approaches, and how varied they can be. Broadly speaking, many researchers refer to research as being either "quantitative" or "qualitative", with the newer "mixed methods" work integrating these two approaches to have a combined quantitative/qualitative study with multiple phases (Bryman, 2012). For some technology researchers, including myself, this reference to either qualitative or quantitative was the extent of the knowledge imparted about research design, with an automatic assumption that the researcher would be conducting an experimental quantitative study and so no more detail was required on the broader topics of research design.

However, I would now argue that the world of research design is actually much richer than this simple quantitative/qualitative distinction. Michael Crotty presents a model that is influential in the field. Whilst many researchers define the various parts of a research design in different ways, there is also a certain simplicity to the model described by Crotty (1998). Crotty (1998) breaks research down into four interconnected elements:

- Epistemology—The theory of knowledge
- Theoretical Perspective—The philosophical stance
- Methodology—The plan of action
- Methods—The techniques employed

Each of these elements contributes to the next, so that a researcher with a clear methodology should be able to trace backwards to a corresponding theoretical perspective and epistemology. Similarly, a researcher with a clear epistemology will be able to select an appropriate theoretical perspective

Table 4.1   Examples of different types of research

Epistemology	Theoretical perspective	Methodology	Methods
Objectivism Constructionism Subjectivism (*and their variants*)	Positivism (and post-positivism) Interpretivism • Symbolic interactionism • Phenomenology • Hermeneutics Critical inquiry Feminism Postmodernism etc.	Experimental research Survey research Ethnography Phenomenological research Grounded theory Heuristic inquiry Heuristic inquiry Action research Discourse analysis Feminist standpoint research etc.	Sampling Measurement and scaling Questionnaire Observation • Participant • Non-participant Interview Focus group Cases study Life history Narrative Visual ethnographic methods Statistical analysis Data reduction Theme identification Comparative analysis Cognitive mapping Interpretative methods Document analysis Content analysis Conversation analysis etc.

Source: Crotty (1998)

and methodology. One of the key tenets of the work by Crotty (1998) is that this connection between the elements clearly exists, in that a path can be mapped between a particular item in any of the four elements and a corresponding item in the other elements.

As noted above, there are differences in the use of terminology depending on the source. However, whilst these different elements can often have different labels, Crotty's (1998) model serves as a useful approach to looking at social research methods. In particular, Crotty (1998) provides details of various items within each of the elements that help to unpack a researchers thinking (Table 4.1).

Arguably, the most important of these is epistemology, which Crotty (1998, p. 3) defines as "the theory of knowledge embedded in the theoretical perspective and thereby in the methodology". Epistemology is important because it influences the question: "What kind of knowledge do we believe will be attained by our research?" (Crotty, 1998, p. 2). Different epistemologies lead to different theoretical perspectives, methodologies, methods and so on.

Using Crotty's (1998) outline, by using a different epistemological lens to look at the world, enables a choice of a different methodology, which in turn requires a different theoretical perspective. Experimental research suggests a positivist theoretical perspective and an objectivist epistemology; however, research using (say) grounded theory will mean a symbolic interpretivist theoretical perspective is required, aligning to a constructionism epistemology. This means a change in thinking, a shift for the researcher in terms of not only methodology, but also a challenge to their internal theory of knowledge.

Considering the two theoretical perspectives noted in the title specifically, Crotty (1998) defines positivism as "The March of Science", noting that it offers "assurance of unambiguous and accurate knowledge of the world" (p. 18). He provides a history of the term growing out of the use of the term "posit", meaning to position something as fact. Finally, he links the term very clearly to science, noting that positivists are "great lovers of science" and that the world addressed by positivism is not the real world but, instead, the scientific world steeped in objectivity, validity and generalisability. Put another way, the text is arguing that for positivists there is only one way to see the world, the "factual" way (as they see it), a literal truth that is not affected by interpretation.

In contrast, with regard to interpretivism, the approach put forward by Crotty (1998) is to build a case for interpretivism as a theoretical perspective steeped in culture, contrasting the natural science approach to "explaining" with the social science needed for "understanding" and working towards an understanding that there is a perceived fundamental difference in the subject matter of social science and natural science research (Crotty, 1998).

On the basis of this case, Crotty (1998) describes Symbolic Interactionism as a historical stream that has "borne [interpretivism] along" (Crotty, 1998, p. 71). Quoting the work of George Mead, Crotty (1998) builds the case that symbolic interactionism postulates that we "owe to society our very being as conscious and self-conscious entities, for that being arises from a process of symbolic interaction" (p. 74). He then links this theoretical

perspective (in Crotty parlance) with the broader epistemology of constructionism, which is the view that objects do not have meaning of their own
(as in objectivism) but instead are assigned meaning contingent on human
practice and in their interaction with us as human beings.

Put another way, the text is arguing that an individual is made up of
their experiences and, further, that to truly understand an individual we
must put ourselves in their place and understand that the symbols with
which they have interacted with to become who they are, as well as relating to rituals, culture and language as certain kinds of symbols. In this way,
Crotty (1998) indicates that symbolic interactionism can share close ties
with an ethnographic methodology.

Finally, Crotty (1998) also notes that the approach to developing an
epistemology can often be different, depending on the research training
received. He notes that for those studying "quantitative" methods, the
thought process often starts with method, working backwards to derive
an epistemology that grows out of the methods that these researchers are
trained to use. In contrast, those investigating a "qualitative" method often
start with epistemology or theoretical framework, working downwards
from these elements to determine a methodology and method out of the
overarching framework.

As noted, this has presented quite a challenge for me in my own personal journey as I moved from Technology to Education. Coming from a
predominantly quantitative background, I had to begin to understand this
model of a more complex research design, and a more complex view of the
world. More interestingly, I have had to realise that a more complex view
actually existed, as my training prior to my discipline change did not even
recognise that this different design existed! In fact, when I first started my
career as a researcher, I was focused solely on a positivist approach, although
I did not know it at the time. The next section discusses this in more detail.

TECHNOLOGY AND THE POSITIVIST EPISTEMOLOGY

As noted above, if we take the position that technology researchers work
with quantitative data and methods, then it is possible to use Crotty (1998)
to work backwards to determine and track a methodology, theoretical
framework and epistemological position. For example, when I completed
my PhD in Information Technology, I used a sampling and measurement
method, which suggests an experimental methodology, a positivist theoretical perspective and, finally, an objectivist epistemology.

However, the more interesting part of this case study is not the epistemology I used, but, rather, the ease with which I accepted that epistemology (and related components) as the only way to do research in my discipline. Using textbooks such as *Introduction to Business Statistics* by Weiers and *The Basic Practice of Statistics* by Moore (Weiers, 2008; Moore, 2004), we were taught the basics of statistics and statistical methods, but very little on the choice of methodology we would use, or the overarching epistemology. This suggests that statistical methods were seen as the only legitimate way of knowing the world and presenting "good" research.

Rather than being asked to select an epistemology and theoretical framework and then apply a method (as per Crotty [1998]), the assumption appeared to be made that we would all use the same methodology and that only the details of the data analysis needed to be learned. This set me up well for the work I was doing, which was predominantly experimental and very quantitative, but provided very little methodological grounding. In fact, a review of the journal paper I published during my doctorate shows a very short methodology section focused solely on the parameters of the experiment and not at all on the methodology (Cowling & Sitte, 2003). While this put me in a good position to complete my doctoral studies, it left me with a very narrow view of research design and a doctorate that, whilst good for quantitative research, had limitations for qualitative work, something that would only become apparent to me almost ten years later as I moved from one discipline to another.

TAKING THE POSITIVIST TO EDUCATION

It is clear from a review of the literature that social research methods require a deeper and more nuanced understanding of research than the approach typically followed in a more experimental field, where the overarching motivations and positions for the work are assumed and subsumed in favour of the importance of the experiment (Bryman, 2012). Rather, to interact with society, it seems important to have an understanding not only of the work to be conducted, but also the rationale for the work and the motivation behind it, including an understanding of how the researcher views the world. Here, the focus of the research is on understanding the interaction of human behaviour, rather than following an experimental design to test a hypothesis.

Despite this, it would be wrong to assume that all technology work is positivist, or that all education work is interpretivist. For instance, positivist work exists in the education field, especially from researchers with a background in "quantitative" research (see, for example, Muijs, 2010). Similarly, in the area of information systems (a sub-discipline of the broader Information & Communication Technology discipline), researchers have completed non-positivist studies (Myers, 2015). Yet despite this, based on my experience, it would not be unreasonable to suggest that for many technology researchers, quantitative research is the norm and qualitative research is unusual. This is because in certain disciplines, quantitative research approaches are seen as the legitimate approach and other types of approaches can be labelled as subjective and not "true" research.

Also not surprisingly, my own experience was definitely along these lines. Moving from an experimental PhD, I found myself taking a greater interest in learning and teaching and the process of educating students. After some time focused solely on teaching, I wanted to answer certain questions that were emerging from my own practice as an educator. I wanted to know how to better engage with students, and how engagement and attendance (for instance) were linked. However, as I started to venture down this path, I maintained a particular approach to how I might investigate these questions.

My first publication in the education space was a conference paper looking at how attendance and engagement were correlated (Cowling, 2012). Rather than interviewing students or taking a survey, I fell back on my research training and decided to look at data relating to the attendance of the students. Using Excel and other statistical modelling tools, I sought to analyse correlations and cross-tabulations in the data, using this to make my conclusions. The paper was well received, especially by the Dean of Business and Informatics at the time, who had a background as a statistician. But my research did not look to the core of the issue, but rather, it looked at a pattern among the numbers to explain student motivation, which influenced the conclusions I was able to draw.

My second attempt to move into this space was with a colleague, looking at the use of Twitter as a mechanism to increase feedback in the classroom (Cowling & Novak, 2012). By this stage, I was starting to realise that pedagogy was more important than technology, so the project was initially driven by a desire to increase feedback from "shy" students and then bolster their feedback with the technology (in this case Twitter). Although we conducted a survey with all students, the way the data was analysed was predominantly statistical, with reporting on the percentages for each student on each question and very few open-ended rich qualitative questions. And again, although the results were interesting, we were struggling to get to the underlying motivations of the students.

Upon completion of this project I felt I had made a contribution to knowledge, but had not really reached the core of what actually made students want to use technology in the classroom. It was at this stage that I finally realised that perhaps I was not asking the right questions. My research knowledge was more limited than I realised, and if I was going to make a contribution in this space I would have to broaden my knowledge so I could really start to consider student motivation and other factors. This is consistent with the transformative learning theory as described by Cranton (2002), which discusses how an event (such as my completion of the Twitter project) can show an individual that they hold a limited or distorted view. Through the application of what Cranton (2002) outlines as emancipatory knowledge, this event allows the individual to critically analyse their views and potentially transform how they make meaning of the world. The next section discusses this critical event and the ramifications to my work.

EDUCATING THE TECHNOLOGIST ABOUT EPISTEMOLOGY

Unfortunately, pursuing a positivist approach for education research can only take a researcher so far. I discovered this in my own work after several attempts to apply a positivist approach to education technology work, but subsequently found that I was not getting to heart of the real questions I wanted to ask. This is because if the research approach involves individuals and qualitative data, then the methodology has to change, resulting in a change to the basic epistemology used. For instance, if grounded theory is used as a methodology, then Crotty (1998) suggests that theory is more appropriately placed in the broader concept of interpretivism, specifically symbolic interactionism. He then links this theoretical perspective (in Crotty parlance) with the broader epistemology of constructionism, which is the view that objects do not have meaning on their own (as in objectivism) but instead are assigned meaning contingent on human practice and in their interaction with us as human beings. This is in stark contrast to my previously positivist leanings and quite a change in "head space".

The critical event that occurred for me, in line with the work by Cranton (2002) on transformative learning theory, was the realisation that I needed to make the change outlined above, understanding that my epistemology was just one of many and that there were other views of the world. I quickly realised that this would require analysis of not only my own epistemology, but also how that linked to the other facets of the Crotty (1998) model that I was using (theoretical perspective, methodology, method) to answer my research questions. I decided that I would investigate interpretivism as a mechanism to widen my epistemology and hence my theoretical perspective and other aspects. This is supported in the literature, with Chinn et al. (2011) arguing that epistemological perceptions must be broadened to help with cognition. In fact, looking at the literature, the use of interpretivism appears to be a common way to approach research design in education and educational technology (O'donoghue, 2006).

Through this new understanding of a different view on research design, I was able to approach my research questions with a new lens. Rather than looking to analyse data, I was able to take a more nuanced approach to how students experienced technology in the classroom and how their thoughts and feelings with technology might affect their acceptance of it, especially as they relate to the ability of the technology to become a part of the classroom rather than a "bolt on".

The beginnings of this change in epistemology can be seen in papers I published after this critical event, such as the paper I wrote at the end of 2014 that looked at models for the integration of social networking into the fabric of the classroom (Cowling, 2014). However, other work I was involved in continued to be dominated by the positivist approach. Working with colleagues, or with PhD students, or simply on existing projects, I found that my newfound epistemology could not always apply, and that I was instead forced to adopt a positivist approach.

And I found that, rather than being distressed by this, I was excited, because in some cases positivist work was more appropriate, and I was still steeped in this epistemology, despite the changes that my journey had wrought. So, in what could be framed as a second critical event, I began to ask myself, was Crotty (1998) perhaps too narrow and was it possible to have a wider, multi-epistemological view of the world, depending on the research question being asked? The following section discusses this final critical question in more detail.

DEVELOPING A MORE COMPREHENSIVE PERSONAL EPISTEMOLOGY

Crotty (1998) defines epistemology as your own personal theory of knowledge. Extending from this definition, it is perhaps reasonable to assume that each person can only have a single viewpoint on this theory. Through my journey, however, I discovered that it was possible to have multiple viewpoints depending on the situation, with my position in life now supporting both a positivist viewpoint as well as an interpretivist viewpoint, depending on the research that I was doing.

There are comments in the literature that support this idea of multiple viewpoints. Hofer and Bendixen (2012) argue for a personal epistemology that places each individual on a spectrum, choosing from a range of different ideas to fit them into a space as more positivist or interpretivist. However, the work by Hofer and Bendixen (2012) suggests that this spectrum is immutable and that a personal epistemology is unlikely to change, a fact that my own experience disputes. Similarly, work by Muis, Bendixen and Haerle (2006) outlines the domain specific and domain general epistemologies for different disciplines, using empirical studies as a guide. However, it also assumes that these domains are immutable and that a particular discipline will always have a particular epistemology and that researchers within that area will maintain a consistent (and myopic) set of beliefs.

Having said this, there is work in the literature that suggests that change is possible, even if that change is a one-time event. For instance, work by Howard, McGee, Schwartz and Purcell (2000) looked at how the epistemology of teachers could be changed through the application of constructivist training techniques to allow a great appreciation of the use of ICT. And work by Pintrich, Marx and Boyle (1993) represents an example of a body of work that looks at a one-time conceptual change in students as a result of the study process. However, in both cases, this change is not represented to be fluid, but, instead, a work of time and context that is then irreversible.

Rather, using this work on personal epistemology as a guide, combined with my own experience, I have come to the conclusion that a single viewpoint of epistemology may not be appropriate. This is because different research asks different questions—and so requires different theories of knowledge and different types of thinking. Rather than having a single epistemology, or a single chance to change epistemologies throughout their lifetime (moving along the spectrum outlined by Hofer and Bendixen [2012]), a researcher should perhaps instead have a selection of different epistemologies depending on the research question that they wish to answer.

Of course, this can be hard work—I originally ventured into the technology field because I have a leaning towards the view that everything is scientific and determined by objects (positivism). However, if I wish to investigate questions outside of this worldview, then I need to acknowledge that Education and exploring my area requires a shift—towards recognising that the way of the world is determined by the way we look at it (interpretivism). It is only by making this shift that I can answer the research questions that I need to answer as an educational technologist.

Perhaps my experience demonstrates that the original model by Crotty (1998) needs to be extended. Whilst the key components can remain, it should be acknowledged that there is a spectrum of epistemologies from which a researcher can draw, and that attaching oneself to one epistemology does not necessarily remove one from pursuing other epistemologies, depending on the research question that is being asked. Rather than a myopic view, perhaps the Crotty (1998) table should be seen as a toolbox from which researchers can select different epistemologies (and hence frameworks, methodologies and methods) as they seek to answer different questions, potentially arising from different disciplines. The key then becomes to equip researchers with these tools through careful training, alerting them to the toolbox that is available rather than slotting them into a particular epistemology based on their discipline. For my own work, this would have made the transition described above much smoother, as I moved from a technology researcher to an education researcher.

CONCLUSION

Research is a complex endeavour. Regardless of the work that we are doing, the design of your research and the choice of questions you answer can be complex. Even worse, my own personal case demonstrates that, whilst a researcher can become an expert in their field, this does not mean that they have the breadth of research design experience to be a researcher in any other field and, in some cases (particularly with positivist work), may not even realise that the field of research design is wider than they think.

Sources such as Crotty (1998) can give us some greater insight into this process of research design and the epistemologies, theoretical frameworks, methodologies and methods that exist within different types of research. However, even they can be simplistic, assuming that a researcher will follow a single line, have a single epistemology and way of thinking. In my case as a researcher, whilst this was the case initially, a change in focus led to a need to change my research approach, with a critical event occurring when I finally realised that this was the case.

Through resources such as Crotty (1998), I was able to change my epistemology, but then realised that I would still need to embrace my original epistemology in some cases. Rather than moving from one box to another, I expanded my viewpoint to include multiple different epistemologies. The research work on personal epistemology gave me some guidance in this area, but left me wondering how it all fit with Crotty's (1998) original ideas.

I finally came to the conclusion, through another critical event, that each of us can move within the spectrum of epistemology. Rather than selecting a side, we can choose a place to begin in the spectrum, but positioning ourselves to move around depending on the research questions we need to answer. It is through this that we can make the methodological manoeuvres required to become diverse, well-balanced researchers, developing a toolbox of different epistemologies for different situations. In the world of education technology research, this is important to allow us to bridge the gap between technology and education.

REFERENCES

Bryman, A. (2012). *Social research methods.* Oxford: Oxford University Press.

Chinn, C. A., Buckland, L. A., & Samarapungavan, A. L. A. (2011). Expanding the dimensions of epistemic cognition: Arguments from philosophy and psychology. *Educational Psychologist, 46*(3), 141–167.

Cranton, P. (2002). Teaching for transformation. *New Directions for Adult and Continuing Education, 2002*(93), 63–72.

Crotty, M. (1998). *The foundations of social research.* Crows Nest, NSW: Allen & Unwin.

Cowling, M., & Sitte, R. (2003). Comparison of techniques for environmental sound recognition. *Pattern Recognition Letters, 24*(15), 2895–2907.

Cowling, M. A. (2012). Student attendance as a measure of academic success. *Proceedings of Hawaii International Conference on Education,* Hawaii, USA, 5–8 January.

Cowling, M. A. (2014). Models for the successful integration of social networking into the studies of digital native students. *Proceedings of ISANA International Education Association 25th Annual Conference,* Adelaide, SA, 2–5 December.

Cowling, M. A., & Novak, J., (2012). Tweet the teacher: Using Twitter as a mechanism to increase classroom engagement. *Proceedings of ISANA International Education Association 23rd Annual Conference,* Auckland, NZ, 4–7 December.

Hofer, B. K., & Bendixen, L. D. (2012). Personal epistemology: Theory, research, and future directions. In K. Harris, S. Graham, & T. Urdan (Eds.), *APA educational psychology handbook, Vol. 1, Theories, constructs, and critical issues* (pp. 227–256). Washington, DC: American Psychological Association.

Howard, B. C., McGee, S., Schwartz, N., & Purcell, S. (2000). The experience of constructivism: Transforming teacher epistemology. *Journal of Research on Computing in Education, 32*(4), 455–465.

Moore, D. (2004). *The basic practice of statistics* (3rd ed.). New York: W.H. Freeman and Company.

Muijs, D. (2010). *Doing quantitative research in education with SPSS.* Thousand Oaks, CA: Sage.

Muis, K. R., Bendixen, L. D., & Haerle, F. C. (2006). Domain-generality and domain-specificity in personal epistemology research: Philosophical and empirical reflections in the development of a theoretical framework. *Educational Psychology Review, 18*(1), 3–54.

Myers, M. D. (2015). Qualitative research in information systems. *MIS Quarterly* (21:2), June 1997, pp. 241–242. *MISQ Discovery*, archival version, June 1997, http://www.misq.org/supplements/. *Association for Information Systems* (*AISWorld*) *Section on Qualitative Research in Information Systems*, updated version, last modified: April 13, 2015, www.qual.auckland.ac.nz

O'donoghue, T. (2006). *Planning your qualitative research project: An introduction to interpretivist research in education.* London: Routledge.

Pintrich, P. R., Marx, R. W., & Boyle, R. A. (1993). Beyond cold conceptual change: The role of motivational beliefs and classroom contextual factors in the process of conceptual change. *Review of Educational Research, 63*(2), 167–199.

Sinatra, G. M., & Chinn, C. A. (2012). Thinking and reasoning in science: Promoting epistemic conceptual change. In K. R. Harris, S. Graham, T. Urdan, A. G. Bus, S. Major, & H. L. Swanson (Eds.), *APA educational psychology handbook, Vol. 3: Application to learning and teaching.*, (pp. 257–282). Washington, DC, US: American Psychological Association, viii, 668 pp. (pp. 257–282). Washington, DC: American Psychological Association. http://doi:10.1037/13275-011 [pp. viii, 668].

Weiers, R. (2008). *Introduction to business statistics* (6th ed.). Ohio: Cengage Learning.

CHAPTER 5

A Bricoleur Approach to Navigating the Methodological Maze

Reyna Zipf

INTRODUCTION

For the novice researcher, navigating through the myriad constructs of research processes is akin to finding your way through a maze constructed of tall hedges. At first, all pathways look similar, some appear to provide a shortcut or easy way out, while others appear convoluted with twists and constant switchbacks. Sometimes you feel you are lost, wandering in the maze. Eventually though you find your way out of the maze, but only after exploring many pathways, some dead ends and occasionally cutting a hole in the hedge to join two previously separate pathways together. During my doctoral journey I found myself trapped in the methodological maze. I was researching a nebulous and esoteric concept that had as many definitions as misconceptions. The problem I faced was finding a methodological pathway through the maze to an elusive destination outside the maze. My solution came in the form of a *bricoleur* approach to my research. The bricoleur uses whatever is at hand to complete a task. The researcher-as-bricoleur uses 'whatever strategies, methods, or empirical materials ... are

R. Zipf (✉)
School of Education and the Arts, CQUniversity Australia,
Rockhampton, QLD, Australia

© The Author(s) 2016
B. Harreveld et al. (eds.), *Constructing Methodology for Qualitative Research*, DOI 10.1057/978-1-137-59943-8_5

59

at hand' (p. 3) to produce a bricolage, a construction whose pieces harmonise and fit together to make a cohesive whole. As a bricoleur I could take advantage of serendipitous opportunities to further the research goals. The researcher-as-*bricoleur* stance enabled me to manoeuvre between and through pathways in the methodological maze and make meaning for my research project; it was the tool by which I cut holes and joined pathways in the maze hedge.

This chapter has two purposes. The first is to take you on a tour of the methodological travels that led me to a bricoleur approach and the second is to empower you to find your own approach to navigating the methodological maze for your research.

The chapter discusses how a *bricoleur* approach enabled a nebulous concept, creativity, to be researched in a complex setting, secondary school science lessons. The journey I travelled to arrive at a *bricoleur* stance is presented and the methodology critiqued. I begin at the start of my methodological travels, entering the maze. My travels in the maze are then discussed. Next, how I emerged from the maze and arrived at my methodological destination is outlined. I conclude by discussing the notion of a researcher-as-*bricoleur*, and what it offers the qualitative researcher.

ENTERING THE MAZE—*RISKY BUSINESS*

Entering the methodological maze is risky business whether you are an experienced researcher or a novice. For the experienced researcher there is the temptation to resort to what you know and have done in the past. To try something different increases the risk of 'failure' and creates unknowns that will need to be dealt with. Although failure is inexplicitly linked with learning and innovation (Lundin, 2009), the experienced researcher is often reluctant to let go of the known and try new ways. New ways can be risky business.

For the novice researcher confronted with a plethora of new terms and methodologies, the risks are both personal and professional. Personal risk stems from fear of appearing lacking if not conversant with the language that is methodology. Fear of being revealed as an imposter in the world of 'real' researchers keeps the novice silent when they have questions aplenty about methodology. The novice can mistakenly think everyone else 'gets it.' Seeking elucidation from supervisors is risking the self.

Professional risk for the novice stems from fear of getting it wrong, that is choosing a methodology that does not 'work.' This positivist perspective of methodology shaped my initial forays into the literature. I believed there was one correct way of conducting my research and I had to find it, get it right, or the research project would be a disaster. Melodramatic maybe, but the fear of failure was very real at the time. For both personal and professional reasons entering the methodological maze is risky business for the novice researcher.

INSIDE THE MAZE: *NAVIGATING YOUR WAY*

Once inside the methodological maze you are not initially navigating your way through, rather you are exploring the maze. This exploration was for me an important foundation for developing the skills and knowledge to be able to later navigate through the methodological maze. Time constraints, inevitable in any research project, eventually put a stop to exploration and force you to navigate a way forward. To assist the navigation process I adopted Denzin and Lincoln's (2000) five phases of research activity below and used them as a roadmap with which to navigate through the methodological maze.

Phase 1—the researcher as a multicultural subject

Phase 2—theoretical paradigms and perspectives within which the research is situated

Phase 3—research design and strategy

Phase 4—methods of data collection and analysis

Phase 5—interpretation, presentation and criteria for judging creditability of findings

When entering the methodological maze there is a tendency to take off down one pathway, and commit to quantitative, qualitative or mixed method. The decision about which path to follow appears, at first encounter, straightforward. Yet, the decision is saturated with pre-existing values and perspectives about what constitutes 'good' research. Research is immersed in values; some readily apparent and easily acknowledged, others so deeply held they are invisible (Denzin & Lincoln, 2005). While travelling down the chosen paradigmatic pathway, doubts arise which lead to reflection and raise the question, why quantitative, why qualitative or why mixed method. The question forces you to retrace your steps to the beginning of the maze. You are back at Denzin and Lincoln's (2000) Phase 1. I realised that my study was value-laden. It took account of the views, values and perspectives of researcher and participant. This was problematic and the first step to dealing with it was to understand my position as a multicultural subject in the research.

Now I was ready to move onto Phase 2 and consider theoretical paradigms. When designing a research methodology, decisions concerning theoretical paradigms are essentially about the nature of the research; is it quantitative, qualitative or does it have features of both? The decision is a subjective one based on researcher interpretation and judgement and requires consideration of the nature of the research and its goal. The type of research you intend and its purpose underpin paradigm decisions. I found further exploration into research type and purpose was useful at this point. I considered the following research types.

Descriptive—How are things now?

Historical—How were things then?

Experimental—What would happen if …?

Correlational—What is the relationship between … and …?

Developmental—How has … changed over time?

Examination of research types enabled me to see that my research was concerned with 'description' and 'correlation.' I went back to my initial research questions and interrogated them as to their purpose and usefulness. The research questions that eventually guided the project were:

1. Why is creativity important in science education? (*Significance*)
2. What are the nature and characteristics of creativity in science education? (*Definitional*)
3. How do secondary science teachers perceive that creativity can be promoted in secondary school science? (*Pedagogical*)
4. What are the challenges secondary science teachers' perceive to implementing a creativity-focused science education in secondary schools? (*Contextual*)

Including the research purpose in italics focused attention on the goal of each question. Such focusing helped shape and consolidate the research direction. The research questions, and their italicised purpose, acted as a set of directions. I recommended navigating through the maze.

Having decided upon qualitative research, attention now turned to Denzin and Lincoln's (2000) Phase 3. Qualitative research has many paradigms with both distinct and overlapping characteristics. Major paradigms include positivism, post-positivism, critical theory, constructivism and participatory views. To navigate through the paradigms I drew flowcharts teasing out characteristics of each. Understanding the evolutionary nature of qualitative research allowed reconciliation of the blurred boundaries I found between methodologies. The evolutionary trail also led me to the notion of researcher-as-*bricoleur*. Denzin and Lincoln (1998) claimed that 'The multiple methodologies of qualitative research may be viewed as a bricolage, and the researcher-as-*bricoleur*' (p. 3). The notion of a bricoleur appealed as it embraced eclecticism and that would be advantageous for research where it would not always be possible to predict what was going to happen. A researcher-as-*bricoleur* draws from 'whatever strategies, methods, or empirical materials ... are at hand' (p. 3) to produce a bricolage, a construction in which pieces harmonise and fit together to make a cohesive whole. As a *bricoleur* I could take advantage of the blurring of disciplinary boundaries between paradigms.

My decision to adopt a bricoleur approach was a deliberate one. It was my navigational tool. The path for my research, indeed any research, is obscure. My research was eclectic, data sources were diverse, the location was complex, and participant actions and thoughts were neither pre-ordered nor clear-cut. A bricoleur stance enabled me to take advantage of miscellaneous and ephemeral instances, and hence was a legitimate approach. It was essentially a pragmatic approach that ensured I was not constrained by the very process designed to further the research goals. A bricoleur stance enabled me to navigate the various pathways throughout the maze and where necessary create a hole in the maze hedge to join two or more previously separate pathways.

The hole in the maze hedge I cut created a pathway between case study, phenomenology and grounded theory. The research was essentially a qualitative case study (Yin, 2003) that drew on the essences of phenomenology (Cohen et al., 2007) and the techniques and reasoning of grounded theory (Cohen et al., 2007) to further the research agenda. Case study can readily alloy to other qualitative strategies to form a blended strategy. An alloy is composed of a main ingredient combined with other elements depending on the attributes desired in the final product. Using the metaphor of a metal alloy, case study is the main ingredient of the methodology and phenomenology and grounded theory form the minor elements. Neither phenomenology nor grounded theory is used in its purist form. This approach, which I called grounded phenomenological case study, used the essences of phenomenology and grounded theory methods to describe and understand the phenomenon of creativity in secondary school science. Figure 5.1 depicts the approach using the alloy metaphor.

Case study
(Basis of the alloy)

Phenomenology
(Contributes focus on essences)

Grounded theory
*(Contributes focus on theory
emerging from data)*

Grounded, phenomenological case study
(New alloy with added strengths)

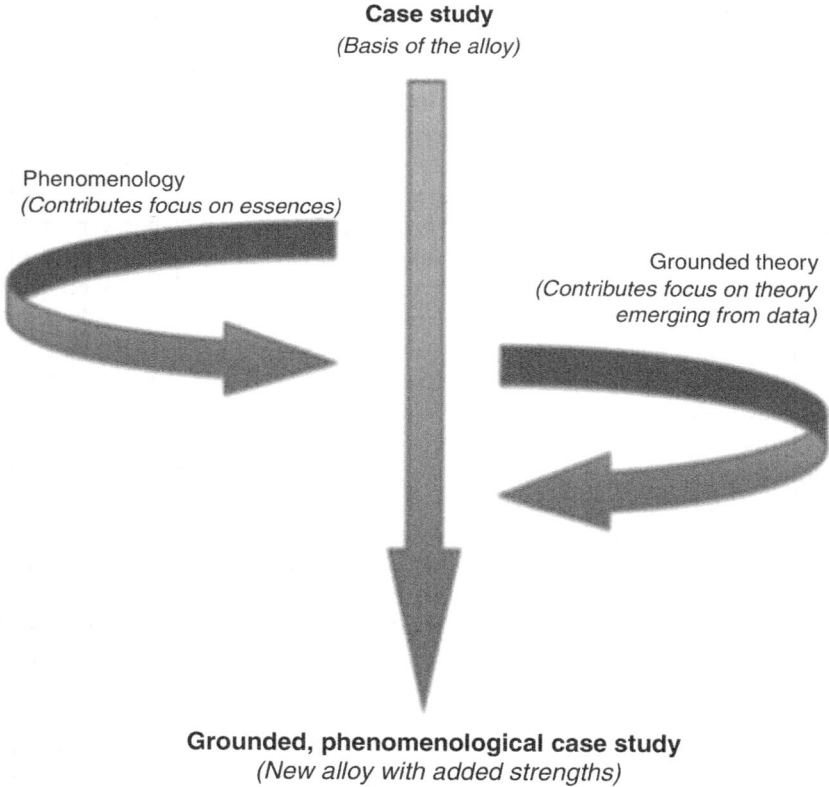

Fig. 5.1   Graphic of research strategy

Grounded, phenomenological case study was used opportunistically as befitted a bricoleur stance. The blend of methods carried the caveat that flexibility was intrinsic to the approach to enable unexpected opportunities that furthered the research goal to be acted upon. This was crucial to Phase 4 of the research process (Denzin & Lincoln, 2000), determining methods of data collection and analysis. A bricoleur approach allowed planning for, and expecting, the unexpected with data collection. I had navigated my way through the methodological maze, albeit by joining previously separate paths, but I was not out of it yet!

EMERGING FROM THE MAZE: *NEGOTIATION WITH SELF*

Emerging from the methodological maze requires negotiation with self. This is the province of Denzin and Lincoln's fifth phase of the research process, the interpretation, presentation and criteria for judging creditability of findings. I realised that judging the worth of my research strategy was my concern. It was not about my supervisor or an examiner judging the research strategy, but it was about negotiating with myself and what I would accept as credible and valid. I had to first justify the methodological pathway I had taken to myself, and that entailed examining deeply held axioms and holding them up for critique and negotiation. Blended methods have mixed popularity among qualitative researchers and reading the literature pulls you in different directions. Once I accepted that a grounded, phenomenological case study was permissible I could then construct an argument, and a defence, for it.

Negotiating Case Study

I start with the contribution of case study to the 'alloy.' Case study has been variously described as a process, an object or an end product. Part of emerging from the methodological maze was negotiating that in this research case study was going to be both a strategy and an object for study. My case study was a 'process' as it would be concerned with investigating a specific phenomenon, creativity, in its real-life context—secondary science lessons. Cohen et al.'s (2007) definition of case study as an 'investigation into a specific instance or phenomenon in its real-life context' (p. 170) lent support. Merriam (2009) argued that if the boundaries of the phenomenon being studied cannot be defined, it was not a case. Again negotiation with self was called for. I resolved that this study was bounded by its focus on creativity in secondary school science. Creswell (2007) described case study as both an approach and an object. This aligned with the intent of my research strategy and lent further support.

Case study has characteristics that both distinguish it and allow it to work in harmony with other strategies. The focus on vivid description of events and the narrative approach aligned with phenomenological goals of exploring the meaning of participants' lived experiences around creativity. Case study blends description and analysis of a phenomenon in its real-life context by using multiple evidence sources about the 'case' (Yin, 2003) and this was important in order to get to the essence of creativity in secondary school science. Focus on description and analysis was crucial, as the research questions required both description and interpretation to be resolved (Robson, 2002). Case study research is, by nature, 'richly descriptive, because it is grounded in deep and varied sources of information' (Hancock & Algozzine, 2006, p. 16). It provided the flexibility I desired for data collection. Case study 'employs quotes of key participants, anecdotes, prose composed from interviews ... that bring to life the complexity of the many variables inherent in the phenomenon being studied' (Hancock & Algozzine, 2006, p. 16). This was an additional reason for choosing it.

Case study is 'strong on reality' (Cohen et al., 2007, p. 256). Focus on the 'reality' of teaching for student creativity in science lessons and describing these instances was crucial. Case study allows theories and concepts to constantly evolve and this would facilitate a realistic representation of educational phenomena (Robson, 2002). In addition, case study is exegetic and iterative, which made it ideal for understanding and capturing the nature and complexity of teaching for student creativity in science lessons.

Case study is not without weaknesses and the acceptance and willingness to work with these weaknesses is part of negotiation with self. Data results may not be generalisable, issues with cross-checking can arise, and every step of the research process is open to bias. As Cohen et al. (2007) stated, case study is 'prone to problems of observer bias, despite attempts made to address reflexivity' (p. 256). It is close, subjective and descriptive and the integral involvement of the researcher means that a distant, objective stance is not feasible or desirable (Hancock & Algozzine, 2006). How you deal with these issues forms part of the process of negotiation with self.

Case study research offered a valuable methodological tool for understanding and adding to knowledge about creativity in secondary school science. I accepted its limitations, and dealt with them as the insights it provided into the research problem justified its use. I had successfully negotiated the adoption of case study with self. The negotiation of phenomenology to the grounded phenomenological case study 'alloy' is now explained.

Negotiating Phenomenology

I negotiated the use of phenomenology to lend emphasis to the lived experiences of participants and their interpretation. The purpose of phenomenology is describing and understanding 'the essence of lived experiences of individuals who have experienced a particular phenomenon' (Lichtman, 2010, p. 75). I negotiated that in this study, the phenomenon was creativity in secondary school science, and the focus was the essence of teacher pedagogies that promoted creative thinking by secondary school students. Phenomenology involves 'moving from very specific and detailed statements about the phenomenon, or even examples of the phenomenon, ultimately to the essence of the phenomenon' (Lichtman, 2010, p. 77). I anticipated that opportunities for student creativity in science lessons might share essences, and negotiated that the research task would involve describing the essence of science lessons that promoted student creativity.

Phenomenologists attempt to suspend beliefs and assumptions about the phenomenon under study to avoid preconceptions influencing determination of the essences (Merriam, 2009). Although believed critical to seeing the experience for what it is, I acknowledged that researchers are inescapably part of the world they are researching and participants' thoughts and actions change in response to our presence (Cohen et al., 2007). Suspension of beliefs and assumptions implied at an aloof stance that was not consistent with my positioning as a researcher. Again, negotiation with self was required. I negotiated that being aware of my beliefs and assumptions was feasible, and consistent with the dialogic relationship (Cohen et al., 2007) aimed for. My goal was to determine the essences of science lessons that involved creative thinking opportunities for students. I believed acknowledging, and seeking to understand, my part in the research, rather than trying to eliminate preconceptions from my interactions would achieve this.

The contribution of phenomenology to the case study alloy was the focus on the essences of pedagogies that develop and nurture student creativity in secondary school science. Having negotiated the role of phenomenology, I will now focus on negotiating the contribution of grounded theory to the case study methodology.

Negotiating Grounded Theory

Grounded theory is a 'qualitative research approach from which theories may emerge' (Lichtman, 2010, p. 244). It emphasises theoretical sampling and the use of open, axial and selective coding techniques (Lichtman, 2010). Grounded theory allows the theory that explains the phenomena to emerge from the data and be derived inductively (Cohen et al., 2007; Hancock & Algozzine, 2006). I negotiated the addition of grounded theory to my phenomenological case study as the study was not testing a pre-set theory; data would be collected and then theory derived through inductive reasoning (Cohen et al., 2007).

Grounded theory aims at increasing complexity through inclusion of context rather than distilling down (Flick, 2009). In common with case study, it embraces multiple data sources in order to identify the relationships between concepts (Corbin & Strauss, 2008).

My negotiation with self was premised on the view that grounded theory had more points in common with case study and phenomenology than points of difference and it had much to offer the purposes of the study. Uppermost being that in common with case study and phenomenology, grounded theory offered the promise of arriving at what was relevant without loss of complexity. Grounded theory must align comfortably with the research and the researcher as it requires a 'tolerance and openness to data' (Cohen et al., 2007, p. 492). The researcher must be open-minded with regard to data and theory generation and be prepared to accept, if not embrace, changing emergent categories (Cohen et al., 2007) and this resonated with the bricoleur stance I had taken.

Coding and constant comparison techniques of grounded theory promised a systematic approach to data analysis I was unable to resist. Coding enabled like themes in the data to be identified, retrieved and compared to further understanding of the phenomenon (Cohen et al., 2007). Constant comparison between data sources would further determination of disconfirming cases, an important step in the illumination of creativity. As creativity is such a nebulous concept, determining 'what it is not' was going to be as important as determining 'what it was.'

I was aware that Glaser (2004) argued strongly that grounded theory should not be combined with other qualitative data analysis methodologies. Glaser believed that mixing other qualitative methodologies with grounded theory had 'the effect of downgrading and eroding the GT goal of conceptual theory' (p. 2). Indeed, Glaser criticised Morse (1994) for her 'phenomenological grounded theory' approach and maintained that classic grounded theory was not the same as 'piecemeal' combinations of grounded theory and qualitative methods. I negotiated that this would not be a classic grounded theory methodology as espoused by Glaser. It would be a case study strengthened and enhanced by the contribution of grounded theory techniques and reasoning. Drawing on my science background to construct the metaphor of an alloy that explained the blended research strategy enabled successful negotiation of my methodology with self and I could now move forwards.

Arriving at Your Destination: Researcher-as-*Bricoleur*

A bricoleur approach had enabled me to arrive at my methodological desti-nation: case study combined with the essence of both phenomenology and grounded theory methods. A bricoleur is 'a person who can skillfully and professionally complete a range of different tasks' (Wicks, 2010, p. 60). The researcher-as-*bricoleur* draws from 'whatever strategies, methods, or empirical materials … are at hand' (Denzin & Lincoln, 1998, p. 3) to pro-duce a bricolage, a construction whose pieces harmonise and fit together to make a cohesive whole. As a *bricoleur* I was able to take advantage of the blurring of disciplinary boundaries between paradigms to further my research aims. Bradley (2014) claimed that a bricoleur does not know where they are going or where they will end up, but they do produce a *bricolage* in the end. Adopting a bricoleur stance was not a 'whatever goes' approach for me, it is a deliberate decision and required knowledge and understanding of the range of methodological options available to the qualitative researcher. As a *bricoleur*, I could negotiate the justification of grounded phenomenological case study.

The metaphor of a metal alloy and the researcher-as-*bricoleur* picking and choosing whatever was required to progress the research was apt. Case study was the main ingredient in the methodological alloy. Phenomenology and grounded theory played a minor part, but their inclusion strength-ened the overall research strategy through the properties they brought to the blend. The job of the bricoleur was to monitor and adjust, where necessary, the balance of the ingredients for the methodological alloy so that the research aims could be realised. As Kincheloe (2004) noted, a bricoleur had to be prepared to learn from failure and adapt and change in response. King (2009) defined creativity as 'the ability to see beyond the obvious, shift perspectives, and explore ideas in new ways' (n.p.). In keep-ing with the subject of my study, grounded phenomenological case study was a research strategy designed to see beyond the obvious and explore creativity in secondary school science in a new way.

Whilst there are communal understandings between some para-digms, there are also axioms that are not shared (Lichtman, 2010). The researcher-as-bricoleur must be familiar with all paradigms in order to draw from them without compromising the creditability and cohesiveness of the research (Denzin & Lincoln, 2005). Cohen et al.'s (2007) notion of 'fitness for purpose' (p. 71) guided methodological decisions. There

is a plethora of data collection and interpretive activities for the methodological bricoleur to draw from. With choice comes decisions and taking
a bricoleur stance necessitates being 'adept at performing a large number
of diverse tasks, ranging from interviewing to intensive self-reflection and
introspection' (Denzin & Lincoln, 2000, p. 6). A bricoleur stance demands
the researcher judges which research activities are most suitable and fit,
and will progress the research purpose (Kincheloe, 2004; Lévi-Strauss,
1962/1966). Kincheloe (2004) aptly coined the researcher-as-*bricoleur*
as a methodological negotiator, one who is committed to eclecticism of
methodological tools. I would add that they are also a methodological
navigator and explorer.

CONCLUSION

Methodology is ultimately based on, and derived from, paradigms; equally
'paradigms have implications for methods' (Punch, 2009, p. 16). This
chapter has described the methodological journal I travelled during my
doctoral study. How I navigated and negotiated a path through the methodological maze is explained. Key to navigating through the methodological maze was the adoption of Denzin and Lincoln's (2000) five phases of
research activity as a roadmap to the maze. Central to negotiation of the
methodology was the researcher-as-*bricoleur* stance I adopted. A bricoleur
stance enabled the research strategy, grounded phenomenological case
study, to be negotiated and justified. Using the metaphor of a metal alloy
aided the blended strategy to be explained from a bricoleur standpoint.
Case study was the main ingredient of the alloy with phenomenology and
grounded theory contributing desirable traits that would strengthen the
metal alloy and make it fit for the research purpose. Denzin and Lincoln
(1998) claimed that 'The multiple methodologies of qualitative research
may be viewed as a bricolage, and the researcher-as-*bricoleur*' (p. 3). I used
a bricoleur approach to create new pathways in the methodological maze,
which enabled me to reach my methodological destination, grounded
phenomenological case study.

The approach to navigating through the methodological maze presented in this chapter is based on the author's own experiences and as such
depicts the end destination for my journey. A bricoleur approach facilitated my methodological journey allowing me to navigate and negotiate
my way to a methodological destination that I believed would progress
the research questions. Your journey will have similarities and differences

to mine. Navigating through the methodological maze requires courage. Arriving at a methodological destination requires methodological negotiation. The journey's end sees the methodological navigator and negotiator arrive.

References

Bradley, G. (2014, June). Six characters in search of an author: A qualitative comedy in the making. Qualitative Inquiry, 20(5), 659–667.

Cohen, L., Manion, L., & Morrison, K. (2007). *Research methods in education* (6th ed.). London, UK: Routledge.

Corbin, J., & Strauss, A. (2008). *Basics of qualitative research: Techniques and procedures for developing grounded theory* (3rd ed.). Thousand Oaks, CA: Sage.

Creswell, J. W. (2007). *Qualitative inquiry and research method: Choosing among five approaches* (2nd ed.). Thousand Oaks, CA: Sage.

Denzin, N. K., & Lincoln, Y. S. (1998). Entering the field of qualitative research. In N. Denzin & Y. Lincoln (Eds.), *The landscape of qualitative research: Theories and issues.* Thousand Oaks, CA: Sage.

Denzin, N. K., & Lincoln, Y. S. (2000). The discipline and practice of qualitative research. In N. Denzin & Y. Lincoln (Eds.), *Handbook of qualitative research* (2nd ed.). Thousand Oaks, CA: Sage.

Denzin, N. K., & Lincoln, Y. S. (Eds.) (2005). *The SAGE handbook of qualitative research* (3rd ed.). Thousand Oaks, CA: Sage.

Flick, U. (2009). *An introduction to qualitative research* (4th ed.). Thousand Oaks, CA: Sage.

Glaser, B. G. with the assistance of Judith Holton (2004). *Remodelling grounded theory.* Forum Qualitative Sozialforschung/Forum: Qualitative Social Research, 5(2), Art. 4. Retrieved on January 28, 2011, from http://www.qualitative-research.net/index.php/fqs/article/viewArticle/607/1315

Hancock, D. R., & Algozzine, R. (2006). *Doing case study research: A practical guide for beginning researchers.* New York: Teachers College Press.

Kincheloe, J. (2004). Introduction: The power of the bricolage: Expanding research methods. In J. Kincheloe & K. Berry (Eds.), *Rigour and complexity in educational research: Conceptualizing the bricolage* (pp. 1–22). Maidenhead, UK: Open University Press.

King, J. (2009). *The code of authentic living: Cellular wisdom.* Fort Collins, CO: Beyond Success LLC.

Lévi-Strauss, C. (1962/1966). *The savage mind.* Chicago, CA: University of Chicago Press.

Lichtman, M. (2010). *Qualitative research in education: A user's guide* (2nd ed.). Thousand Oaks, CA: Sage.

Lundin, S. C. (2009). *CATS: The nine lives of innovation* (2nd ed.). Springhill, QLD: Management Press.

Merriam, S. B. (2009). *Qualitative research: A guide to design and implementation*. San Francisco, CA: Jossey-Bass.

Morse, J. (1994). "Emerging from the data." Cognitive processes of analysis in qualitative research. In J. Morse (Ed.), Critical issues in qualitative research methods (pp. 23–41). Thousand Oaks, CA: Sage.

Punch, K. F. (2009). *Introduction to research methods in education*. Thousand Oaks, CA: Sage.

Robson, C. (2002). *Real world research* (2nd ed.). Oxford, UK: Blackwell.

Wicks, D. (2010). Bricoleur. In A. J. Mills, G. Durepos, & E. Wiebe (Eds.), *Encyclopedia of case study research* (pp. 60–61). Thousand Oaks, CA: Sage. doi:10.4135/9781412957397.n25.

Yin, R. K. (2003). *Applications of case study research* (2nd ed.). Thousand Oaks, CA: Sage.

Manoeuvring Through the Maze of Methodology: Constructing the Research-Ready Embodied RHD Student

Teresa Moore

INTRODUCTION

Teaching research methodologies is both a joy and a challenge. Big words such as epistemology, ontology, axiology and methodology can paralyse the novice researcher who just wants to do the project, run some numbers and see their findings change the world. Introducing students to the conceptual and abstract nature of qualitative methodologies broadens the intellectual landscape for both novice and experienced researchers to think differently and become intimately part of their research project. Some of these students are manoeuvring new pathways and epistemological understandings, while others are manoeuvring the maze of methodological choice previously unknown. The purpose of the chapter is twofold: firstly to interrogate my own practice as both a supervisor of Research Higher

T. Moore (✉)
School of Education and the Arts, CQUniversity Australia,
Rockhampton, QLD, Australia

© The Author(s) 2016
B. Harreveld et al. (eds.), *Constructing Methodology for Qualitative Research*, DOI 10.1057/978-1-137-59943-8_6

73

Degree (RHD) students and as a teacher of RHD students who are supervised by other academics. The second purpose of this chapter is to examine the course as preparation of students in building research capacity.

To do this I will present an overview of RHD student preparation, namely the institutional requirements, policy, procedures and the methodology course that some students are required to take as part of their research journey. Using an auto-ethnographic approach, I reflect on my own practice and epistemology as a researcher and course coordinator as I manoeuvre the methodological maze along with students. I critically appraise the role of the course in developing research capacity and the construction of the "research-ready embodied RHD student" at CQUniversity (CQU). Finally, I examine the intersection of supervision, personal growth as a supervisor and course coordinator and student preparation, through what I have learned from RHD students as they manoeuvre abstract concepts such as epistemology, ontology and methodology.

Becoming a RHD Student at CQU

According to the official website, CQU provides a diverse array of programmes and degrees to more than 30,000 students ranging from Certificate to postdoctoral qualifications. The university is also a leader in distance education with approximately half of this number of students doing their programmes through the online/distance mode. This means that technology underpins the operation of teaching and learning, administration and communication. CQU is also very proud of the fact that the student cohort contains one of the highest ratios of students from low socio-economic backgrounds, mature age backgrounds, Indigenous backgrounds as well as students who represent the first-in-family to attend university, at both undergraduate and postgraduate levels.

The research sector of CQU is also growing with Excellence in Research Australia rankings rated at or above world standard in the following areas: agriculture, applied mathematics, nursing, medical and health sciences (http://www.cqu.edu.au/about-us/history). These areas also represent a particular epistemological positioning in relation to research, namely a scientific or positivist approach to research. In 2014, the School of Education and the Arts was shown to have the largest number of postgraduate RHD students (personal communication). The broad research focus in this school covers creative writing to education to social science research. Within the School of Education and the Arts, postgraduate students are able to join the following RHD programmes: Master's by Research (MEd CA73), Doctor of Philosophy (PhD, CD61), Doctor of Education (EDD, CQ16) or Doctor of Professional Studies (DProf, CU56). Students are able to study as either on-campus or distance students.

Supervisors of RHD students can request that their students be enrolled into EDED20289 The Research Process. Students within the Doctor of Professional Studies programme do a separate course as part of the six Professional Research Tasks. Those students who are doing the Doctor of Education programme can have EDED20289 considered as one of the required research tasks. Any postgraduate student is able to do the course to develop research capacity if relevant skills and knowledge have not been evidenced through prior transcripts or documentation.

THE RESEARCH PROCESS—HISTORY AND STRUCTURE

The course has been offered since 2007 with a varied number of students each term. The course was designed to introduce Master's and doctoral students to a range of qualitative methodologies and associated research process. The course is only offered in the distance mode. There is a weekly tutorial session scheduled which is a "live discussion" via the Blackboard Collaborate mechanism within the Moodle 2.7 site. These sessions are recorded so that students unable to make the live session can revise the discussion in preparation for the next discussion.

The actual curriculum content has been divided into ten topics. The first four topics are what I consider the thinking phase—or headwork. Here the students engage with situating themselves within their research by examining how they individually understand and connect with their world, challenging what is seen as "valid" or "legitimate" knowledge and ways of knowing, disrupting the notion of value-free research and where they see their research as contributing to their chosen discipline. Into this discussion are drawn aspects of ethics and politics where students are asked to consider what counts as evidence and who benefits from their research work.

One of the more difficult sections of the course concerns the discussion around ontology and epistemology. Often students have not had the time or previous experience to engage with philosophy and although this does not form a huge part of the course, it is often the part that causes the most angst. Here students are asked to interrogate the nature of reality as they see/experience this and then to explain how they know what they know.

The second major part of the course focuses on analytic methods. As some methodologies have specific analytical tools, I have put this part of the research process adjacent to the methodology phase. I work from a position where I do not believe we can necessarily separate methodology and analysis. Working from a particular epistemological position, some methodologies become a more comfortable fit for the researcher. Then, out of this methodological position, certain data collection tools align with corresponding analytical tools or methods. The students spend two to three weeks working on this section by doing the actual organising, coding and categorising activity with data that is supplied to them.

The third section of the course covers information literacy and literature review. This is fairly standard with most methodological approaches where the students discuss the ways that literature can support their project, can make visible any gaps in the field of their research or offer alternative ways of investigating their topic area. Looking at the topic area or phenomenon could be considered as the heart-work or where the passion for the research lies. The last section attends to the research design and data collection methods and presentation—the fieldwork component.

Having learnt of some of the obstacles that some students experience in order to reach their goals, I have made certain discussions explicit within the final topic of the course. One of these discussions concerns the supervision process and the day-to-day conduct of being an RHD student. I feel it is important for the students to acknowledge and work with the multiple positions they find themselves in, in relation to the institution. Some students are new to the university but others are staff. In both cases, as an RHD student, people must know where and to whom they can go when they need to talk about issues arising from their candidature or when crossing borders from one role to another (Braidotti, 1994). It can be within the intersection of subject positions of student and staff member that ethical dilemmas and transgressions can occur. These may be unintentional purely because the student has not recognised the boundaries between the role as a staff member and their position as an RHD student. This also relates back to my own epistemological positioning of multiple subjectivities, nomadism and post-structural feminism, thus acknowledging the multiple hats that people wear (Braidotti, 1994).

In this discussion, I remind students, and myself, that we all have lives beyond the RHD programme. It is important that both students and supervisors are aware without the need to be inquisitive or invasive that taking this journey, whether as part of the course and then later within their programme, that RHD work has to be factored within the lifespan. Otherwise completion is likely not to occur. We do not ask people to set aside family for three to six years, or to stop work or not feed their families; therefore, doing an RHD course/programme has to be squeezed within an existing life, as part of manoeuvring the maze of not only methodology but of life in general.

METHODOLOGY

In this discussion, I draw on the tenets of auto-ethnography as a framework to reflect and comment on my own practice within the Research Process course (Chang, 2008). Here data sources include reflection of my lived experience as a lecturer, plus the textual artefact—the course materials and online site. Auto-ethnography is a research methodology that exposes vulnerability, fosters empathy, can be therapeutic (Custer, 2014) and I would further argue seeks to validate subjectivity and performativity. Within this methodology the researcher explores not only how they know the world but also their way of being in that world (St Pierre, 2013).

I see myself as a carrier of particular culture, namely, a white middle-class migrant academic woman who has identified as a feminist. This means that I view, and hold critical views, about the world through the lens of being female. There has been a century of feminist practice in Australia coinciding with the phases of the feminist movement. There is a history of suffragette advocacy near the beginning of the twentieth century, the rise of the Femocrat (Wearing, 1996), women's health centres (WHCs) and trade union advocacy representing liberal, radical and socialist positions with second wave feminism and finally the turn to post-structural and postmodern positions associated with third wave feminism. It was during my own doctoral journey that I connected to where I saw myself within feminism and see this as a critical instance in my intellectual growth.

At the time I was a volunteer at the local WHC, an explicit feminist space, and got to know many women from the local area. The local WHC offered a safe environment for women to manoeuvre the dimensionality of their lives and for me to learn about this place that I had moved to as a migrant. It was here that I began to understand the issues surrounding lots of women living in a regional/rural area. I got to know about funding issues and political stances and developed a deep admiration for the women within this feminist space. Places and spaces such as the WHC are sites for resistance and re-negotiation of powerful discourses that position women in narrow social and gender norms. Some women had abusive partners, others lived in poverty; most of the women had children and busy lives but these women were not victims, they were survivors and leaders. The staff and volunteers also had competing interests of work, family, community advocacy and tertiary study. In other words, we were different but had similar beliefs and values around the status of women—same and different. I saw among these women conflicting issues but enduring hope for the enhancement of women's lives. I then realised that we were different creatures at different times and with different people, but the space of the WHC enabled everyone to manoeuvre and shape the direction of personal goals, to understand multiple worlds and how they intersected. I did not see myself as a radical 'man-hating' lesbian or a socialist trade union fighter. I was interested in politics but again felt the Australian liberal position wasn't me either. Perhaps now I could see how my epistemological understanding and engagement to my world aligned more closely to a post-structural feminism. This is something that I have carried into other aspects of my life.

While powerful discourses and self-surveillance can constrain changing discourses, there is also the possibility of change and resistance. Foucault's notion of resistance allows for flexible and optimistic space grounded in women's everyday struggles and experiences (Wearing, 1996). I would argue that this does not relate just to women, it is also applicable to men and children. Opening up counter-narratives enables new identities, resistance to dominant ways of thinking and speaking and the possibility of transformation. Thus similar to my work in a WHC, using an auto-ethnographic approach to interrogate my practice as an educator can challenge assumptions and encourage me to connect to self, beliefs and practice; it is dangerous, risky and emotional work.

DISCUSSION: CONSTRUCTION SITES

Universities have always placed high value on research, noted in particular to the status given to GO8 universities that are research focused. In recent years, this pendulum of status has swung back towards valuing teaching within tertiary institutions. During this time, curriculum dealing with doctoral programmes has being hotly debated (Green, 2012). With the introduction of Australian Qualifications Framework (AQF) guidelines institutional quality control concerning graduate outcomes and attributes are influencing the building of research capacity among enrolling RHD students, thus requiring the creation of a new student identity—the post-graduate research student (Green, 2005). There has been an increasing emphasis on research training where the researcher acquires specific skills and knowledge, therefore the role and purpose of research training is to produce particular kinds of bodies that do legitimate research, however what happens when the construction of legitimate research is challenged by alternative discourses and construction of alternate subject positions?

The subject positions "academic lecturer" and "course coordinator" are sites to explore teaching and learning discourses and cultural productions around "teaching research". I am both a supervisor of RHD students and the lecturer/course coordinator of the Research process course. These invite similarities and differences within the academic role, thus the wearing of multiple hats. This multiplicity is enhanced when my own RHD students are required by the Office of Research to do the course as an elective.

The concept of a nomadic subject (Braidotti, 1994) is useful to highlight the complexities and differences among academics. As Braidotti (1994, p. 5) states:

> Though the image of nomadic subjects is inspired by the experience of peoples or cultures that are literally nomadic, the nomadism in question here refers to a kind of critical consciousness that resists settling into socially coded modes of thoughts and behaviour.

In other words, this is a consciousness that is fluid, partial and temporal as it flows within lived experiences, shaping and being shaped as transformation occurs. I also wear the hat of learner within the course and within the supervision process. As Halse (2011) contends, doing a doctorate is a learning process for the students, but it also has an impact on the supervisor's learning and knowledge development. I have learnt much from my students in the way they want to approach research work, learning at the postgraduate level and of course, learning about their lives as multiple beings. I have also learnt that students have many responsibilities, they are not just a student on my course; they have other responsibilities as well.

Students are usually someone's mother, father, sister, teacher, lecturer, carer and friend. They too wear multiple hats and this requires crossing borders from one world to another. Sometimes the borders are not clear cut or highly visible. Sometimes life can get in the way of research and research can get in the way of life, so what is important is to recognise this and factor it into the whole journey. In recent years, there has been a move towards more collective models of supervision and RHD support (Malfoy, 2005). The notion of making cohorts of students by grouping students into an elective course at the beginning of research programmes is one way of achieving this collective support. This means that students at similar levels gain from peer and social support rather than remaining within the confines of a discipline that often reinforces isolation. There has also been an increase in workplace managers and senior leaders enrolling into doctoral programmes, who are able to bring years of experience in the academic arena and these relationships are challenging a more traditional novice/expert relationship among supervisor and student (Malfoy, 2005).

DISCUSSION: HAVING SPACES AND PLACES TO MANOEUVRE

One of the aims of the course has been to prepare students to undertake a research project leading to a thesis/dissertation outcome. This means the teaching and learning about research in general and in the assessment, linking to the particular. While this does not take anything away from the role and guidance of the student's supervisor, the course was proposed as a way of introducing students to research aims and to bring students up-to-speed with the process of research. The other aim of the course is to develop research capacity. This is done through a focus on developing terminology and access to the jargon often associated with academic research. It is hoped that once students have created a glossary of terms they become immersed within particular academic and research discourses. Building capacity also means understanding the role and place of research, what makes research legitimate, and what guides "good" research and, of course, to do research.

By including a range of qualitative methodologies in the design of the course, I signal a number of approaches to investigating a research question, problem or curiosity. However, to engage with qualitative research, the researcher needs to be able to locate their 'self' within the research process. This means "seeing" the place of ethics and politics within the field of research. In other words, ethics is not something tacked on just before the data collection phase. Stepping back further, the questioning of how the researcher connects to their world needs to be made explicit, thereby introducing a critical dimension to what they are doing. This is why I ask the students to share within the group what they see as "reality" and then "how do they know this". Therefore, the structure of the course reflects the possibility of exploring personal, critical, transformative events. It hopefully reflects my own position where I see multiple realities constructed from experience, history and socialisation. The students bring with them different views of "the world", which in turn, can then be shown as "different worlds". This is a challenge for many of the students as the link to research is not readily visible.

Choice of Assessment Content, Discussion

Through tutorial discussions and the use of different examples, I present different ways of investigating research questions having asked the students to share their area of interests. One way of demonstrating multiple positions is to manoeuvre the wording of research questions to show how different dimensions of a topic can be investigated through asking different research questions, which highlights different approaches. This does two things: firstly, it challenges the positivist approach as the only way to do legitimate research and, secondly, offers pathways to consider "what it is that students really want to know" from their research. Occasionally, students realise that they are not asking the "right" questions in relation to investigating a phenomenon or curiosity.

Green (2012) talks about the representation in and through curriculum and a semiotic view of curriculum. For me, this means that what is presented within the Research Process course is representative of the kinds of "research bodies" we wish to produce. The course provides the opportunity for collaboration among students, peer-to-peer support, skill development and challenges. While the explicit learning outcomes of the course—examine the key features of a research process; explore selected phases in the research process and critically appraise a number of research methods—are general, within the Moodle site, the topics indicate a more specific focus on self, assumptions, research as a journey and a site of critique, multiple discourses and multiple representations of research.

Within the Moodle site, the curriculum content is organised in specific ways for the students to read, do individual activities to clarify the reading material, to consider my summaries, to pose questions or comments and then to engage in various forms of discussion. I encourage the students to be involved with the live tutorial discussions and to also use the discussion forums. I realise from my own experience as a novice researcher that sharing comments of what you plan to do and how you are thinking about this kind of "stuff" is really confronting. This is even more so when you are doing it within a group that you do not know. One of the positive aspects of distance education and online interaction is that you, as the student, can remain partially anonymous, in that students know names but we do not see each other in the flesh, so to speak. The discussions are audio-only recordings and these discussions are mediated through a screen. I attempt to reduce the power relationships between student/lecturer by sharing personal insights and experiences as a novice researcher and by stating upfront that this is a safe environment to bring questions. I also refer to questions that I have encountered from different classes to enable students to see (hopefully) that no question is silly and that many students have similar queries. As Wearing (1996) states, power and resistance can be transcribed through multiple sites such as the body, discourses, artefacts, subjectivity and knowledge. These are sites where power and resistance is negotiated, subverted, shifted and transformed. So I would argue that the Moodle site is both a place and space for students to manoeuvre positions, thoughts and commentary. It is a space designed for manoeuvring among the different methodologies and to re-design or articulate RHD projects. Through discussion and engagement of the materials, I hope that the student experiences similar manoeuvring and perhaps transformational engagement in that ontological and epistemological space.

Scaffolding Across the Four Assessment Pieces

There are four assessment items within the course. The first assignment deals with recognising methodological approaches. In this assessment, the student discusses a methodology of choice, including the history, philosophy and theorising, then the student looks at two studies using this methodology, critiquing the methodology in action. This critique enables students to demonstrate knowledge and understanding of the methodology, and link the discussion to understandings of ontology, epistemology, axiology and methodology. This is an initial step into being able to recognise a particular approach within a study. Students think about the trustworthiness and credibility of the findings in light of the approach used.

The second assessment involves coding some interview data where the student then creates the person or subject position from the data. Here all students get to choose an interview transcript to code. In the third assignment, the student presents a writing exercise by comparing and contrasting six research articles associated with their research topic area that can then be used as part of a larger literature review. In the last assignment, students choose a funded government report, again aligned to their own area of interest, where they overlay their knowledge and understanding of the research process, distinguishing and appraising the processes as described within the report. Again there is a focus on the trustworthiness and credibility of the entire study. By staging these assignments the research process is both a scaffold and examination of, and for, specific phases. The student has space to apply personal learning to the area of interest that will be the focus of individual RHD projects.

Constructing the Qualitative RHD Student

Students on entry to this course can be broadly categorised into three main groupings: those who have limited knowledge concerning research practices, those who have fixed ideas about research which may not necessarily be correct and those students with previous research experience who bring specific ontological and epistemological beliefs to the course. Students are enrolled into the course for various reasons but usually it is to expand their knowledge and understanding of qualitative research. Often students have not engaged with tertiary level study since undergraduate days and come into course when deciding to upgrade their qualifications with a Master's by Research degree. These students generally have had limited exposure to recent research in their field of interest and may have developed a possible researchable curiosity by noticing something within their workplace. Occasionally, this grouping may include students who require a further qualification for a promotion to a management or senior position within their workplace.

Some students may have had prior exposure to research through doing a Master's by coursework programme and are wanting to engage further into tertiary study for both personal interest and workplace reasons. There are also some students who have had previous Master's or doctoral experience with quantitative methodology. A change in workplace direction or roles often contributes to teachers and educators moving from their primary discipline into teaching areas associated with that discipline, for example, from an IT discipline into the teaching and learning associated with IT.

The third grouping consists of students who have some anecdotal knowledge of research but this is a rather fixed view on research as one particular type. There is also use of the word "research" to mean information gathering and looking for resources. This grouping come to the course with fixed ideas about what they are going to do, often "have the answer" to their proposed research and are just setting out to "prove their point".

Transformation of Students

Supervision is a practice that can be viewed as surveillance of RHD students, also surveillance of supervisors through institutional policies and procedures (Halse, 2011) and as Green (2005) asserts, postgraduate research supervision is about the production of identity as well as the production of new knowledge. He suggests that it is also "unfinished business" (Green, 2005, p. 152). Others such as Willison and O'Regan (2007) suggest that it is only about skill development. These days supervision can be seen as more than the traditional relationship of sage and lonely student (Boud & Costley, 2007). It has moved towards new structures containing supervision teams, provision of in-house courses, learning activities such as specific workshops and institutional monitoring. These activities serve to produce a new subject position— the postgraduate research student. This new subject position is constructed of multiple subjectivities, fluid epistemological and ontological stances and histories. This "student" comes with angst, emotions, established thoughts, beliefs and norms. Crotty (1998) talks about the bewilderment expressed by research students, fledgling researchers and even seasoned researchers when they wade into the array of methodologies and methods available. He states:

> These methodologies and methods are not usually laid out in a highly organised fashion and may appear more as a maze than as pathways to orderly research. There is much talk of their philosophical underpinnings, but how the methodologies and methods relate to the more theoretical elements is often left unclear. To add to the confusion the terminology is far from consistent in research literature and social science texts. One frequently finds the same term used in a number of different, sometimes even contradictory, ways. (Crotty, 1998, p. 1)

Many RHD students invest enormous amounts of time, money and emotional resources in their studies (Service, 2012) but this may also depend on the particular discipline. Students undertaking programmes within disciplines such as IT, Engineering or Physics usually work within a positivist paradigm thus enabling them to remain separate or distant from their research. This emotional detachment reinforces a scientific and experimental design focus to research. This is not the same when considering qualitative research approaches.

Part of the emotional response described by Service (2012) can be related to subjectivity and identity. This could be more so in the case of experienced researchers as they have developed an academic identity based on previous PhD work or study; some of my experienced students have used quantitative approaches or experimental designs before considering qualitative approaches. I am not arguing that qualitative research designs are the only way to do research, what I am saying is that when dealing with human participants as part of the research process, then approaches designed to apply to natural environments are inappropriate. I am also not against numbers, I find Australian Bureau of Statistics (ABS) data to be very useful and use it with the knowledge of specific assumptions around the collection of this data.

Dealing with human subjects demands a more intimate attachment, the positioning of "I" as an authority within the text and recognition of the self within the research process at every stage (Service, 2012), this being contrary to quantitative approaches. This can challenge the personal identity of not only the novice researcher, but also the experienced researcher when moving into qualitative research paradigms. While data collection is a "natural" stage where the novice researcher can feel anxious, emotional turmoil can begin when novice and occasionally experienced researchers begin to confront challenges and assumptions related to qualitative research approaches and examination of ontological and epistemological beliefs (Service, 2012). Malfoy (2005) highlights the role of talk when students are struggling (and "whinging") over different aspects of their candidature. This is not necessarily something to be alarmed at, but rather an opportunity for supervisors and educators to see the ways in which research students juggle multiple identities.

As the course coordinator of the course I have learnt much from the students in both how they manoeuvre the methodological maze and how they negotiate conflicting, competing or challenging personal epistemological positions. It has been a challenging journey for me at times, and a joyful one because through the intersection of multiple subject positions and lively discussions, a site of resistance to dominant research discourses has been established on the Moodle site for the course EDED20289, along with the co-construction of a new identity—that of the "research-ready embodied RHD student" or as Green (2005) described earlier, the new "postgraduate research student" who can go into a supervision relationship with less of a power imbalance, armed with confidence to talk about their proposed research.

CONCLUSION

Positivist approaches to research have historically been perceived as dominant or patriarchal discourses that maintain notions of objectivity, an indifferent subject and a universal truth. This serves to "de-legitimise" alternative ways of knowing and approaches to research. Unfortunately, qualitative approaches to research have often been seen as "soft" science, subjective and having less rigour. Running in parallel are discourses that associate qualitative research with women's positionings to patriarchal discourses. By associating qualitative approaches to the construction of women as subjective, soft and feminine, there is a subversive narrative being used to reinforce positivist epistemology and ontology as the only legitimate way to "know" truth. Offering a course in qualitative research methodologies can be seen as a site of resistance to the dominant patriarchal discourse of positivism as the only way of "knowing", thus introducing a counter-narrative.

The purpose of my course is to expand the repertoire of knowledge of the RHD student and to transform this person into a "research-ready embodied RHD student" able to make informed decisions about the design and implementation of research projects at CQU. My role is to give the RHD student tools and skills to critically analyse data, to gain an understanding of what influences their interpretation of findings and how they may view the research literature and interpret the work of others, thus building research capacity. Becoming a "research-ready embodied RHD student" and also the supervisor/lecturer of this new subject position is more than skills development and being an advisor. It is about knowing the student, being able to meet the needs of the student and recognising your own position within this process of "becoming".

In this chapter, I have highlighted that there are multiple approaches to research and argue these are linked to how we view "reality". Discussions around assumptions relating to qualitative and quantitative research approaches can challenge the images and identities held by RHD students, both novice and research-experienced. Taking my research training or preparation course challenges the student to recognise or make visible their "self" within the research process. This new identity is something they can take into new projects and journeys post the RHD phase. It is hoped that there is acknowledgement of research as a journey of "self" as much as a journey into the topic/discipline. In this way, the Research Process course is just one of the many cartographies (Braidotti, 1994) or intellectual navigation points on a journey; perhaps a journey that never ends.

REFERENCES

Boud, D., & Costley, C. (2007). From project supervision to advising: New conceptions of practice. *Innovations in Education and Teaching International, 44*(2), 119–130.

Braidotti, R. (1994). *Nomadic subjects.* New York: Columbia University Press.

Chang, H. (2008). *Autoethnography as method.* Walnut Creek, CA: West Coast.

Crotty, M. (1998). *The foundations of social research.* Crows Nest, NSW: Allen & Unwin.

Custer, D. (2014). Autoethnography as a transformative research method. *The Qualitative Report, 19*(21), 1–13.

Green, B. (2005). Unfinished business: Subjectivity and supervision. *Higher Education Research & Development, 24*(2), 151–163.

Green, B. (2012). Addressing the curriculum problem in doctoral education. *Australian Universities Review, 54*(1), 10–18.

Halse, C. (2011). "Becoming a supervisor": The impact of doctoral supervision on supervisors' learning. *Studies in Higher Education, 36*(5), 557–570.

Malfoy, J. (2005). Doctoral supervision, workplace research and changing pedagogic practices. *Higher Education Research & Development, 24*(2), 165–178.

Service, B. (2012). Keeping the faith: How reflective practice can turn emotional turmoil into a positive outcome in the context of doctoral study. *Reflective Practice, 13*(2), 169–182.

St Pierre, E. (2013). The posts continue: Becoming. *International Journal of Qualitative Studies in Education, 26*(6), 646–657.

Wearing, B. (1996). *Gender the pain and pleasure of difference.* Melbourne: Addison Wesley Longman Pty Limited.

Willison, J., & O'Regan, K. (2007). Commonly known, commonly not known, totally unknown: A framework for students becoming researchers. *Higher Education Research & Development, 26*(4), 393–409.

Elements of a Fusionist Ontology: Paradigmatic Choices in Understanding the Reasons for Career Change

Rickie Fisher

INTRODUCTION

This chapter explores "becoming" as a paradigmatic methodological construction for career change secondary school teachers. A fusionist ontology is developed to reflect this linking of "being" while also "becoming". For the career change participants in this study, not dissimilar to a novice researcher, becoming secondary school teachers could be explained in terms related to whatever they had previously been; that is, their previous career engagements, experiences, and prior states. The fusion between what may have *been* and what may *become* is dynamic. Much like the career change participants, novice researchers too manoeuvre through the maze of methodology in their journey to define and understand their past and present social realities.

In the style presented in the most elementary framework of the research process, the chapter follows the research journey and the manoeuvres made along the way. That is, considering the critical first step of identifying

R. Fisher (✉)
School of Education and the Arts, CQUniversity Australia,
Rockhampton, QLD, Australia

B. Harreveld et al. (eds.), *Constructing Methodology for Qualitative Research*, DOI 10.1057/978-1-137-59943-8_7

89

a research topic worthy of pursuit along with related research questions and research aims. For both novice and established researchers, this initial step is critical in providing the foundations for the ontological, epistemological, methodological manoeuvres made to attain the investigation's aims and purposes, and other manoeuvres congruent with the researcher's situatedness and axiology. These manoeuvres are discussed in the context of grounded theory research undertaken to construct the core category of *becoming* to understand the reasons and experiences of those taking up secondary school teaching as a new career (Fisher, 2012). This theory is founded upon the reasons and past experiences recounted by career change participants and how these had impacted upon their becoming secondary school teachers. The manoeuvres undertaken within a fusionist ontology served to explain how whatever may have *been* in the past social realities of the career change participants is ultimately fused to their *becoming* a secondary school teacher.

In discussing the fusionist ontology, the chapter also provides a perspective on the further development of a novice researcher undertaking a postgraduate research project. That is, the transitory phase of *being* the researcher together with whatever else the researcher may have previously *been* in themselves become fused to impact the novice researcher's own *becoming* an investigator more experienced in the manoeuvrings between methodological choices and the novice researcher's emerging axiological stance.

MAKING THE FIRST MANOEUVRE: FORMULATING A RESEARCH TOPIC

For the novice, as for all researchers, locating a topic, question, or "problem" to be investigated is a critical first step impacting upon the manoeuvres taken through other paradigmatic choices: ontology, epistemology, methodology, and axiology. Three questions underpin the choice of a research topic:

- *Is it viable?* Can sufficient information be generated either through secondary materials and/or primary research methods to address the topic and related research questions that it contains to satisfy the aims of the investigation? Questions of viability also reflected something of the researcher's axiology and partiality for a qualitative approach to understanding more fully the social realities of career change participants.

- *Is it worthwhile?* Decisions need to be made in terms of whether the research will contribute further to existing knowledge either through new knowledge or the further verification of existing knowledge through filling an identifiable gap.
- *Can interest in the research be sustained?* Is it a topic in which the novice researcher has sufficient interest to "see it through" within the prolonged period of a doctoral candidature?

Each of these questions had a positive answer in making the decision to research the reasons and experiences of participants who had decided to make the change to a new career as a secondary school teacher.

In assessing the viability of the research topic and the manoeuvres required to recruit participants, I was in an advantageous position. Although a novice researcher, as both programme coordinator responsible for initial student intake and programme lecturer, I had ready access to students and alumnae of a graduate diploma pre-service teacher education programme that regularly enrolled career changers seeking to become secondary school teachers. With the approval of university authorities I was able to access student record data such as age, gender, previous undergraduate qualifications. Such data enabled me to identify potential participants in terms (age and previous qualifications) that indicated they were individuals intent on making a career change into secondary teaching. While gender was not a factor of central interest in this investigation, its inclusion would result in a potentially useful gendered "mix" of women and men should their reasons and experiences of career change seem to differ to any extent in the stories that they shared with me. The viability of participant recruitment seemed assured. In basing the research on a grounded theory approach, close relationships between researcher and participants were essential as they constructed the social realities of their career change experiences; the research also seemed viable. I had developed professional relationships with graduates of the programme, several of whom "stayed in touch" as they commenced their new secondary teaching careers. At another level, the research struck a personal chord. I was also a career changer who had been a secondary school teacher and was in the process of "becoming" an academic.

In gauging whether the research was worthwhile, and remaining mindful of the cautionary wisdom contained in the seminal works on grounded theory of concerning the place and timing of a literature review, I followed the advice of Charmaz (2006) and undertook a preliminary literature search. This early manoeuvre served to locate my study in the general field of career change research and also in the more specific field of research in career change into secondary school teaching. This preliminary literature search identified four apparent "gaps" that confirmed the research topic as potentially worthwhile:

1. Only limited distinction had been made in previous studies between recruitment into primary rather than secondary pre-service teacher education programmes while other studies had considered recruitment into the teaching profession in general terms.
2. Only a limited number of previous studies had drawn the link between career change and entry into the secondary school teaching profession.
3. Few studies had been concerned with postgraduate pre-service teacher education as a pathway into secondary school teaching by career changers.
4. Providing insights into career change into secondary school teaching could prove useful in the recruitment of such teachers. This may have value when there are predicted shortages of suitably qualified staff at the secondary school level in some specialist teaching areas based on the collusion of three causal factors.

- Policy changes to Australia's national requirements for accreditation of pre-service teacher education that will see two-year postgraduate pre-service teacher training programmes replace the current one-year programmes.
- The movement of Year 7 classes into secondary schools in Queensland from 2015.
- The projected staffing shortfalls resulting from ageing and retirement trends (Arlington, 2012); difficulties in retaining teachers in a highly stressful occupation (Milburn, 2011); the growing pool of individuals who are intent on changing careers (University of Sydney, 2011); and, knowing why people seek new careers as secondary school teachers.

Finally, as a novice researcher, I needed to convince myself, and also my supervisors, that my interest in the research topic could be sustained. At a personal level, in my own "becoming", I needed to pursue a higher degree qualification. Having been a career changer myself, I felt some empathy with those seeking to make a similar change in becoming second-ary school teachers and I acknowledged that this and my leanings towards qualitative research methodologies were fundamental to my values and axiological perspectives. Serendipitously, at a professional level, as pro-gramme coordinator I was responsible for initial student intake decisions and in that process had come to know a little of the reasons and experi-ences of career changers through the student entry processes. Equally, as programme coordinator, I was required to provide information that was also ongoing as part of the formal programme accreditation process with the Queensland College of Teachers and this necessitated tracking student intakes, progress, in-school supervised placements and workforce entry upon graduation.

Convinced that the research topic was viable, worthwhile, and sustain-able, I then undertook the first manoeuvres to develop the two interre-lated aims:

1. To explain the reasons that had influenced people's decisions to change careers and become secondary school teachers.
2. To develop an understanding of the experiences of a cohort of career change participants while students of a particular pre-service teacher education programme, including aspects they had found more chal-lenging, as well as aspects they considered had supported and enhanced their career change ambitions while developing their new professional identities as secondary school teachers.

While it is the first of these aims that provides the substance of this chapter in terms of my ontological, epistemological, methodological, and axiological manoeuvres, the two aims were addressed concurrently throughout the investigation.

ONTOLOGICAL MANOEUVRES: ELEMENTS OF A FUSIONIST ONTOLOGY

With the research topic broadly established, two further points needed to be considered. First, it was obvious that the investigation was centred on the notion of change and its antecedents and precursors in the form of participant reasons and experiences that led them to make a career change. Secondly, and given the preliminary review of the literature undertaken, as a novice researcher I became increasingly convinced that a qualitative

methodology would be appropriate founded on an interpretive constructivist epistemology and multiple social realities. I needed then to make
further manoeuvres to establish the ontological, epistemological, and
methodological components of my chosen research paradigm.

The ontological perspective asks questions about the nature of reality
(Denzin & Lincoln, 2005). Given that career change was at the forefront,
I sought an ontology that aligned with this. My further manoeuvres demonstrated what I termed "the fusionist ontology" served to inform this
investigation and the interpretations placed on the accounts of the past
reasons and experiences provided by participants making a career change
into secondary teaching. The fusionist ontology shares much in common
with a critical realist ontology, itself originating in the works of Aristotle's
perception of a fusion between "being" and "becoming" (Blasch & Plano,
2003). The Aristotelian view sought to reconcile being and becoming,
with individuals experiencing the dynamics of a change process from the
realm of mere theory (i.e., of becoming) to what becomes the reality (i.e.,
of being).

The fusion between being and becoming that Aristotle sought to
establish as an alternate ontology, was adopted and elaborated by
Driesch (1914). Trained as a biologist (Webster & Goodwin, 1996),
Driesch argued that pre-existing states form systems that can be understood in accounting for further change or morphogenesis. As Webster
and Goodwin (1996) indicate, in Driesch's view, "particular forms
can only be explained by means of historical narrative" (p. 36); that
is, becoming could be explained by earlier phases of development. In
Driesch's (1914) ontology, becoming can be regarded as if any prior
phase was the "reason" of a later phase and the "consequence" of an
earlier one. A fusionist ontology reflects an "atomist view" or the "thesis of pre-formation" that claims "there must be some least amount
of being … that already contains … the determinacy that makes 'living sensible'" (Morris, 2008, p. 69). This also reflects Driesch's background in embryology and the study of embryogenesis. The key to the
fusionist ontology is to claim that all that an embryo might become is
found at the moment of conception. Hence, becoming rests on what
may have previously been. Such a claim has been critiqued by Merleau-
Ponty (as cited by Morris, 2008) who argued what might become "is
not explained by the pre-existence of possibilities", is not regulated by
what may have been, but rather situations that allow "other forces to
come into play" (Merleau-Ponty, as cited by Morris, 2008, p. 76).

Blasch and Plano (2003) argue that the state of "being" for any individual contains and includes the precursors and antecedents to a reality that is yet to exist in the state of "becoming", an argument not unknown to critical realism with its identification of causal mechanisms and structures. Wenger (1998) developed this ontological perspective further in suggesting that the self and self-identity are characterised as "a 'constant becoming' that defines who we are" (p. 149). These dynamics of "becoming" form the basis of the postmodernist views of Foucault (1982, and cited also in Martin, 1988) in stating that, "The main interest in life and work is to become someone else that you were not in the beginning". Butler (1987) notes that some two centuries beforehand, Hegel had theorised about "becoming" in very similar terms. Hegel depicted reality (i.e., "being") as relatively stable at any point in time. However, this stability, as Butler (1987, p. 49) interprets Hegel's philosophy, disguises an "inherent movement in 'being'—rather than being, we are always 'becoming' … Becoming implies growth and change … we are always 'becoming', what the self was is lost, but that self is now something new that it was not before" (Zaborskis, 2011, p. 1).

Adopting a fusionist ontology became an attractive option in an investigation aimed at interpreting the reasons and previous experiences that had influenced decisions to become secondary school teachers when contemplating possible new careers. After attaining relevant qualifications in order to pursue their previous careers, participants had then decided to embark on new careers in becoming secondary school teachers. They had also been involved in and had prior experiences of formal and informal training. For some, at least in part, these accounted for their decision to seek new careers as secondary school teachers. Whatever they had been, aspects of their previous lives became fused to their reasons for becoming secondary school teachers. The fusion between what may have *been* and what may *become* is dynamic.

Congruent with all of this, in considering my axiological stance, of necessity I needed to acknowledge that I was not a neutral observer. Moreover, I was mindful of those post-structural notions of becoming with its emphasis on historical perspectives. That is, that the reasons for, and experiences of, change are best explained by those with experiences of the change processes, rather than causes related to social and cultural structures. Given this, I remained alert to my "second-hand" role as researcher to *interpret* the reasons and experiences contained in their career change stories that my research participants shared with me. At its base, my fusionist ontological stance allowed me to appreciate that in the reasons and experiences of change there are multiple social realities. This had direct implications for the further epistemological and methodological manoeuvres that I made.

EPISTEMOLOGICAL APPROACH TOWARDS MULTIPLE SOCIAL REALITIES

As the ontological perspective became clearer it also became apparent to this novice researcher that epistemologically multiple social realities constructed by participants contained the requisite knowledge of their reasons and experiences of career change. Multiple social realities are constructed by individuals or groups, acknowledging that "realities exist in the form of multiple mental constructions, socially and experientially based, local and specific, dependent on the persons who hold them" (Hollinshead, 2004, p. 76). "Ontologically speaking, there are multiple realities or multiple truths based on one's construction of reality" (Sale, Lohfeld, & Brazil, 2002, p. 45). While such a perspective underpins the interpretive constructivist paradigm, it is has come to be shared with critical realism. The critical realist ontology developed in the works of Bhaskar (1978, 1979, 1986) and also by Sayer (1992, 2000) and Maxwell (2004a, 2004b) considers "the REAL are the causal mechanisms and structures that produce actual events, a subset of which then is empirically observed" (Klein, 2004, p. 131). It was the "REAL" that I sought to capture through my methodological manoeuvres.

METHODOLOGICAL MANOEUVRES AND A GROUNDED THEORY APPROACH

The investigation was purposefully qualitative in order to place the reasons for, and experiences of, career change into secondary school teaching in the foreground for further analysis, interpretation, and theorising. A qualitative methodology was chosen because I considered a quantitative approach would not provide full accounts of the reasons for, and experiences of, changing careers. More specifically, the investigation was located within an interpretive constructivist paradigm and a grounded theory approach so that an explanatory theory could be constructed from the accounts provided by the research participants, those who were in the best possible positions to provide authentic stories of career change. The research participants were 19 adults who held other tertiary-level quali-fications, who had experienced other careers, who possessed a wealth of life and other experiences, and who had recently taken up appointments as secondary school teachers following their successful completion of a particular postgraduate pre-service teacher education programme.

The rationale for choosing a grounded theory approach reflected my intention to establish authentic data from participant accounts. The explanatory theory constructed using inductive reasoning was firmly founded on their "multiple realities" (Lincoln & Guba, 1985, p. 37). This approach focused on a particular group of individuals becoming second-ary school teachers at a particular point in time within a particular context that defined the research setting. In the year prior to that in which data were gathered, the participants had graduated from a pre-service teacher education programme, and were some five months into their new careers as secondary school teachers when they were interviewed.

In making methodological manoeuvres, I was aware that a grounded theory approach was not the only available methodology for collect-ing, sharing, and constructing knowledge concerning the reasons for, and experiences of, career change into secondary school teaching among those who participated in this investigation. However, a grounded the-ory approach was consistent with the epistemological perspective that knowledge is constructed on the basis of the multiple realities of people experiencing a given phenomenon that happens to be under investiga-tion (Charmaz, 2006). In collaboration with the participants, I sought to understand their multiple realities of career change reasons and expe-riences that formed the basis for constructing the explanatory grounded theory of "Becoming".

Deciding on a grounded theory approach positioned me as the key research instrument and in a research partnership with the participants. This offered me the advantage of being able to work closely with the empirical data as it emerged from the semi-structured interviews of about one hour that I completed in an informal, conversational discussion with each participant. It also allowed me to develop a "closeness" with the data throughout the transcription and coding of those interviews, and the interpretation of the stories that participants shared that were at the foundations of the constructed grounded theory. In implementing the designed methodology, I maintained a reflexive journal to record my own reflections upon the participants' stories as they unfolded. Such affinities with participants and close proximity to the data their stories provided also allowed me to identify a point of saturation, a point at which further interviews were not adding any "new" information to that previously gathered.

While grounded theory methodologies have become widely used in a range of disciplines including health sciences, business, and education, my preliminary search of the literature identified only two studies of relevance in career change that had also employed a grounded theory approach. Haggard, Slostad and Winterton's (2006) American study adopted a grounded theory approach in attempting to understand some of the challenges of second career teachers. The key points of difference between that study and this investigation were that they focused on second career teachers who had been in their teaching positions for longer than my participants; and they were not specifically concerned with second career secondary school teachers. Tigchelaar, Brouwer and Korthagen (2008) also used a grounded theory approach in their Dutch study of change in the context of second career teachers entering the teaching profession. While that study shared some common features with this investigation in examining the reasons for career change into teaching, clearly it was not connected to Australian career changers and their experiences.

In adopting an interpretive constructivist grounded theory approach, I constructed a theory that would provide some explanation of the reasons behind a person's decision to become a secondary school teacher as their new career, and some understanding of their career change experiences. Despite its limited application to the wider field of career change into secondary school teaching, a grounded theory approach has become one of the most widely accepted research strategies for generating new theories in fields for which extant theories are either limited or yet to exist.

THE FINAL MANOEUVRES TO "BECOMING"

Faced with a large amount of information contained in the verbatim transcriptions of the semi-structured, informal interviews, further manoeuvres were required in order to "make sense" of what participants had articulated as their reasons for career change, and their past experiences that had prompted their career change decisions. Following the advice of Charmaz (2006), an initial open coding phase was undertaken. This involved naming each word, line, or segment of data in breaking down, examining, comparing, conceptualising, and categorising empirical data (Strauss & Corbin, 2005). The purpose of open coding is to develop general insights into the content of the empirical data before proceeding to more detailed focused coding and beginning to build the explanatory grounded theory that such empirical data support.

Axial coding was undertaken to refine the open coded categories. As suggested by Strauss and Corbin (2005), the purpose of axial coding is to reassemble data that may have been fractured during open coding, to then put the data back together in new ways by making new connections between categories and any subcategories. This involved continually relating subcategories to a category, comparing categories with the collected data, exploring the density of the categories by detailing their properties and dimensions, and exploring variations in the occurrence. In these ways, constant comparison became a continuous cycle of collecting and analysing data and provided a "method of analysis that generates successively more abstract concepts and theories through inductive processes of comparing data with data, data with category, category with category and category with concept" (Charmaz, 2006, p. 187). Through constant comparison among and between participant responses, the categories could be grouped around possible themes. This manoeuvre aligned with Glaser and Strauss' (1967) view that constant comparison involves labelling a concept that portrays an underlying meaning that assists in categorising and sorting empirical data. As new information is collected and coded, it is compared to already existing data, categories, and emergent themes and, where necessary, new categories created.

As a further analytical manoeuvre, theoretical sampling enabled continual re-examination of empirical data in light of the developing categories. The initial sorting and coding of the empirical data gave shape to tentative groupings and categories. Theoretical sampling involved delving further, "seeking and collecting pertinent data to elaborate and refine categories in [the] emerging theory" (Charmaz, 2006, p. 96). The properties and categories of the theory were continuously compared across the data until no further variations were apparent (Glaser, 2007). At that point, I considered the categories were sufficiently "saturated". I also followed Charmaz's advice to diagramise the categories to "integrate [your *sic*] the emerging theory" (Charmaz, 2006, p. 96).

From all of this, "Becoming" was constructed as the core category of the explanatory grounded theory. "Becoming" was not a term constructed by the investigator, but an in vivo term used by participants whose voices were foregrounded throughout this investigation. All participants at some stage used "Becoming" to describe their career change as exemplified in the following excerpts from the transcribed interviews:

Becoming a teacher was so important to me.
For me becoming a teacher was a personal choice.

In using "Becoming" to denote the core category of the constructed grounded theory, I followed Glaser (1978) and Charmaz's (2006) approach in using gerunds to emphasise actions and processes within the phenomena under investigation. "Becoming" implies a pre-existing state of having *been*, from which change proceeds. The research participants were in the process of *becoming* secondary school teachers having *been* occupied in a previous career. There was a fusion between what they had *been*, and what they were *becoming*. And, what they had been and had previously experienced served to explain their reasons for their career change.

A number of contributing factors emerged to illustrate what had attracted the career change participants to a new secondary school teaching career. Five themes were identified that emphasised factors that had influenced their decision to become a secondary school teacher through the attraction of teaching as a new career. Through the fusionist ontology, for some participants, their reports of having *been* engaged in a previous career included their recognition of "forces" that had "pulled" them towards their *becoming* a secondary school teacher as a new career:

- Enjoyment and satisfaction from teaching and how teaching would satisfy the need for personal fulfilment.
- Helping young people learn and the reward and satisfaction this would provide.
- Always wanting to be a secondary school teacher, a want some had held from a young age and now sought to fulfil after various obstacles had intruded, or other opportunities and options had initially caused them to embark on non-teaching careers.
- Family and lifestyle factors along with the appeal and practicality of working during school hours while rearing their own family.
- Influence of significant others including family members or friends who are, or had been, teachers, as well as former teachers who had inspired and attracted them to become a secondary school teacher.

Additionally, to understand their reasons for deciding upon a new career in secondary school teaching, participants referred to three interrelated prior experiences that may have prompted their career change decisions. For some, these past experiences included events and circumstances that had "pushed" them away from their previous career and into teaching. Within the fusionist ontology, these themes emphasised what the career changer had *been* or experienced prior to *becoming* a secondary school teacher influenced their career change decision:

- Dissatisfaction with previous careers including the lack of fulfillment.
- Previous formal (paid) and informal (unpaid/volunteer) teaching or training experiences that had provided some of the skills and insights into the nature of teaching-related roles.
- "Life experiences" together with age and maturity were assets in new careers as secondary school teachers.

IMPLICATIONS

The implications of this investigation are threefold:

- On a theoretical level, the development and implementation of a fusionist ontology provided a world view aligned to those of Driesch (1914), and the later historical emphasis of post-structuralists that there are explanatory linkages to be found between what may have been, and what may become. The past provides a series of antecedents that help explain what may be, and what may become. Such linkages were clearly apparent in the stories of those who participated in this investigation as they spoke of their past experiences and the related reasons for making a career change. For them, *becoming* a secondary school teacher reflected the multiple social realities of their past that were their antecedents of change.
- On a pragmatic level, at a time when education authorities continue to report deficits in staffing the teaching profession, understanding the reasons and how past experiences may influence individuals to make a career change into secondary school teaching better informs those authorities in their staff recruitment campaigns.
- Contextually, unlike other studies into career change into teaching, this investigation is distinguished by its focus on career change into secondary school teaching with an Australian focus. Given the predominance of quantitative studies among the existing literature, this investigation is also distinguished by its qualitative research methodology.

CONCLUSION

This chapter has provided a further example of investigations illustrating how researchers manoeuvre through the maze of methodology to make meaning for their research projects. As a novice qualitative researcher, making methodological manoeuvres required me to return to the fundamental elements of any theoretical paradigm: ontology, epistemology, and axiology, all of which influence the choices of methodology, and the manoeuvres made within research methods to address the underlying questions of the research project.

Acknowledging that all change is dynamic, contiguous, and continuous, in addressing the first of two underlying research questions (namely, to explain the reasons that had influenced people's decisions to change careers and become secondary school teachers), this investigation adopted a "fusionist ontology". This provided a lens focused on the precursors and antecedents of change. That is, what may once have been provides the foundations of what may become. The perspective of this ontology informed the manoeuvres I made through qualitative research methodologies to acquire and then interpret the historical narratives of a group of 19 career changers *becoming* secondary school teachers. True to its fusionist foundations, the investigation has demonstrated that whatever the research participants' multiple social realities and past experiences may have *been*, these provided understanding of their reasons for making their career change decisions.

REFERENCES

Arlington, K. (2012, February 1). Teacher shortage looms as many approach retirement. *The Sydney Morning Herald*. Retrieved from http://www.smh.com.au/national/education/teacher-shortage-looms-as-many-approach-retirement-20120131-1qrfg.html

Bhaskar, R. (1978). *A realist theory of science*. Hassocks: Harvester Press.

Bhaskar, R. (1979). *The possibility of naturalism*. Brighton: Harvester Press.

Bhaskar, R. (1986). *Scientific realism and human emancipation*. London: Verso.

Blasch, E. P., & Plano, S. (2003). Ontological issues in higher levels of information fusion: User refinement of the fusion process. In *Proceedings of the Sixth International Conference of Information Fusion* (pp. 634–641). Cairns, QLD. Retrieved from http://www.dtic.mil/cgi-bin/GetTRDoc?Location=U2&doc=GetTRDoc.pdf&AD=ADP021721

Butler, J. (1987). *Subjects of desire: Hegelian reflections in twentieth century France*. New York: Colombia University Press.

Charmaz, K. (2006). *Constructing grounded theory: A practical guide through qualitative analysis*. Thousand Oaks, CA: Sage.

Denzin, N. K., & Lincoln, Y. S. (Eds.) (2005). *The SAGE handbook of qualitative research* (3rd ed.). Thousand Oaks, CA: Sage.

Driesch, H. (1914). *The history and theory of vitalism*. London, UK: Hesperides Press.

Fisher, R. J. (2012). Becoming: An explanatory grounded theory of secondary school teaching as a new career. PhD thesis, Central Queensland University, Rockhampton. http://hdl.cqu.edu.au/10018/1005799

Foucault, M. (1982). The subject and power. *Critical Theory, 8*(4), 777–795.

Glaser, B. G. (1978). *Theoretical sensitivity. Advances in the methodology of grounded theory*. Thousand Oaks, CA: Sociology Press.

Glaser, B. G. (2007). *Doing formal grounded theory: A proposal*. Mill Valley, CA: Sociology Press.

Glaser, B. G., & Strauss, A. L. (1967). *Discovery of grounded theory: Strategies for qualitative research*. Chicago, IL: Aldine.

Haggard, C., Slostad, F., & Winterton, S. (2006). Transition to the school as workplace: Challenges of second career teachers. *Teacher Education, 17*(4), 317–327.

Hollinshead, K. (2004). Ontological craft in tourism studies: The productive mapping of identity and image in tourism settings. In J. Phillimore & L. Goodson (Eds.), *Qualitative research in tourism*. London, UK: Routledge.

Klein, H. K. (2004). Seeking the new and the critical in critical realism: Deja Vu? *Information and Organization, 14*, 123–144.

Lincoln, Y. S., & Guba, E. G. (1985). *Naturalistic inquiry*. Newbury Park, CA: Sage.

Martin, R. (1988). Truth, power, self: An interview. In L. H. Martin, H. Gutman, & P. H. Hutton (Eds.), *Technologies of the self: A seminar with Michel Foucault*. Amherst: University of Massachusetts Press.

Maxwell, J. (2004a). Causal explanation, qualitative research, and scientific inquiry in education. *Educational Researcher 33*, no. 1.

Maxwell, J. (2004b). Using qualitative methods for causal explanation. *Field Methods, 16*(3), 243–264.

Merleau-Ponty, M. (1995). La nature: notes, cours du Collége de France. Paris: Seuil. Translated by Morris, D. (2008). The time and place of the organism: Merleau-Ponty's philosophy in embryo. *Alter: Revue de phenomenology, 16*, 69–86.

Merleau-Ponty, M. (2003). Nature: Course notes from the Collège de France. Translated by R. Vallier. Evanston, IL: Northwestern University Press.

Milburn, C. (2011, March 7). More teachers, but fewer staying the course. *The Melbourne Age*. Retrieved from http://www.theage.com.au/national/education/more-teachers-but-fewer-staying-the-course-20110304-1bhuv.html

Morris, D. (2008). The time and place of the organism: Merleau-Ponty's philosophy in embryo. *Alter: Revue de phenomenology, 16,* 69–86.

Sale, J. E. M., Lohfeld, L. H., & Brazil, K. (2002). Revisiting the quantitative-qualitative debate: Implications for mixed-methods research. *Quality and Quantity, 36,* 43–53.

Sayer, A. (1992). *Method in social science: A realist approach* (2nd ed.). London: Routledge.

Sayer, A. (2000). *Realism and social science.* London: Sage.

Strauss, A., & Corbin, J. (2005). *Grounded theory methodology: An overview.* In N. K. Denzin & Y. S. Lincoln (Eds.), *Handbook of qualitative research.* Thousand Oaks, CA: Sage.

Tigchelaar, A. E., Brouwer, C. N., & Korthagen, F. A. J. (2008). Crossing horizons: Continuity and change during second career teachers' entry to teaching. *Teaching and Teacher Education, 24*(6), 1530–1550.

University of Sydney Workplace Research Centre. (2011). Australia at Work Five Year Study 2007–2011 [Fact Sheet #9]. Retrieved from http://sydney.edu.au/business/workplaceresearch/news/2012/australia_at_work_study

Webster, G., & Goodwin, B. (1996). *Form and transformation: Generative and relational principles of biology.* Cambridge, UK: Cambridge University Press.

Wenger, E. (1998). *Communities of practice: Learning, meaning and identity.* New York: Cambridge University Press.

Zaborskis, M. (2011, August 4). *How becoming of you* [Web log post]. Flexner Book Club Blog. Retrieved September 9, 2011, from http://flexner.blogs.brynmawr.edu/

We Cannot Do This Work Without Being Who We Are: Researching and Experiencing Academic Selves

Sarah Loch and Alison L. Black

INTRODUCTION

In this chapter, we experiment with ways to speak our lives in the academy as we question what counts as research and what should and could be the work of researchers. As we do this, we confirm the notion that we cannot do the work of research without being who we are. Our chapter emerges from a body of shared communication which seeps deeply into our lives— our work in education, our values, identities, histories, domesticities, and professional and personal experiences. In assembling our chapter, we use aesthetic methodologies of story and image to explore our thinking, feeling and manoeuvring through the expectations and requirements of academic life and the everyday happenings of being human. Researchers

S. Loch
International Research Centre of Youth Futures, University of Technology Sydney, Sydney, NSW, Australia

A.L. Black (✉)
School of Education, University of the Sunshine Coast, Maroochydore, QLD, Australia

© The Author(s) 2016
B. Harreveld et al. (eds.), *Constructing Methodology for Qualitative Research*, DOI 10.1057/978-1-137-59943-8_8

interested in the human experience have long been attracted to inquiry approaches that possess aesthetic qualities (Dewey, 1934; Eisner, 1997). Aesthetic representations and visual methodologies support inquiry and voice, and promote personal and professional connections to ways of knowing and to internal and tacit narratives.

For us, these methodologies have opened doorways to deep experiences, thinking and reflection. Acknowledging and responding to our own and each other's ways of knowing and living have created nurturing, reciprocal spaces of disclosure/exposure which we make public and invite others to share.

Our chapter gives attention to the place of the personal in researching qualitatively. Many academics feel significant pressure to produce research, receiving dogged messages about what counts as research, its impact, preferred audiences and outcomes. Our chapter explores not only the manoeuvring we do to be producers of research, but also our conscious appreciation that we cannot do this work *without* being who we are. Who we are cannot be separated from how we are being produced as researchers through the methodological choices we make. Exploring the potency of listening, collaborating and connecting for research and understanding, we encourage consideration of the risk and value of adventuring with others into public and research arenas to access and speak out loud the experiences of our lives.

DECIDING WHAT RESEARCH IS

It is the researcher who decides what research is or might be.
  (Rhedding-Jones, 2005, p. 18)

Jeanette Rhedding-Jones offers that research should be about topics that matter, questions that are useful and inquiries that are interesting. Remembered for her commitment to 'thinking more-than' (Otterstad et al., 2014, pp. 1–2), we write alongside Rhedding-Jones as two female academics based in different universities on the east coast of Australia. We have only met in person once but for two years have been conversing and acquiring ways to communicate our scholarship and thinking through Skype and emails; chapters, articles and theorists; image, poetry and stories. We came together through a writers' workshop for a book now published (Trimmer, Black, & Riddle, 2015) and through a string of emails

Fig. 8.1   Our string of emails has become a cat's cradle for our work in academe (Ali Black, Digital artwork, 2015)

which became a cord, then a rope, then a cable and which we have now twisted into an ever growing cat's cradle of our working, writing and living lives (Fig. 8.1).

This chapter finds us engaging with poststructural writers like Laurel Richardson (2008, 2010), Jane Bone (2008, 2009) and Susan Finley (2010); others who use auto-ethnographic writing to question further 'the kind of researcher you want to be' (Rhedding-Jones, 2005, p. 148). Writing together is helping us to consider this question as we 'come out' as philosophers, as Rhedding-Jones suggests. Rhedding-Jones points to the importance of researchers going 'beyond simple description and into knowledge' (1996, p. 33) and into spaces where 'fluidity not seen in traditional academic writing' (1995, p. 494) picks up speed.

A question in this chapter is how do we create conditions which will allow such flow to happen? One way is through our attention to texts which nestle inside one another and through the creation of supportive relationships which bring attention to what the other sees as less important. For example, we write emails outlining the most potent experience of our day, with our 'academic writing' attached. We send a text alerting the other to the latest version we have uploaded to Dropbox, conscious it will likely be read amongst backgrounds of meetings, lectures and deadlines, physical exhaustion, medical appointments, sick children, sadness or engagement with grief. We conduct a Skype call about a new writing project against backdrops, including kids' drawings on office walls and views out of the other's window. These situations have led us to question who we are as researchers and why our own life experiences ought to have a place in our work. Our communication is motivated by the desire to secure more authentic information about each other and about our lives. Our methodologies evolve with the realisation that conventional forms of research/writing constrain and hide what we seek to understand about ourselves and each other as researchers and people.

Such textured/textual pieces, now scattered through this chapter, dialogue our queries about what counts as research and what counts when researching. They are part of our web of manoeuvres through personal and professional binaries. They are our realisation that the meanings of our lives cannot be laid in a drawer until 'the work' is over.

* * *

Ali to Sarah: (July 2014) *Hi Sarah, great to see you in my inbox as always. Yes, have been trying to work on this—contribution is slow and my Endnote dropped off so I got side-tracked trying to reinstall that. Then for some reason I googled dad and found he is on Wikipedia which just chilled me and made me feel sick as they list the charges incorrectly and my mum's full name in the spouse section. I was relieved to see I wasn't there. See, I feel ashamed. He sent me a link to join him on Linked-in last week and I just ignored it. Perhaps the sharing of my father story [in our planned writing about our fathers for an upcoming paper] is fickle as I don't name him, can't …*

I read the document where you put all our conversations together. I love how real this has become, so much more important than writing a chapter, the becoming of a friendship, yet keeping our writing alive and purposeful.

* * *

Sarah to Ali: (September 2014) *Hi there Ali, This attached article looks really interesting for the way we will approach our father piece/peace/pierce. Father's day this weekend isn't it?*

I am keen to get into this head space soon but I have been writing all those Year 12 references and they are almost done now. Keen to lose myself again in our collaborations!

* * *

Ali to Sarah: *(January 2015) Hi Sarah, I can't sleep and wanted to write to you. It is my birthday in ten minutes, but an hour ago I received a phone call to say my dad has died. He was overseas. Don't know any details. I feel numb. He has forgotten to ring me my last two birthdays, and was adamant he would ring me tomorrow! The kids and I got to speak to him a few days ago and we all said I love you. So that is good. I'm not sure what to say, but given you have lost your dad and we have been in this space of reflecting and writing about our father stories, I wanted to commune with you.*

***

Sarah to Ali: *(February 2015) Hi Ali, Did another IVF during the week. We have one vial of sperm left so end is in sight. But this embryo was a 4 cell when frozen. Upon defrosting it started to eat itself and was down to 3 cells when we entered the room, and by the time the lab technician was loading it into the catheter it was only 2 cells which is 'unviable'. I had to sign forms to say I knew it was unlikely to implant.*

***

Sarah to Ali: *(April 2015) Hi Ali, I've got a new abstract together and new title. I should have time tomorrow as well but if you want to adjust and just send it back tomorrow some time, that's fine with me. Sorry. I'm a bit distracted. After your lovely email, so pertinent, I got a very high hormone reading on the weekend which implied a pregnancy might be happening, couldn't believe it, and spent 2 days scarily happy, but hopes dashed again. I am really OK but just don't get why this can't work.*

***

This chapter represents another strand in our 'deterritorialising' and 'reterritorialising' collaboration (see the beginnings in Black & Loch, 2014) as we allow our views on what matters as research to be changed and moved outwards by the continual sluicing of sharing back and forth with one another. Deterritorialisation, described by French poststructuralists Gilles Deleuze and Félix Guattari (1987, p. 53), is found in actions such as 'waves or flows [which] go from the central layer to the periphery, then from the new centre to the new periphery, falling back to the old centre and launching forth to the new'. This movement uses its every slosh to pick up and pull in new layers of experience previously positioned on outer edges.

Fig. 8.2 How important is it to take time to sit with our views about what speaks meaningfully to us, and then to connect with another and be moved (transformed) by the sharing back and forth? (Ali Black, Personal photo 2011, Using image to connect with what reterritorialising might involve)

Before we met, we, singularly, felt more on the outer, with responsiveness from the other playing a big part in fostering our desire to keep adventuring. Our experiments with aesthetic ways and forms of communicating and representing experience and knowing—poetry, image, reflection—began taking greater shape in our writing but we were unsure how others would receive these texts. Our early communication drew attention to what we thought important to mention and to what we glossed over. In this chapter, our writing shares attempts to adventure into areas conventionally glossed over. These methodologies speak meaningfully to us, and support our assembling of experience, expression and communication (Black & O'Dea, 2015; Black & Loch, 2014; Loch, 2014) (Fig. 8.2).

How important is it ...?
    What kind of researcher do I want to be?
    Waves and flow, back and forth.
    I'm watching.
    What kind of research matters to me?
    Waves and flow, back and forth.
    I'm watching you. I'm watching with you.
    Can I be who I am? Can I be seen?
    Waves and flow, back and forth.
    I see footprints, rock pools, movement, and undulating sand.

I hear a beating heart, the crash (and sighs) of surf, or is that you?
What is it for if not for connecting?
Our human ways of living, knowing and telling?
Waves and flow, back and forth.
I'm watching. I'm watching with you.
Eventide. Tidings.
I sit with what matters.
The sea is sucking back. Beginning again.
I sit with what gives me meaning.
Thoughts become lost in rhythmic bands.
Contemplation. Reflection.
Waiting. Watching. Being. Listening.
Noticing.
Your feet make patterns. Sand on your hands.
Connecting.
I'm here. All still. The earth in place.
A new way of seeing.
Looking inwards. Looking outwards.
Only the sea and its sailors can see your face.
Can see the change, brought by this space.
Waves and flow, back and forth.
I watch you and I sit with you.
I see anew too.

This chapter is also written for others. We aim to provide a point of connection for others interested in researching with 'self-positioning' (Rhedding-Jones, 2005, p. 18) through asking questions of their own becoming. To our readers, we extend an invitation to sit with us in this nurturing, responsive and reciprocal space of disclosure and exposure, and ponder with us the importance of aesthetic tools for finding, using, hearing and comprehending experience and voice (Black, 2015). As with our previous writing (Black & Loch, 2014), we invite consideration about the risk and value of adventuring to speak stories out loud into public and research spaces.

THE RISKS OF ADVENTURING TO SPEAK OUT LOUD

Sarah to Ali: (October 2013) I have been thinking how prayer is used as a language during times of gaps and transitions that often do not have other language. I am not religious or possibly spiritual, or perhaps I am, but I don't use prayer in my life. However, I am interested in recalling my father and understanding the role he played in getting me 'here: becoming-researcher,* *academic'. I have noticed that through my poststructuralist engagement in writing (which I'm looking forward to working with you to expand), this writing space becomes a type of prayer in my life. Writing of the personal and making connections across difficult spaces seems to be happening through writing which is 'prayer-like'. So, if we were to write about father figures, I might use a type of academic prayer to manage this. I have a feeling what I would write would be unlike the other writing voices I have learnt to use.*

* * *

<u>*Ali to Sarah:*</u> *(March 2014) It has meant so much to have you take the time to share how my stories have stayed with you. So often in my work I feel that 'what really matters' is not valued. I have observed how one's worth is determined with a glance—with a scroll down a CV to see how many publications we have and how much grant money we have brought in. Such narrow lenses. I think I struggle with the question of where being human sits in all of this educational work. Where do we value the person, each other, interactions, living an ethic of care, learning as a process of sharing experience? We shouldn't have to set aside those things that give us meaning for competitive, heartless processes. Who is research for in the end? Does the research count or is it the research dollars—the greater the dollar the greater the assigned 'value'? Where does all the money go? How does any of it make any real kind of difference? Are lives improved? Anyone's lives? Researchers or researched? So, these are the things I grapple with.*

With universities deploying huge infrastructure to ensure research outputs count and can be counted, spaces for experimental inquiry are receding and becoming less viable for researchers to explore (Honan, Henderson, & Loch, 2015). It takes courage and conviction to approach research differently when careers and livelihoods are placed at risk. Of an alternative ethics, Laurel Richardson (2008, p. 1) writes encouragingly to those who adventure: 'You are the ones who chose to act differently, to respond to your callings, to build community, to welcome others.' And, what happens when we really pause to consider the purpose of research? Jeanette Rhedding-Jones (2005, p. 148) stresses that change is 'a crucial quality of research' and 'seen personally, research is about surviving the workplace and then transforming both it and yourself'. So, what happens when the kind of researcher we want to be is bound up in who we are and our lived experiences? What happens when we want the purpose of our work to support this deep exploration of the meaning of life, of 'what life is for' (Kronman, 2007)?

Writing together has supported our understanding of how the 'whole' of who we are and the 'whole' of our experiences influence everything (Palmer,

Fig. 8.3 Writing with you Sarah connects me to something deep, to myself, it is like communion (Ali Black, Personal photograph, digitally modified 2015)

2009). As we engage in our 'academic' work together, we slip in fragments of our lives: IVF, relationships with fathers, domesticities, struggles and joys. And in this everydayness is a reminder of what research means for us—engaging with the lives and stories and experiences of others, and being changed by these, understanding things about others and ourselves that we would not have been able to—without—this interaction and relationship.

Writing collaboratively with support for the aesthetic and sensual means more than just telling each other happenings; it is reaching into something deep, like communion. Similarly, Jane Bone explores 'everyday spirituality' (2009) and 'spiritual withness' (2008) in educational writing and research processes where the potency of being with and thinking with those being researched allows her 'own memories and personal narrative … [to] closely engag[e] with the stories of others' (2008, p. 354). Bone (2009, p. 150) draws attention to ways that writing research 'supports a reconceptualisation of endings whereby an ending is simply opening up another possibility and supporting new directions', which is a thought to which we respond. Thinking about ourselves as researchers, we raise our sensitivity towards 'the process of dwelling with the data' (Finlay, 2014, p. 9) by first of all looking around our own interactions to think about what research is and how it becomes ours (Fig. 8.3).

Research Through Relationship

Our adventuring along this path thinking about what research is and how it becomes ours began with a paper about feeling compelled to respond to one another's writing (Black & Loch, 2014). We were surprised by what happened here, by the ease of opening up, the warmth of writing for someone who wanted to respond and the value of creating safe spaces to welcome others. Our multiple positions as writer–reader–thinker of one another's stories help these spaces form. Our individual voices became stronger as we read—'That matters! I want to join with you in speaking!'

Reflection on becoming through relationship shows us that responsiveness is central, as is trust and time. Tentative at first, we have developed a rhythm of sharing and responding, although in the responding, we do not always know what to say. Roles blur as there are many different ways to respond. Even silence registers a response when words are inadequate. But we like the feeling of being called to respond; of mattering in someone else's dialogue and the energy of (e)motion that stirs us to connect to another's varied life threads. Storying and responding with and to others are how we want to work, write and research.

Our we-ness or two-ness is a factor we pause to consider. Writing with an unwavering 'we' implies a twinness with two voices speaking from a shared embodiment. Of course, we are different. Sarah has only recently become an academic after being a middle school teacher and taking a break to become a parent. Ali has given many years to academia across three universities. Others who write in collaboration have suggested the value of keeping 'difference alive in the text' by 'giv[ing] expression to … multiple singularities' (Wyatt et al., 2014, p. 132). But here we dwell on the intensity of how the connection feels and why we experience its force as productive and enabling. We have not experienced conflict in our relationship (for thoughts on conflict between collaborative writers, see Wyatt & Gale, 2011), instead in collaboration we enjoy 'our mutual becomings … expand[ing] creatively and unexpectedly' (Myers, 2014, p. 43) and seeing how the other does things, manages life and academia. A feature of our exchange, however, is unevenness in the intensity, volume and rhythm of our communications. There can be one-sidedness, fast and slow, differences of moods and different needs and goals. Our differences chip away irregularly at our shared projects—one of us waiting and pushing on alone, the other caught up elsewhere, then returning, rejoining. There are periods of equanimity where a calm and easy back and forth deterritorialises us with the rhythm of Deleuze and Guattari's waves. At these times, we move in flows of sharing which in their own time will eventually be interrupted. Accepting an unevenness of collaboration offers different size spaces through which we learn more about the other and ourselves. We find ourselves shifting into expansive places of fellowship and kinship, discovering and rediscovering our common humanity (Boyle, 2011).

Manoeuvring Through What Cannot Be Laid in a Draw Until 'The Work' Is Over

Allowing another to see the items squirreled away reactivates and repairs our connections to parts of us open to damage from zombifying work cultures that prefer emotionless workers who meet targets and get on with it (Palmer & Zajonc, 2010; Ryan, 2012; Whelan, Walker, & Moore, 2013). We work to connect so that we and those around us do not shut down; to collectively engage in discovery (Finley, 2014); in stories already underway and ceaselessly occurring.

Sarah, her PhD and becoming academic: *I look back over my journey to becoming academic and I don't find much coherence except the dissonance of lining up a PhD that came to being through dedication and sacrifice, and a journey to parenthood pockmarked by failure. The excitement of the next attempt, the nervous knowledge that it is highly likely to fail, and hoping it won't. And I don't actually have any fertility problems. It seems I just find it harder to do than university degrees. This haze of ups and downs has marked this 'becoming academic' period of my life* (Fig. 8.4).

* * *

Ali, her PhD and becoming academic: *Sarah, there really is a sense of understanding between us, a place of connection about real things that are generally those 'unspokens'. I like your open interweaving of life and becoming academic. In it I recognise that this is my story too.*
What I find intriguing is that whilst there is enormous interweaving, I did not feel able to acknowledge the personal realm in the professional realm in my becoming academic. There has been a definite sense that the personal must stay

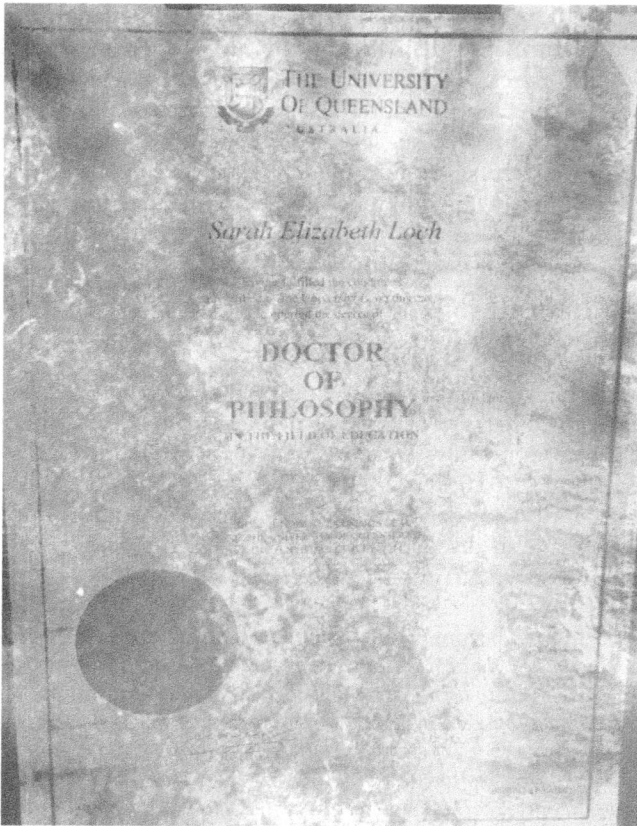

Fig. 8.4 A PhD journey pockmarked by failure? (Ali Black, Digital artwork, based on Personal photo offered by Sarah Loch, 2015)

personal and hidden. Yet, that is impossible. As we are coming to understand, we simply cannot do this work without being who we are. As I reflect back on the first five years of my 'becoming academic' I am startled. During these five years I began my PhD (studying part-time while working full time), my first marriage completely broke down and my husband left me, my grandmother died days after that, and I was visiting my imprisoned father most weekends. My mother moved from our family home into a retirement village and I moved into a house where I subsequently got burgled three times. I got divorced and started a new relationship. My mother had several serious operations. I moved house four more times,

Fig. 8.5 What is the cost (to our research, to expanding our understanding of the world, to our own sense of wholeness) if we compartmentalise life and work to veil the full dimensions of our own humanity? (Ali Black, Digital artwork, 2015)

got married, and negotiated the blending of families. And in the year our son was conceived and born, my PhD was completed and conferred.

So many dramas, emotions, unspokens. It simply is not possible to compartmentalise life and work—and something essential is lost in the trying (Fig. 8.5).

CONTEMPLATION

Contemplate.

I enter this space thinking about how much has changed since I began writing with Ali. I am now living out what I wanted: a full time position as a lecturer in a university, PhD acquired, a more experienced parent, juggling full time work and parenting with more fluency.

Jagged fluency.

My IVF experience continues. The further we go, success-less in this second-time-round, the closer we come to the end. I have resolved this means my boy is my only child and he has no siblings. This doesn't mean I didn't try. It just means we are the loving parents of one child. But everything about this situation stings. Is this something to write about here? Is it relevant, interesting? Does it belong? The potency of this wave of sharing is that through this becoming-ending of my too-long IVF journey, I am finally feeling settled again, not always as yearning. It is allowing me to become 'professional' again.

Research.

Was I ever less professional because I was more personal? Why am I falling into binaries when it is within in-betweenness that I am found? But when you are in-between, although this may be the desired place for disruptive, philosophical thinking, it is not really so nice. There's some benefit in being agile, flexible and responsive, but there's also benefit in drawing nourishment along the roots and lines already established. Slippage.

I'm a professional body and a parent who leaves on the dot to get back home to her child.

I can barely bring language to that feeling—do you know it? Having your body in one place, but bolting with that splintered sick feeling to the car to get home to your baby and to be yourself again. In terms of 'extending to others an invitation to also dwell, join and contribute', I will try to find expression for these intermeshes of personal and professional. It may become visual? Perhaps this photo below... (Fig. 8.6).

Pause.

A new way of seeing.
Looking inwards. Looking outwards.
Waves and flow, back and forth.
I watch you and I sit with you.
I see anew too.

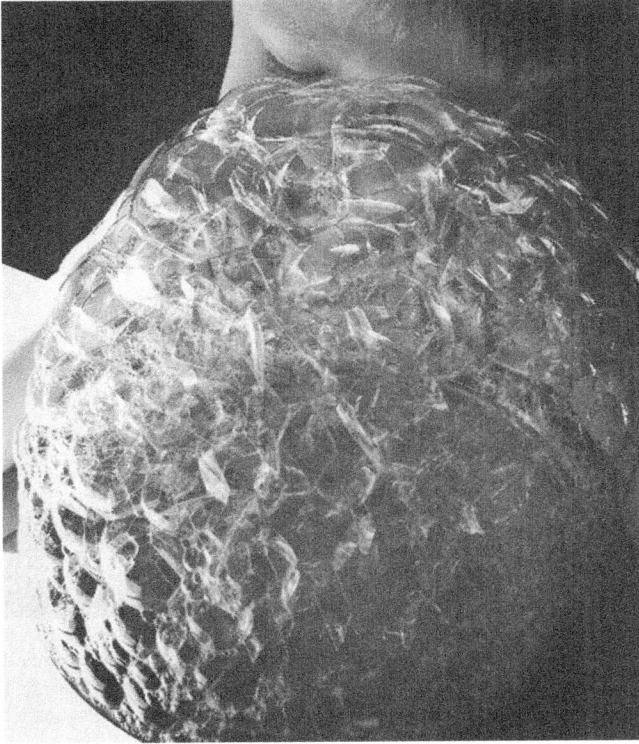

Fig. 8.6 My four-year-old son loves 'doing science' and he's made a brain out of air. He blows bubbles using a straw in a bowl of water and his creation begins to overflow. What do I see? What else should I be doing with my time? The intermesh of personal/professional. (Sarah Loch, Personal photo, 2015)

Through collaborative adventure, our ideas about inquiry are shared in ways we hope will be useful to others who are also querying who they are in their research and how their stories can matter.

We hope work like ours will help more researchers to find ways to tell their academic communities how they do the work they do and who they are whilst they do it. There is richness in connecting with others but we must not forget why we research. It is not just a game of citations, funding, getting in the best journals; it is about engaging with the lives and stories and experiences of others, and being changed by these, understanding

Fig. 8.7 What is at the heart of our research if we are not there? A call to live beyond the divided academic life (Ali Black, Digital artwork based on Personal photo offered by Sarah Loch, 2015)

things about others and ourselves that we would not have been able to without this interaction, without these methodologies.

In terms of methodology, beyond manoeuvring around the personal/professional binary, we urge something more; a methodology that, through continued and varied use, becomes ever more mindful. We have found writing, art, poetry and representations of thinking helpful in contemplating, exposing and disclosing the heart of our humanness. We have found that venturing together informs our research by giving us skill in recognising and saying what matters to us, and we have developed sensitivity towards the ways we speak about ourselves as well as others. We invite the reader to dwell with us, to contribute and adventure with us, to speak out loud the experiences of a multitude of lives into diverse research arenas (Fig. 8.7).

REFERENCES

Black, A. L. (2015). Authoring a life: Writing ourselves in/out of our work in education. In M. Baguley, Y. Findlay, & M. Kerby (Eds.), *Meanings and motivation in education research*. London: Routledge.

Black, A. L., & Loch, S. (2014). Called to respond: The potential of unveiling hiddens. *Reconceptualising Educational Research Methodology*, 5(2), 60–75. doi:10.7577/rerm.1221

Black, A. L., & O'Dea, S. (2015). Building a tapestry of knowledge in the spaces in between: Weaving personal and collective meaning through arts-based research. In K. Trimmer, A. L. Black, & S. Riddle (Eds.), *Mainstreams, margins and the spaces in-between: New possibilities for education research*. London: Routledge.

Bone, J. (2008). Creating relational spaces: Everyday spirituality in early childhood settings. *European Early Childhood Education Research Journal*, 16(3), 343–356. doi:10.1080/13502930802292122.

Bone, J. (2009). Writing research: Narrative, bricolage and everyday spirituality. *New Zealand Research in Early Childhood Education Journal*, 12(1), 143–152.

Boyle, G. (2011). *Tattoos on the heart: The power of boundless compassion*. New York: Free Press.

Deleuze, G., & Guattari, F. (1987). *A thousand plateaus: Capitalism and schizophrenia* (B. Massumi, Trans.). Minneapolis: University of Minnesota Press.

Dewey, J. (1934). *Art as experience*. New York: Capricorn Books.

Eisner, E. W. (1997). The new frontier in qualitative research methodology. *Qualitative Inquiry*, 3(3), 259–273. doi:10.1177/107780049700300301.

Finlay, L. (2014). Embodying research. *Person-Centered and Experiential Psychotherapies*, 13(1), 4–18. doi:10.1080/14779757.2013.855133.

Finley, S. (2010). "Freedom's just another word for nothin' left to lose": The power of poetry for young, nomadic women of the streets. *Cultural Studies ↔ Critical Methodologies*, 10(1), 58–63. doi:10.1177/1532708609351158.

Finley, S. (2014). An introduction to critical arts-based research: Demonstrating methodologies and practices of a radical ethical aesthetic. *Cultural Studies ↔ Critical Methodologies*, 14(6), 531–532. doi:10.1177/1532708614548123.

Honan, E., Henderson, L., & Loch, S. (2015). Producing moments of pleasure within the confines of an academic quantified self. *Creative Approaches to Research*, 8(3), 44–62.

Kronman, A. T. (2007). *Education's end: Why our colleges and universities have given up on the meaning of life*. New Haven, CT: Yale University Press.

Loch, S. (2014). *Unfolding becoming: An invitation into the future imaginings of middle school girls, interlaced with my own journey to researcher*. (PhD), University of Queensland, St Lucia.

Myers, C. Y. (2014). A "terribly inefficient" production: Unsettling methodologies with children through Deleuzian notions of time. *Reconceptualising Educational Research Methodology, 5*(2), 34–45.

Otterstad, A. M., Osgood, J., Bloch, M., Taguchi, H. L., Sandvik, N., & Montserrat Fonseca Bustos, M. (2014). Editorial Special Edition. *Reconceptualizing Educational Research Methodology, 5*(2), 1–4.

Palmer, P. J. (2009). *A hidden wholeness: The journey toward an undivided life.* San Francisco: Jossey-Bass.

Palmer, P. J., & Zajonc, A. (2010). *The heart of higher education: A call to renewal.* San Francisco: Jossey-Bass.

Rhedding-Jones, J. (1995). What do you do after you've met poststructuralism? Research possibilities regarding feminism, ethnography and literacy. *Journal of Curriculum Studies, 27*(5), 479–500. doi:10.1080/0022027950270502.

Rhedding-Jones, J. (1996). Researching early schooling: Poststructural practices and academic writing in an ethnography. *British Journal of Sociology of Education, 17*(1), 21–37. doi:10.1080/0142569960170102.

Rhedding-Jones, J. (2005). *What is research? Methodological practices and new approaches.* Oslo: Universitetsforlaget.

Richardson, L. (2008). Foreword: You changed my life. *Creative Approaches to Research, 1*(1), 1–2.

Richardson, L. (2010). Jeopardy: A grandmother's story. *Symbolic Interaction, 33*(1), 3–17. doi:10.1525/si.2010.33.1.3.

Ryan, S. (2012). Academic zombies: A failure of resistance or a means of survival? *The Australian Universities' Review, 54*(2), 11.

Trimmer, K., Black, A., & Riddle, S. (Eds.) (2015). *Mainstreams, margins and the spaces in-between: New possibilities for education research.* London: Routledge.

Whelan, A., Walker, R., & Moore, C. (2013). *Zombies in the academy: Living death in higher education.* Bristol: Intellect Books.

Wyatt, J., & Gale, K. (2011). The textor, the nomads and a labyrinth: A response to Graham Badley. *Qualitative Inquiry, 17*(6), 493–497. doi:10.1177/1077800411409880.

Wyatt, J., Gale, K., Gannon, S., Davies, B., Denzin, N. K., & St. Pierre, E. A. (2014). Deleuze and collaborative writing: Responding to/with "JKSB". *Cultural Studies ↔ Critical Methodologies,* 1–10. doi:10.1177/1532708614530313.

Show and Tell: A Practice-Led Methodological Solution for Researchers in Creative Writing

Leanne Dodd

INTRODUCTION

This chapter presents a case study of the author's experiences in transitioning from the role of creative writing practitioner to that of practice-led researcher of creative practice. A key challenge facing students engaged in this transition is that 'creating' is different from 'researching and writing about the creative process'. Scrivener (2000, p. 8) proposes that the language of theory is at odds with [the language of] creative production. The case study sets out to resolve this dichotomy by demonstrating how these competing modes of writing can be complementary when assuming strategic risks to combine them in creative research writing. The impetus for the 'Show and Tell' design is to develop a methodology tailored to creative writing practitioners that values the imagination and the intellect. While practitioners may contribute new knowledge to the research com-

L. Dodd (✉)
School of Education and the Arts, CQUniversity Australia,
Newmarket, Brisbane, QLD, Australia

© The Author(s) 2016
B. Harreveld et al. (eds.), *Constructing Methodology for Qualitative Research*, DOI 10.1057/978-1-137-59943-8_9

munity gained through experimentation in practice, this is often inter-mingled with an equally important personal agenda to use research to produce enriched creative work. This methodology design aims to grant practitioners a legitimate way to pursue this agenda while meeting the definition and goals of academic research.

The rationale is introduced by uniting with the author on a journey through the maze of methodological literature to establish a framework for the methodology design, which both engages with and arises from individual creative practice. The chapter then explores the need to moti-vate the practitioner/researcher and cultivate intellectual curiosity to keep engagement high enough to complete the research project. Ways in which the 'Show and Tell' approach can achieve this are examined alongside a dis-cussion on mitigating the risks involved in resisting dominant discourses.

The final section invites the reader to develop a personal 'Show and Tell' approach by observing an evidence-based case that takes into account the practitioners' prior learning and acquired knowledge and offers ways to integrate this into writing up the research. By forming a dynamic rela-tionship between the competing notions of 'show' and 'tell' which are demanded of creative and academic writing, respectively, the methodol-ogy design pays attention to the practitioner's personal creative agenda while adhering to the conventions of scholarship.

THE ROAD NOT FOLLOWED

Two roads diverged in a wood, and I—
  I took the one less travelled by,
  And that has made all the difference.
Robert Frost (1920, p. 9)

Rationale

Setting out on the journey into the maze of post-graduate research lit-erature, it was intimidating to find many books written from a mind-set of pain. The first two pages of a Google search on thesis-writing books illustrate this by offering the following warning terms: daunting, dreaded, formidable, uphill, overwhelming, pressure, wrestle, stuck, challenging. The existence of such descriptions demonstrated a need to challenge this pain mind-set. Creative writing practitioners generally partake in writing as a pleasurable endeavor so the opportunity arose to envision ways to extend this passion into research writing. What eventuated is a show *and* tell approach.

Many creative writing practitioners will attest that 'Show, don't tell' is the number one rule of the practice. Sword (2012, p. 99) claims that it 'is the mantra of the novelist'. This is an evocative metaphor as this writing rule is customarily drilled into the minds of creative writers during professional training, and subsequently recalled throughout the writing process. Telling is to be avoided unless there is a justifiable reason to impart information quickly. To understand the difference, telling employs a simple abstract description: *Marley was terrified as the door closed loudly*. Alternatively, showing is achieved by the use of specific action-oriented language: *Marley felt her body go rigid as the door slammed shut*. While this description does not plainly state that Marley is terrified, or that the door was loud, it allows the reader to see these states through concrete actions, and more importantly, to be engaged in the story. As a formally trained creative writing practitioner bringing a working knowledge of the creative writing process to my academic research, 'Show, don't tell' was a key device in my creative writing toolkit.

Relying on Candy's (2006, p. 2) definition that practice-led research takes the nature of practice as its central focus, bringing the concept of 'Show, don't tell' into the realm of academia seemed appropriate for my practice-led creative writing project. One motivation to transition from pure practice to the research of practice was to enhance my practice outcomes by creating a hybrid crime novel that aligned the narrative strategies of trauma and crime fiction, thereby representing trauma more innocuously for the benefit of readers and writers. This presented an opportunity to add a new subset of trauma fiction and/or a new sub-genre of crime fiction to the canon of existing literature, which could make an original contribution to knowledge. 'Original contribution to knowledge' is defined by Central Queensland University (2010, p. 9) policies as:

> a subject area in the form of new knowledge through discovery or application of existing knowledge by the exercise of independent critical thinking, as evidenced by a substantial body of new work.

Having researched the narrative strategies used in trauma fiction and exercised independent critical thinking to apply them to a new work of hybrid crime fiction in original and innovative ways, this project seemed to fit within the context of this definition. As a novice researcher, who had been distanced from the academic world for almost 20 years, my rudimentary belief was that my creative work would be embedded with new knowledge and that in its own right, it would be of scholarly benefit to other practitioners in learning new creative writing processes.

Venturing deeper into the maze, Candy's (2006, p. 2) discussion about the importance of distinguishing between practice-led research and pure practice signposted the next turn:

> [T]he outcomes of the practice must be accompanied by documentation of the research process, as well as some form of textual analysis or explanation to support its position and to demonstrate critical reflection.

While it was correct to assume that the process of creation is intrinsic to the creative work, the knowledge about the process does remain trapped in the mind of the creator unless it is released in some way. It is much like a new animal born at the zoo but shielded from public view; we know this knowledge is there, but how do we access it? Strand's (1998, p. 51) report had earlier theorized that the possibility of research 'exists only when the worker pauses in one of these activities and says "what if?"' This knowledge is not available to the reader unless an explanation of that knowledge is exhibited. This draws a parallel with Candy's claim that practice must be accompanied by critical reflection to be considered as research. My research methods needed to harness and record my individual insights into the creative process and make them accessible to others.

Framework

Further meandering revealed that many post-graduate creative arts programs mandated the submission of an accompanying exegesis to the creative work. Even so, there was no clear direction for my project. The exegesis has been defined in simple terms as a document that sits alongside the creative work and explores the ideas in the non-academic work using traditional academic discourse (Arnold, 2005, p. 41). Fletcher and Mann (2004, p. 6) propose that the purpose of the exegesis is 'to present the research framework: the key questions, the theories, disciplinary and wider contexts of the project'. They also claim 'These things are not necessarily evident…in the creative work itself.' Arnold (2005, p. 41) observes a more recent evolution in the creative arts exegesis: a rising incidence of reflective writing, 'in which the contribution to knowledge becomes insights into the individual creative process with reference to ideas in the relevant literature'. While further research revealed that not all types of reflective writing have been readily accepted across the academy as academic in nature (Bourke & Neilsen, 2004), this offered a method that warranted further exploration.

Examining exegetical works in the creative arts, approaches to their focus and subject matter seemed inconsistent with no commonly applied methodology. To compound this, no generally agreed exegetical approach existed between institutions. Among examples encountered, Candy (2006, p. 1), from Sydney University of Technology, outlines a 'structure of a practice-based doctoral thesis [with] a short description of the expected content of each chapter', including a full template which serves to straightjacket students into a generic format. Nash (2011, p. 5), from University of the Sunshine Coast, argues against developing a standard methodology. Suggesting that creative writing 'sit[s] on the fringes of any number of disciplines', he sets out a kaleidoscope method of picking theory from other disciplines related to the variable themes and content area of the creative work. Scrivener (2000, p. 2), from Coventry University, UK, defines two different types of creative projects, 'problem-solving' and 'creative-production', which require different exegetical approaches. Although further progress had been made, the path ahead was far from clear.

It transpired that the 'research' was to be found in the relationship *between* the creative work and the exegesis. Candy (2006, p. 9) validates the existence of this relational space when she explains that 'the text describes the innovation embodied in the artefact but cannot be fully understood without reference to and observation of the artefact', where 'artefact' refers to the creative work. Based on Candy's earlier requisites for 'linguistic description', and Arnold's for 'traditional academic discourse' in the exegesis, it was natural to deduce that the two components called for two different styles of writing. Kroll (2002, p. 1) refers to this as '*the schizophrenic nature*' of the creative writing thesis. My creative practice was governed by the rule of 'Show, don't tell'. The academic writing style, where the main purpose is to 'tell', was in conflict with this style.

Direction

A fork in the road loomed ahead. Scrivener (2000, p. 2) contends that many researchers/practitioners face this dilemma, aspiring that research enhance their practice, and not subordinate it. The route most traveled seemed to follow the two paths in isolation, producing a creative work and an exegesis in disjointed writing styles. As the creative work was my primary outcome from a practitioner's stance, my quandary became how to write up the exegetical component without allowing my creativity to suffer. This was made problematic by my findings that, traditionally, more emphasis has been placed on the exegetical component by examiners of creative arts degrees. Bourke and Neilsen confirm this when they state creative writing is 'a discipline whose principal concern is with the development, critique and articulation of process rather than product' (2004, p. 12). While my stance was not uncommon, the risks of challenging the conventions of academic writing needed to be approached in a strategic way. Rather than taking these two isolated roads, the dare to poke my head through the dividing hedge was overpowering. The 'Show and Tell' methodology design elects to merge the two paths, with creative practice as its central focus. It manoeuvres between the two writing styles in such a way as to form a dynamic relationship between the competing notions of 'show' *and* 'tell'. Before outlining the methods chosen to enact this vision, it is worth taking a side-track to look at the significance that the 'Show and Tell' methodology approach may have for creative writing practitioners and for the academy, and why in the earlier words of Robert Frost, 'that has made all the difference' for my research writing.

A ROUTE OF ONE'S OWN

I am rooted, but I flow.
   Virginia Woolf (2015, p. 59).

Significance

The creative writer aspires to uniqueness of voice. In 1922, Virginia Woolf wrote in her diary that individuality, not popularity, was her only interest. 'I'm to write what I like; & they're to say what they like' (cited in Pankin, 1987, p. 104). Woolf's idealistic goal of finding her unique voice and following her own route, regardless of the critical response, is perhaps reflected in the thoughts of many a creative writer. In a conversation with Dr. Jo-Ann Sparrow, former DCA candidate from University of Sunshine Coast, she confirmed that finding the unique voice for her doctoral exegesis was the most difficult part of her research journey but an achievement that was highly commended by her examiners (J. Sparrow, personal communication, 4 March 2015). While following one's own route may be a valiant stance for any creative writer, Kroll (2002, p. 5) reminds us that for those undertaking a post-graduate research degree, formal 'evaluation must happen at the end of the process'. From this perspective, it makes sense to simply compose the exegesis in an academic writing mode to satisfy the requirements of the university.

Returning to the motivations of the practitioner, however, it becomes evident that there is a need for a methodology tailored to creative writing practitioners conducting academic research. As previously discussed, the creative ambitions of the writer may overshadow other considerations. Vella (2005, p. 2) argues that keeping the arts degree creative is paramount to avoid the danger of the practitioner becoming 'disenfranchised from their own practice'. While these ambitions may appear self-serving, they do in fact hold value for the community. Kroll (2002, p. 2) claims that creative writing 'provides entertainment and intellectual stimulation, but in a larger sense it preserves and promotes our heritage'. Tapping into the natural drive of the writer to entertain, stimulate and inform can promote a passionate engagement for the duration of the project. This is important in terms of student gratification but it also promotes student commitment and consequently, retention. Milech and Schilo (2004, p. 8) recount their experiences with creative writing students at Curtin University in Perth, Australia. Even their best students displayed unwanted attitudes ranging from reticence and lack of confidence to outright hostility toward the prevailing methods of academic writing. They deduce that creative writing students need the freedom to explore their research question in creative and academic modes of writing, which results in a 'bimodal' thesis (p. 11). Since student retention is generally linked to government funding, Australian institutions have every incentive to sustain students' enthusiasm throughout their course of study.

While this issue is frequently explored in the Australian context, some international studies can help pave a way forward. In Canada, for example, Piers Steel, of the University of Calgary's psychology department, has proposed the following formula for calculating a person's ability to complete a task:

$$\text{Utility} = \frac{E \times V}{\Gamma \times D}$$

where E is confidence of succeeding in the task, V is how pleasant it is perceived to be, Γ is how easily the person is distracted and D is time lapse before reward (cited in Pringle, 2014, p. 109). This formula combines highly emotive variables relating to enthusiasm with the best score achieved when the top line is highest and the bottom line is lowest. This formula can be applied to the writing of an exegesis in various ways. For instance, utilizing skills acquired in practice may increase one's confidence of succeeding (E). Second, using the language of creative writing in the exegesis may increase the pleasure rating (V) and decrease the distraction level (Γ) for practitioners who often enjoy, and get lost in, the writing task. With the resulting productivity gains, the reward might also be more quickly attained (D). Steel's formula demonstrates how cultivating a relationship between creative and academic writing styles may result in greater engagement during the exegetical component of the project, and ultimately a better chance of student commitment and retention.

Practitioners/researchers whose practice is deeply rooted in creative writing modes may also struggle to branch out into academic writing modes due to fear or boredom. Davis and Shadle (2000, p. 418), of Eastern Oregon University in the USA, highlight the importance of alternative research methods for creative writing students in order for them to overcome the 'fear of, and boredom with, traditional research writing'. They propose the term "multi-writing" to describe a model which 'often involve[s] choosing among, mixing, and juxtaposing a grand variety of discourses' (p. 421). 'Mixing' and 'juxtaposing' perfectly articulate the basis for combining the two writing styles in the 'Show and Tell' methodology design to provide an alternative to traditional research writing and overcome these issues.

Risks

Before moving on, it is prudent to consider the risk involved in blurring the boundaries between these two styles of writing. A divide continues to exist between analytical, critical or theoretical academic modes of writing and the more expressive modes of creative writing. Kroll (2002, p. 3) alludes to a long history of apprehension among 'segments of academia [who] remain suspicious of creative writing as research'. A risk exists that the 'bimodal' exegesis may not be accepted as meeting academic research criteria.

With risk, however, comes the potential for innovation. Stewart (2001, p. 4) makes the counterproposal that taking control of our discipline by 'appropriating [it's] accepted processes and restructuring them for our needs, may be the way to go'. Virginia Woolf's earlier quote fittingly describes this process. By redefining these structures, the exegesis can be 'rooted' within the parameters of scholarship, while also being allowed to 'flow' into the terrain of creativity. Risks have actually been proposed in not taking this risk. Davis and Shadle (2000, p. 426) express concerns that directing students to rigidly follow convention may risk making them fearful of exploring the unknown. Making a 'contribution to knowledge', however, necessitates striking a passage into the unknown. The aim of the 'Show and Tell' methodology approach is to take strategized risks in this direction in order to innovate a restructured form of academic writing.

Through a practice-led example, the following section outlines selected methods and how they can be tailored to meet the criteria for the 'Show and Tell' methodology design, which attempts to locate research in the domain of creativity and practice in the domain of scholarship.

'SHOW AND TELL' METHODOLOGY DESIGN

Paradigm/Strategy

In designing the methodology, the first step was to identify the appropriate research paradigm and strategy for my project in order to adhere to the conventions of scholarship. My project sought to find ways to represent trauma more innocuously for the benefit of readers and writers in a work of crime fiction. This seemed to sit most comfortably in the interpretive paradigm where the philosophical assumption is that the meaning of trauma is a social construct based on individual experience (Creswell, 2003, p. 8). Creswell (2003, p. 18) aligns the qualitative approach to constructivist perspectives, so a qualitative strategy seemed most fitting.

Yin's (2014, p. 236) description of research design was adopted for the purpose of selecting qualitative methods to configure this strategy:

> *An action plan for getting from here to there*, where *here* may be defined as the initial set of questions to be answered and *there* is some set of conclusions (answers) about these questions.

It followed from this that the design of my 'action plan' or methodology called for methods to collect and analyze data that would ultimately allow me to answer my research question and provide information to test my writing experiments against (Brien, 2006, p. 56). My key research question was: How can trauma be represented in a crime fiction novel so that this work performs functions similar to trauma literature, while still maintaining the popular appeal of crime fiction? Case study was the qualitative method chosen to collect and analyze data about how trauma is currently represented. Reflective writing was the method chosen to make an effective contribution to knowledge by capturing new writing processes that achieved the aim of the question.

Thesis

To locate practice in the domain of scholarship, an academically accepted thesis format was required to write up the results of the research inquiry. Fletcher and Mann (2004, p. 4) observe that 'the generally accepted definition of the creative thesis is where "creative work plus exegesis" equal the thesis'. They saw an opportunity for flexibility in the way this model was not 'uniformly and clearly articulated' across Australian universities. This unintended consequence allowed me the liberty to create a model that combined the creative and academic writing styles in the exegetical component.

Figure 9.1 maps the overarching design of the 'Show and Tell' methodology approach. The outer circle represents the creative thesis. While it contains both the creative work and the exegesis, it aligns with Candy's (2006, p. 2) earlier definition that practice-led research takes the nature of practice as its central focus. The remaining inner circles represent the selected qualitative methods.

The intersecting segments in Fig. 9.1 embody the dynamic relationship between the competing notions of 'show' and 'tell', traditionally separated by the creative and academic writing modes typical of each component. Utilizing this juncture to nurture the relationship between the two thesis components helped me to link the active process of creation with the product. This consequently established the desired creative engagement between them that would locate the research in the domain of creativity.

Methods

The final step in designing the methodology was to tailor the selected qualitative methods to achieve this desired relationship. The design takes into account my prior learning, acquired knowledge and personal creative agenda. As differing creative writing projects may have unlimited outcomes, these methods are presented as possibilities to be mixed and matched with other suitable methods according to the requirements of individual projects.

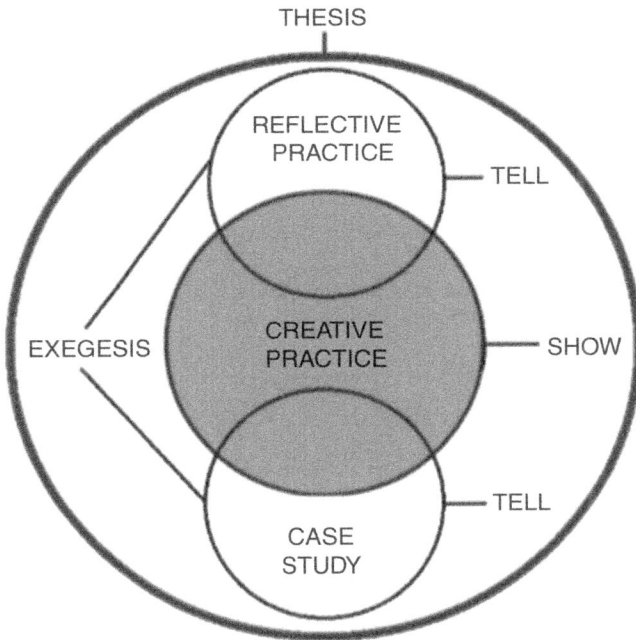

Fig. 9.1   'Show and tell' methodology design

1. Case Study

The first method employed in my research project was a series of case studies. A case study can be seen as the ultimate 'show and tell' method. The *Oxford Dictionary* defines a case study as 'a particular instance of something used or analysed in order to illustrate a thesis or principle'. The case illustrates, or *shows*, a particular real-life situation. The study of the case analyzes, or *tells*, about the situation.

The case study presented in this chapter demonstrates how the two languages, creative and academic, may be combined to develop a relationship with a creative work while following a format that conforms to academic guidelines and places it in the realm of academic scholarship. It first identifies and analyzes the problems of the real-life case with reference to relevant theory, being issues faced by me and other practitioners/researchers in writing up the results of creative research in two writing styles. It then outlines the potential solution as combining these styles, and integrates theory to assess the advantages and disadvantages of this solution. Finally, it offers ways to implement the recommended solution (Monash University Library, 2007).

This chapter enacts examples of the use of 'show' language to describe the case. Action-oriented language is used to describe concrete actions throughout the journey, which allows the reader to 'see' the manoeuvres being made through the metaphoric maze. The metaphor below from section one paints a visual picture and allows the reader to experience the journey and the implied risk in steering from the traditional discourse.

> Rather than taking these two isolated roads, the dare to poke my head through the dividing hedge was overpowering.

Analogies are also used to compare theory to a familiar situation that the reader is more likely to relate to:

> It is much like a new animal born at the zoo but shielded from public view; we are told this knowledge is there, but how do we access it?

Verbs have been carefully chosen to reinforce the metaphors or analogies throughout the text. The verbs 'trapped', 'released', 'exhibited' and 'harness' are employed in association to the zoo analogy above. Following the Woolf quote in section two, 'I am rooted, but I flow', related words are subtly inserted throughout the section, including 'nurture', 'tap into', 'wither', 'deeply rooted' and 'branch out'.

Exercising this creative language in the exegesis can form a relationship with the language crafted in the creative work. Also of significance, the process of writing this academic chapter called upon prior learning and knowledge and had an equivalent impact to that of creative writing in maintaining my engagement throughout the research and writing process. Juxtaposed with this 'show' language, an academic writing mode using the language of 'tell' has been employed when integrating theory into the case study. This process draws a correlation with Stewart's (2001, p. 4) earlier suggestion that 'appropriating [the discipline's] accepted processes and restructuring them for our needs, may be the way to go'.

The case study for my project employs textual analysis of four selected creative works to inform the creation of my hybrid crime novel. Works were chosen that engaged with related social themes about trauma, and employed the narrative strategies of trauma fiction and crime fiction. The case studies for my exegesis are written up using this 'show and tell' technique to achieve my goal of establishing creative engagement between the exegesis and my creative work.

2. Reflective Practice

The second method selected to achieve creative engagement is reflective practice. The aim of this method is to 'show' how theory permeates the creative work as it is produced. Scrivener (2000, p. 9) distinguishes two types of reflective practice. The first he terms 'reflection-in-action', which details surprises and decisions made in the creation process in real time. Bourke and Neilsen (2004, p. 2) argue this type of reflection is of little value in the exegesis as it 'far too easily collapses into narcissism and endless auto-reflexivity'. From this perspective, it is easy to see how this method could lead to writing that has negligible benefit in contributing new knowledge. The importance of reflection-in-action, however, is that new theory can be built through the act of writing. Reflection-in-action describes the 'action of making', which takes into account both planned and unplanned outcomes and the researcher's responses to them. Done well, this may be drawn upon by writers wishing to improve their practice by attempting similar experimentation. Candy (2006, p. 8) provides guiding questions for monitoring and recording this type of reflective practice, which include what was proposed, carried through and how stumbling blocks were addressed. Employing the action language of 'show' in this writing to interpret the creative work in the context of process, rather than detached from it, is another effective way for me to create links between the thesis components.

Debate persists around the scholarly value of reflective writing. Bourke and Neilsen (2004, p. 2) claim reflective writing 'must be examined, critiqued and connected to the act of writing' to achieve its goal. To clear this hurdle, the second type of reflective practice described by Scrivener (2000, p. 10) is drawn upon. 'Reflection-on-action' is driven by a desire to learn from experience. This form of reflection takes place after the action of making. Rather than describing the process, it critiques it while taking into consideration its contribution to, and implications for, the practice as well as the individual practitioner. Candy (2006, p. 8) provides a further set of questions to frame this type of reflection which have guided my reflections of successes/failures, solutions and lessons learned. Bourke and Neilsen (2004, p. 3) term this 'writing *about* writing' which 'can be drawn on by other writers who wish to understand, evaluate or interrogate their *own* writing practices'. In this type of reflective writing, I have allowed the language of 'tell' to take center stage.

Alternating both of these writing styles in reflective practice offers a 'show and tell' approach that brings together theory and practice in a way that satisfies both my motivations as a practitioner and the accepted conventions of scholarship.

CONCLUSION

As creative practice-led research projects increase in number and diversity, it is inevitable that methodological frameworks will continue to evolve. The aim of this chapter is to demonstrate how the competing modes of creative and academic writing can be complementary when assuming strategic risks to combine them in creative research writing. The 'Show and Tell' methodology approach reflects a movement away from the traditional design of the post-graduate thesis while maintaining traditional roots by attempting to restructure its accepted processes.

The preceding evidence-based case study not only voices the experiences of one trained creative writing practitioner and novice academic researcher, but also highlights emerging issues faced by other practitioners in the field. The solutions offered in the context of this project should therefore be informative for those embarking on practice-led research in creative writing. It is envisaged that these recommendations will invigorate the research process for creative students who similarly choose to exercise their own unique voice and to take the road less traveled when undertaking academic research projects.

The exploration of the relationship between the competing notions of 'show' and 'tell' in language offers a space for further experimentation into ways that creative and academic writing styles can be combined in the creative thesis while continuing to meet the definition and aims of academic research.

REFERENCES

Arnold, J. (2005). The PhD in writing accompanied by an exegesis. *Journal of University Teaching and Learning Practice, 2*(1), 36–50.

Brien, D. L. (2006). Creative practice as research: A creative writing case study. *Media International Australia Incorporating Culture & Policy*, (118), 53.

Bourke, N. A., & Neilsen, P. M. (2004). The problem of the exegesis in creative writing higher degrees. *TEXT: The Journal of the Australasian Association of Writing Programs*, Special Issue, 3.

Candy, L. (2006). Practice based research: A guide, vol CCS Report: 2006 V1.0 November, pp. 1–19. *Creativity and Cognition Studies.* Sydney, NSW: University of Technology.

Creswell, J. W. (2003). *Research design: Qualitative, quantitative and mixed methods approaches.* Thousand Oaks, CA: Sage.

Central Queensland University. (2010). *Program rules for the degree of doctor of philosophy.* Version 10. Author.

Davis, R., & Shadle, M. (2000, February). "Building a mystery": Alternative research writing and the academic act of seeking. *College Composition and Communication, 51*(3), 417–446.

Fletcher, J., & Mann, A. (2004). Illuminating the exegesis, an introduction. *TEXT: The Journal of the Australian Association of Writing Programs,* Special Issue 3.

Frost, R. (1920). *Mountain interval.* New York: Henry Holt and Company.

Kroll, J. (2002, April). Creative writing as research and the dilemma of accreditation: How do we prove the value of what we do? *TEXT: The Journal of the Australian Association of Writing Programs, 6*(1). Retrieved from http://www. textjournal.com.au/april02/kroll.htm

Milech, B. H., & Schilo, A. (2004). "Exit Jesus": Relating the exegesis and creative/production components of a research thesis. *TEXT: The Journal of the Australian Association of Writing Programs,* Special Issue 3.

Monash University Library. (2007). *QuickRef27: How to write the case study.* Author. Retrieved from http://www.monash.edu.au/lls/llonline/quickrefs/27-case-study.pdf

Nash, G. (2011, April). The creative writing kaleidoscope. *TEXT: The Journal of the Australian Association of Writing Programs, 15*(1). Retrieved from http:// www.textjournal.com.au/april11/nash.htm

Pankin, S. (1987). *Virginia Woolf and the lust of creation: A psychoanalytic exploration.* Albany, NY: State University of New York Press.

Pringle, H. (2014) The thief of time. *New Scientist: The Collection,* Issue 3.

Scrivener, S. (2000). Reflection in and on action and practice in creative-production doctoral projects in art and design. *Working Papers in Art and Design, vol. 1.* Retrieved from https://www.herts.ac.uk/__data/assets/pdf_file/0014/12281/ WPIAAD_vol1_scrivener.pdf

Stewart, R. (2001, October). Practice vs praxis: Constructing models for practitioner-based research. *TEXT: The Journal of the Australian Association of Writing Programs, 5*(2). Retrieved from http://www.textjournal.com.au/oct01/stewart.htm

Strand, D. (1998). *Research in the creative arts.* Department of Employment, Education, Training and Youth Affairs, Canberra, ACT.

Sword, H. (2012). *Stylish academic writing.* Cambridge, MA: Harvard University Press.

Vella, R. (2005). Keeping the degree creative. *Real Time Arts, Issue No. 68* Aug–Sept.

Woolf, V. (2015). *The waves.* New York: Oxford University Press.

Yin, Robert K. (2014). *Case study research: Design and methods* (5th ed.) Thousand Oaks, CA: Sage.

Articulating the Fact Behind the Fiction: Narrative Inquiry as a Research Methodology for Historical Novelists

Alison Owens

INTRODUCTION

Writers of historical fiction are not conventionally academics, yet research is an important aspect of the groundwork that they complete to build an authentic and credible portrait of an imagined past. Variously described as a 'bricoleur as bower-bird' (Webb & Brien, 2011) or 'magpie' (Pullinger, 2008) approach to research, creative writers of historical fiction conduct research into a period in time drawing on a wide range of data as the needs of the story dictate. This chapter argues that such research can usefully be conceived, pursued and explained as arts-based, and arts-informed, narrative inquiry. As the narrative inquiry approach is deemed 'best for capturing the detailed stories or life experiences of a single life or the lives of a small number of individuals' (Creswell, 2007, p. 55) and encourages the review of diverse categories and sources of data including personal

A. Owens (✉)
School of Education and the Arts, CQUniversity Australia, Donvale, Melbourne, Victoria, Australia

© The Author(s) 2016
B. Harreveld et al. (eds.), *Constructing Methodology for Qualitative Research*, DOI 10.1057/978-1-137-59943-8_10

accounts, it is a promising framework for historical novelists. The chapter explains the relevance of this approach as a methodological manoeuvre for organizing and articulating a novelist's engagement with historical fact in order to create historical fiction.

Further to the somewhat altruistic purpose of examining and explaining the relationship between 'factual' or 'true stories' and creative writing, the question arises of why an historical fiction writer might engage with narrative inquiry, or indeed any formal research, at all? Beyond an enhanced and reflexive understanding of one's own practice, there are multiple benefits flowing from such a project, including the possibility of non-fiction publications in the form of scholarly journal articles, media publications, books, essays and lectures as well as the potential to earn higher formal education qualifications, particularly doctoral status and thereby diversify and expand a writing career. Inferential credibility (as well as publicity) for an author's works of fiction may also flow from such exposition of creative practice. Further to this, developing authors may benefit from the sharing and mapping of creative practice-led research through a narrative inquiry in developing their own skills and options as historical novelists.

THE SIGNIFICANCE OF RESEARCH FOR WRITERS OF HISTORICAL FICTION

Historical fiction is defined by the Historical Novel Society (Lee, n.d.) as any fiction that is written about events in contexts that are 50 years or more in the past. Other efforts at defining the genre suggest a more inclusive timeframe at 25 years or more, or even two to five years in the past (Hoffman, 2002). In addition to focusing on a specific period and place in history, historical fiction is differentiated from non-fictional historical accounts because historical novels

> focus on human consequences of historical events. The human consequences may be embarrassing moments, or humorous happenstance or the loss of life, loved ones and personal property. It can depict humor and irony or personal choices made because of historical events. (Hoffman, 2002, n.p.)

Sarricks (1999) states that historical fiction requires accuracy of historical details, authentic characterization, recognizable storyline, and an 'unfolding' pace to succeed in the genre. This chapter argues that a clearly articulated research methodology, such as that provided through narrative inquiry, can contribute powerfully to the accuracy, authenticity, and recognizability of any fictional account of the past.

Historical fiction has its roots in the conventions of 'realism' established in the eighteenth century with the rise of the novel made accessible to a general reading public thanks to the development of the industrial printing press (Kovarik, n.d.). John Sutherland (2013) notes that Daniel Defoe's *Robinson Crusoe*, published in 1719, marks the start of society's love affair with realism despite the fact that Crusoe's adventures were entirely imagined. Realism entailed an approach to novel writing that has been described as a marriage between the report writing of journalism and literature and which found expression in Defoe's novel and many historical novels to follow. Sir Walter Scott's *Waverley* (1814) depicts the 1745 Jacobite Rebellion and is considered by many to be the first fictional novel set in a period before the life of the writer. Highly successful contemporary writers, such as Ken Follett, Philippa Gregory, and Hilary Mantel, continue the long and rich tradition of historical fiction established over several centuries by such influential writers as Tolstoy, Flaubert, Dickens, Hawthorne, James, and Graves.

It should be acknowledged that while all fiction eventually becomes 'historical' due to the passage of time, historical fiction writers compose a story of lives that are no longer extant, that are lost to us in the everyday sense and therefore resonant with temporality and by inference, underscoring the temporality of the present. By creating for us the rich experience of immersion in a past time, they change the way we understand our present selves in a manner distinct from our responses to contemporary fiction.

Historical fiction is currently enjoying renewed interest referred to as a 'hot genre' (historicalfiction.info, 2014, n.p.) with the novels of many writers, including in the Australian context Colleen McCullough, Peter Carey, Kate Grenville, and most recently Hannah Kent, achieving bestseller status. Nevertheless, contemporary fiction remains the dominant genre of novel publication and readership. In an answer to the question 'why write about the past?', John Cleese has playfully observed 'Well, there is more of it', yet most authors opt to write about the present. Perhaps this is a consequence of the necessity for the extensive and sometimes-burdensome research required to write authentic and convincing accounts of the past. While writers of contemporary fiction may also conduct extensive research, as this is research of the living, they are immersed in a world of relevant data and their selection of available sources is less constrained by the fragmented and often arbitrary preservation of extinct worlds available from surviving sources in public or private historical records.

Well-known authors of historical fiction make the requirement for research clear:

> The writers of historical fictions, just like real historians, do (or ought to do) a huge amount of research before beginning on their works, and then continue doing research until the very end. (Crowley, n.d.)
>
> I read for a year before I begin to write a thing. (Gregory in Akbar, 2013)
>
> As I wrote the novel I took notes about what I was doing—how I was doing the research, what I was finding out, where I was coming to a dead end. I took notes about the 'experiential' research I did. (Grenville, 2005)

Clearly, research informs the writing process for historical novelists but most frequently this research and the manner by which it drives, limits, and shapes the creative process remain 'hidden or unarticulated ' (Carter in Web & Brien, 2011, p. 186). It is not usually evident to readers of historical fiction, for example, which primary, secondary, and tertiary sources were consulted by novelists, how predominantly they have influenced the research process, nor which artistic texts or artifacts may have featured in the process of researching a specific topic, time, and place. Developing a better understanding of the creative process is an important objective for increasing numbers of scholars in the discipline of creative arts practice, and creative practice-led *research* provides a mechanism for this undertaking. Brien (2006) argues that 'it is as researchers that creative writers can provide valuable insights into the creative process and how creativity can be enhanced both in other academic disciplines and the wider community' (p. 53).

Leading researchers in the discipline, Kroll and Harper (2013) describe a range of productive methods to *draw together* critical and creative practice in writing and emphasize that it is particularly important to explain the convergence between the practice of research and the practice of creative writing. The proliferation of creative arts doctorates over the last two decades (Webb & Brien, 2011) is evidence of the growing interest in framing the creative writing process within a theoretical framework that aims to explicate creativity itself.

In order to better illustrate how narrative inquiry research can be adopted to frame and explain a creative writing project, the author incorporates quotes from the exegesis of a current PhD study in creative writing.

The thesis explores the process of researching and writing a novel set in the 1930s in Woolloomooloo, a dockside suburb of Sydney, Australia, where the author's family by marriage has a long history. The project sources a wide variety of data including public records such as local history accounts, maps, newspaper reports, filmed footage, radio broadcasts, photographs and so on as well as creative works of the period including novels, songs, poetry, and painting. Family history data from surviving family members was also sourced in order to build a credible, authentic, and engaging narrative of what the past may have been like for this community. The story is inspired by stories themselves, and much of the 'data' is in the minutiae of the daily life of this family.

> *My father-in-law, who passed away before I met my husband, is and always has been for me, a narrative. A story told in the past tense. A hero swallowed in time but ever-present at the dinner tables of our family gatherings, reaching through time to straighten slumped shoulders or correct poor table manners and intrude on the lives of the living through story. 'If your father were here' is a familiar mantra uttered by my mother-in-law as we eat off the crockery he purchased in Iran, laid out on the rosewood table he had carved in China, overlooked by his paintings of the Sydney foreshore completed after his stroke and hanging on the walls of the comfortable home purchased with the salary he made as an oil explorer. In many respects he is very 'here'.*

So, narrative inquiry offers a 'bower-bird' methodology that embraces manifold sources and forms of data for the purpose of developing a story that can account for the lives of a selected population in a historical era and geographical context.

Research conducted for the purpose of writing an historical novel can be usefully understood as a sub-genre of narrative inquiry that is described as arts-based, and arts-informed, narrative inquiry. Arts-based narrative inquiry (Clandinin & Connelly, 2000) involves field text gathering while arts-informed narrative inquiry refers to research text presentation which may be visual, performative, or textual in the form of prose or poetry. Research begins with an arts-based process of identifying, reviewing, and analyzing relevant resources and texts and develops into arts-informed text construction in the form of a novel, for example, and frequently, an exegesis explaining the relationship between the research and the creative writing process.

I think of this story as a swing with one support rope constructed from 'factual evidence' drawn from available primary and secondary data, and the other from creative moves drawn from the aesthetics and conventions of fiction. So, a romance may blossom where none existed and a couple of bad guys in the family may move into a later generation in order to provide necessary human interest and colour, but they will speak in historically appropriate vernacular, engage in real contemporary issues and attend historically significant events in the transportation available in the era.

Indeed, arts-informed qualitative inquiry is 'burgeoning' as part of 'the postmodern movement involving a search for methodologies offering more authentic representations' (Butler-Kisber, 2010, p. 2). That is, representations that offer readers direct and sustained access to recognizable and convincing voices, perceptions, and experiences of a specific community in time and space. In the context of fiction, such representations are, by definition, not *real* and not *true*, but are 'realistic' and 'truthful' offering the reader a multiplicity of meanings (Leavy, 2015) in contrast to the defined conclusions iterated for the reader in conventional or non-artistic research. It can be argued that while qualitative researchers tend to select representative quotations from interviewees and argue on the basis of these for some generalizable conclusion, fiction writers deploying narrative inquiry create believable stories within which realistic conversations take place leaving the reader free to reflect and conclude as they will. The heavily trodden pathways that writers create between sources that describe an historical event and their fictional account are shared with readers by the creative writer engaging in narrative inquiry research so that readers may ponder not only the meanings of a fiction but also the meanings and implications of the process of fictionalization. A narrative inquiry account of historical fiction writing hence allows the reader a degree of textual reflexivity that generates meanings greater than the sum of the parts. There is the fiction and there is the research and between them is the creative process laid bare.

DEFINING AND JUSTIFYING NARRATIVE INQUIRY AS A RESEARCH METHOD FOR WRITERS OF HISTORICAL FICTION

In the early twentieth century, possible frameworks and processes for research diversified from the traditional and dominant positivist approach in which scientific knowledge was 'assumed to be a direct mirror of reality' (Sexton, 1997, p. 7). Such knowledge was established through processes of experimentation and manipulation in laboratory-based scientific seclusion with the influence of the researcher suppressed or obscured in order to achieve 'objectivity'. An alternative approach to developing our understanding of the world emerged in the Chicago School of Sociology in the form of narrative inquiry as a means of representing life experience (Chase, 2005 in Lal & Suto, 2012, p 4). Such an approach offered sociologists a way of understanding, organizing, and presenting human experience that was not confined to numerical or statistical measures, nor the artificial domain of the laboratory but provided insights developed through sustained engagement with real people in the ordinary contexts of their daily lives.

The narrative inquiry approach is

> underpinned by the ontological assumption that humans organize their experiences, memories, life situations, and events in narrative form and as such the nature of reality is at least in part storied. This ontological stance extends the conventional understanding of narrative from being a representation of experience (or some aspect of it) to narrative being a form of experience. (Bruner, 1991 in Lai & Suto, 2012, p. 6)

Just as a novel, particularly an historical novel, is a public account of a specific community, place, and time, it is also an individual *experience* for a reader. That is, it has repercussions for the reader in how it affects their understandings, perceptions, and feelings. Reading is not a passive exercise and stories are not neutral accounts. If this were the case, novels would be dry, somnambulant matter indeed. The power of stories to both recount and change our lives is recognized in narrative inquiry.

Narrative inquiry is primarily employed for the purpose of understanding human experience(s) rather than solving specific social problems or informing decisions as much applied research seeks to do. In narrative inquiry, 'the stories that people tell are the vehicles through which experiences are studied' (Lal & Suto, 2012, p. 6). This form of inquiry is based largely on the assumption that stories are a form of social action and the telling of stories is one way that humans experience and make sense of their lives (Bruner, 1991; Chase, 2005; Clandinin, 2006; Riessman, 2008; Caine & Steves, 2009; Lal & Suto, 2012). Storytelling is recognized in all cultures as a valuable tool for teaching and learning. Indeed, in cultures with a circular and indirect rather than linear and direct communication style (Bennet, 1993), such as indigenous Australian cultures, storytelling is the preferred methodology for instruction, so beautifully demonstrated in the recent Australian film *Ten Canoes* which adopts traditional aboriginal storytelling to address the complication of sexual lust for the young hero.

However, the role of the storyteller is not conventionally associated with the scientist. In narrative inquiry, this association is critical. Indeed, predominant theorists and practitioners of narrative inquiry, Jean Clandinin and Michael Connelly (2000), have described the traditional tendency to stress the objectivity of the researcher as 'the silent ... perfect, idealised, inquiring, moralising self as a form of self-deception' (p. 62). They go on to point out that narrative inquirers frequently make their relationships with the research participants and subject matter explicit and reflect on these relationships throughout the research as a means of 'verifying' the research through 'transparency', terms that may substitute for 'validity' and 'reliability' as they are deployed in the positivist tradition. The following is an example of the researcher's reflection on their relationship to subject matter:

> *I love fiction. I love Australian fiction. I love historical fiction. I like storytelling. I like hearing stories and have responded to hearing stories of my family by marriage about the patriarch (long dead) who I have only ever known in a 'fictional' sense. I have left wing tendencies and the era of his youth is highly political so the story I tell will align with the working class struggles of the period and location. I am a qualitative researcher and wish to minimise risk—to myself and participants (family)—which pushes me towards fiction. I fear that the story may not align adequately with the competing views of family members about the patriarch's life and so I have built a world around him loosely based on the family facts and heavily augmented and sometimes challenged by historical facts and context derived from published works of fiction and non-fiction.*
>
> *'That didn't happen to him', or 'You didn't include...' are frequent and welcome statements from my husband as I tell him some of the story. The fact is, it could have happened and the other fact is that telling 'everything' that happened is not necessarily a good story.*

It is not only the narrative inquirer who is engaged in the telling of the story of course. Research informants or participants, where they exist, play a crucial and ongoing role in a narrative inquiry study. In a narrative inquiry, relational issues are at the heart of the research process, including the selection and initiation processes for establishing participation and consent through to representation of findings (Clandinin & Connelly,

2000). As Dewey (1934, 1938) argued over 70 years ago and Clandinin and Connelly (2000) have further expounded, continuity and interaction are crucial to understanding and accounting for experience. In narrative inquiry, the relationship between researcher and researched is consistently relevant and forms an important part of the story. For such reasons perhaps, narrative inquiry research has been practiced extensively in the fields of education and health, particularly nursing, where the relationships between teacher and student or nurse and patient are as important as the professional knowledge and skills of the practitioner.

Stories can be told through varied mediums of expression including verbal accounts, but also written accounts, filmed, photographed, painted, or sculpted accounts and data that contributes to details for such stories is available in private and public artifacts, such as maps, police records, government reports, media coverage, advertisements, popular songs and, of course, other stories. Narrative inquiry tends to draw from widely diverse sources of data wherever and whenever the data contributes to the development of characters, location, era, and thematic concerns relevant to a particular study. Where relevant and possible, the personal narratives or stories of individuals who have experience of the phenomena under study, and in the case of historical fiction research, the setting of the story, are invaluable to the narrative inquirer. It is argued that in the case of narrative inquiry interviewing, the interviewer is not only actively listening to interviewees' accounts but seeks to engage the interviewees in the telling of stories (Riessman, 2008; Lal & Suto, 2012) at times deploying cues in changes of context or inclusion of texts (see Keats, 2009) to stimulate memories and the stories that flow from them. The following is an example of such engagement:

> As we wondered through the library exhibits of diaries and surviving personal objects of World War One soldiers, we came across embroidered postcards from France. 'I had forgotten these', exclaimed G. 'Isn't it funny how you forget about things entirely and then when you see them, all the memories come flooding back. I remember when my mother...' It was just like the time we sat together over the old airline suitcase full of family photographs which had not been viewed for years. Many photographs triggered strong memories and elicited stories associated with the various characters and events portrayed. Some photos drew a blank and were dismissed as 'someone or other... who knows'? Part of family history that was not her part. So, central and marginal characters and events emerge from her story triggered by images and objects long forgotten.

In this manner, a historical novelist as narrative inquirer travels 'through time in our memories shifting our imaginings backwards, expanding out our life stories, enabling multiple possible resonances that may connect our storied worlds to others' (Hale Hankins, 1998 in Caine & Steves, 2009, p. 6).

Narrative inquirers are freed from the objective of many qualitative research studies that seek to establish cross-case theories from data in that the research is case-specific. Narrative inquiry is a contiguous practice (Butler-Kisber, 2010) seeking to establish and illustrate connections between data in a specific context rather than seeking definitions. In the case of narrative inquiry conducted as creative practice-led research, the 'connections' of interest are those between factual input and creative, fictional output. In these connections lie new understandings of the triggers for creativity and the rationale for manipulation of 'the facts' for the purposes of fiction.

THE BENEFITS OF A NARRATIVE INQUIRY APPROACH FOR HISTORICAL FICTION

Selecting a narrative inquiry approach for research conducted for the writing of historical fiction is a methodological manoeuvre that makes ontological sense and provides a methodological framework that enables the articulation of the relationship between research work and creative work.

Creswell (2007) identifies four worldviews for qualitative researchers, including post-positivist, constructivist, advocacy/participatory, and pragmatism. The constructivist approach, established through the work of such theorists as Jean Piaget, Lev Vygotsky, and Gregory Bateson, defines reality as socially constructed/created through social practices, interaction, and experiences. Therefore, all constructed meanings represent a particular and non-definitive point of view, and researchers working within the constructivist model accept that there are ' multiple ways of understanding/knowing the world' (Butler-Kisber, 2010, p. 7). So, 'the perspective of the observer and the object of observation are inseparable' (Sexton in Butler-Kisber, 2010, p. 7). Yet such inevitable entanglement of the observer and the observed does not discredit the value of one account of the 'real'. Given such ontological assumptions, it is not difficult to see how a constructivist, narrative inquiry method of research is highly suitable for the historical novelist wishing to articulate the rationale for the authenticity of a story by an examination of how and from what research experiences it was constructed.

Explaining *how* the story has been constructed from a range of sources including the personal stories of relevant informants is essential in establishing the credibility, plausibility, and trustworthiness of any account proposed as a research-based, creative practice-led study conducted as a narrative inquiry.

> Credibility, plausibility, and trustworthiness are all criteria of quality that have been invoked by grounded theorists and narrative inquirers working from post-positivist, constructivist, and constructionist assumptions. Pundits of both methodologies have suggested that the quality of a study can be conveyed through the transparency of the research process. (Riessman, 2008 in Lal & Suto, 2012, p. 12)

Narrative inquiry can provide such transparency and is highly suitable for a creative arts-led research project because judging the quality of a narrative inquiry also includes an appraisal of its aesthetic components and capacity to evoke emotion in the reader/audience (Riessman, 2008). Creative practice-led research most frequently involves the development of a creative/artistic piece of work accompanied and explained by an exegesis. In the generation of these dual and conjoined texts, one creative and the other theorized and empirically based, creative practice-led research can satisfy aesthetic and emotional criteria for constructing the 'real' through both a fictional and a fact-based account of it.

In the last three decades, creative writing theses have proliferated, and a considerable literature has developed in relation to the creative writing thesis and the exegesis (see, for example, *Text Special Issue Illuminating the Exegesis* 2004). There is debate on the benefits and necessity for an exegesis along with significant variation in the purpose, content, format, and length. Dunlop (1999) completed a novel as a PhD researching the teaching of literature and argued for the novel or literary narrative itself 'as a viable mode of representation for research is envisioned in light of the perception that ideas can be reflectively addressed through the arts in order to enlarge human understandings' (n.p.). However, it is conventionally accepted that 'It is the exegesis that "proves" the work is not just art-as-usual, but art-as-knowledge—a part of the doctoral tradition' (Webb & Melrose, 2013).

Boyd (2010) reviews an extensive range of creative writing research in higher degrees and claims that the exegesis should be more than just an explanation or reflection and could be 'a site of experimentation; an opportunity to theorise about creative writing as a discipline' (p. 22). To explicate the process of the research backgrounding and informing a piece of fiction opens a new level of engagement with the creative text for the reader by addressing methodological wonderings about where and how the account is located in terms of the available sources and forms of data.

> Upon receiving research findings delivered through performative texts, visual arts and written stories, one can be left 'stranded' with questions about research assumptions, intentions, data sources and analytical processes. (Lal & Suto, 2012, p. 13)

Narrative inquiry can satisfy the need for some readers of historical fiction to identify the threads of data drawn from research and distinguish them from the creative moves of the novelist in accounting for and responding to this data. It should be made methodologically evident in the exegesis of any creative writing study how the research data informed the creative writing and was transformed in this process from 'data' to 'story'. Fictional strategies that are deployed to fill gaps, disguise and protect identities, and develop an engaging plot can be tracked and explained in order to explicate the normally 'hidden' or 'unarticulated' (Carter in Webb & Brien, 2011, p. 186) creative process. Murphy (2004 in de Mello, 2007) explains the reflexive and integrative creative process:

> I became interested, as I created the fictionalised pieces, in the process of creating fiction in a research framework and what that meant in the process… it became an exploration of moving in and out of worlds, the worlds of the children in the inquiry, the fictionalised world, and the world I inhabited as narrative inquirer. (p. 21)

In this symbiotic pattern of moving between related but distinct texts as they are constructed, as well as once they are completed, a successful exegesis identifies connections and deviations which emerge between 'data' and 'fiction' and seeks to explain these moves and these relationships in terms of 'representing' and (re) creating history.

In the fictional work that emerges from a narrative inquiry, 'truth' is built up from a rich and broad iteration of the experiences, values, behaviors, life events, and artifacts of the target community in their socio-historical context. The inevitably subjective accounts provided by research informants may not be in agreement and may, in fact, be contradictory yet, as Sarah Pollard demonstrates in her recent film *The Stories We Tell*, 'truth may come from editing the facts, whereby an unedited talking head may yield little' (Lambert, 2014, p. 19). Leys argues that philosophers, scientists, writers of history, and writers of historical fiction are essentially establishing truth via 'imaginative leaps':

> History (contrary to the common view) does not record events. It merely records echoes of events—which is a very different thing—and, in doing this, it must rely on imagination as much as on memory ... the historian and the novelist both must invent the truth. (Leys, 2007, p. 43)

It is in mapping and articulating these imaginative leaps that creative practice-led research conducted as narrative inquiry can contribute both an engaging historical novel and important new knowledge about the creative process itself.

CONCLUSION

This chapter has explained the efficacy of narrative inquiry, particularly arts-informed and arts-based narrative inquiry, as a research methodology for creative practice researchers. It has been argued that narrative inquiry provides a suitable ontological, practical, and analytical framework by which writers of historical fiction can provide exegetical rationale for their fictional accounts of the past. Narrative inquiry can account for the role of the researcher in relationship to the researched as well as the relationship between research data and the creative writing process and product. These accounts contribute important new knowledge providing more comprehensive and scholarly understandings of the elusive creative process.

REFERENCES

Akbar, A. (2013). Queens in many shades of grey: How republican Philippa Gregory is sexing up the Royals. *The Independent*. http://www.independent.co.uk/arts-entertainment/books/features/queens-in-many-shades-of-grey-how-republican-philippa-gregory-is-sexing-up-the-royals-8744064.html

Bennet, M. (1993). Towards a developmental model towards intercultural sensitivity. In R. Michael Paige (Ed.), *Education for the intercultural experience.* Yarmouth: ME Intercultural Press.

Boyd, N. (2010). *Strange Loops and Confessions: In search of a creative writing research methodology (exegesis) and AI PI: A novel (creative component).* (PhD), Griffith University.

Brien, D. (2006). Creative practice as research: A creative writing case study. *Media International Australia, 118,* 6.

Bruner, J. (1991). The narrative construction of reality. *Critical Inquiry, 18,* 1–21.

Butler-Kisber, L. (2010). *Qualitative inquiry: Thematic, narrative and arts-informed perspectives.* London: Sage.

Caine, V., & Steves, P. (2009). Imagining and playfulness in narrative inquiry. *International Journal of Education & the Arts, 10*(25), 15.

Chase, S. E. (2005). Narrative inquiry: Multiple lenses, approaches, voices. In N. K. Denzin & Y. S. Lincoln (Eds.), *The Sage handbook of qualitative research* (3rd ed., pp. 651–679). Thousand Oaks: Sage.

Clandinin, D. J. (2006). Narrative inquiry: A methodology for studying lived experience. *Research Studies in Music Education, 27,* 44–54.

Clandinin, D. J. (2007). *Handbook of narrative inquiry: Mapping a methodology.* Thousand Oaks: Sage.

Clandinin, D., & Connelly, M. (2000). *Narrative inquiry: Experience and story in narrative research.* San Francisco: Jossey-Bass.

Creswell, J. W. (2007). *Qualitative inquiry & research design: Choosing among five approaches.* Thousand Oaks: Sage.

Crowley, J. (n.d.). The accu-thump of Googletarity. http://www.powells.com/fromtheauthor/johncrowley.html?utm_source=overview&utm_medium=rss&utm_campaign=rss_overview&utm_content=John%20Crowley&PID=11

de Mello, D. (2007). The language of arts in a narrative inquiry landscape. In D. Clandinin (Ed.), *Handbook of narrative inquiry: Mapping a methodology* (pp. 203–224). Thousand Oaks: Sage.

Dewey, J. (1934). *Art as experience.* Toms River, NJ: Capricorn Books.

Dewey, J. (1938). *Experience and education.* New York: Collier Books.

Dunlop, R. (1999). *Boundary Bay: A novel as educational research.* University of British Colombia.

Grenville, K. (2005). Searching for the secret river. http://kategrenville.com/Searching_For_The_Secret_River

Historicalfiction.info (2014). Writing historical fiction. http://www.historical-novels.info/Writing-Historical-Fiction.html

Hoffman, B. (2002). Historical fiction: Criticism and evaluation. http://web.cocc.edu/cagatucci/classes/eng339/Intro/Hoffman.htm

Keats, P. A. (2009). Multiple text analysis in narrative research: Visual, written, and spoken stories of experience. *Qualitative Research, 9*, 181–195.

Kovarik, B. (n.d.). *Revolutions in communication: Media history from Guttenberg to the digital age.* http://www.environmentalhistory.org/revcomm/

Kroll, J., & Harper, G. (2013). *Research methods in creative writing.* Basingstoke, UK: Palgrave Macmillan.

Lal, S., & Suto, M. (2012). Examining the potential of combining the methods of grounded theory and narrative inquiry: A comparative analysis. *The Qualitative Report, 17*(41), 22.

Lambert, C. (2014). Sweet little lies: Truth and fiction in stories we tell. *Screen Education, 73*, 5.

Leavy, P. (2015). Fiction and the feminist academic novel. *Qualitative Inquiry, 18*(6), 516–522.

Lee, R. (n.d.). Defining the genre. http://historicalnovelsociety.org/guides/defining-the-genre/

Leys, S. (2007). Lies that tell the truth: The paradox of art and creative writing. *The Monthly,* (Nov), 6.

Pullinger, K. (2008, 20 September). How to write fiction: Research. *The Guardian.*

Riessman, C. K. (2008). *Narrative methods for the human sciences.* Thousand Oaks, CA: Sage.

Sarricks, J. (1999). Writers and readers: Historical fiction rules of the genre. *Novelist News,* http://web.cocc.edu/cagatucci/classes/eng339/Intro/Sarricks.htm

Sexton, T. L. (1997). Constructivist thinking within the history of ideas. In T. L. Sexton & B. L. Griffin (Eds.), *Constructivist thinking in counseling practice, research and training* (pp. 3–18). New York: Teachers College Press.

Sutherland, J. (2013). *A little history of literature.* London: Yale University Press.

Webb, J., & Brien, D. (2011). Addressing the "ancient quarrel": Creative writing as research. In M. Biggs & H. Karlsson (Eds.), *The Routledge companion to research in the arts.* London: Routledge.

Webb, J., & Melrose, A. (2013). Understanding the value and the impact of the 'shock': Examining the creative writing doctorate. *New Writing, 11*(1), 134–148.

CHAPTER 11

On Manoeuvre: Navigating Practice-Led Methodology in a Creative Writing PhD for the First Time

Mike Danaher and Margaret Jamieson

INTRODUCTION

This is an evidence-based case study of a shared research journey between the principal PhD supervisor and his student. As the rationale behind this book states, the supervisor and student are negotiating methodological allegiances while developing research expertise investigating and interpreting critically the contextualized social practice within this PhD study. This chapter explores how both the supervisor and student have approached a non-traditional PhD study that involves writing a historical romance novel and accompanying exegesis, where the main aim is to show how oppressed women (some incarcerated) can become empowered through

M. Danaher (✉)
School of Education and the Arts, CQUniversity Australia,
Rockhampton, QLD, Australia

M. Jamieson
School of Education and the Arts, CQUniversity Australia,
Spring Gully, VIC, Australia

© The Author(s) 2016
B. Harreveld et al. (eds.), *Constructing Methodology for Qualitative Research*, DOI 10.1057/978-1-137-59943-8_11

155

both reading historical romance novels and engaging with the heroines in these novels. In this context, oppression refers to women who perceive themselves to be isolated from opportunities, and disadvantaged by feelings of inequality and domination by patriarchal structures. The student is predominantly employing practice-led research (PLR) as the overarching methodological framework for her exegesis. This chapter uses the notion of going on manoeuvre to map their journey together of how they came to terms with practice-led methodology for the first time, and how it can be deployed in this PhD. The chapter also disrupts to some extent the binary opposites (Midgley, Tyler, Danaher, & Mander, 2011) of novice versus experienced researcher and student versus supervisor, and therefore the power relations that these binary opposites encode.

A manoeuvre is a planned and controlled movement involving skill and care, but despite the best-laid plans, there can still be ambushes. The following five stages for going on manoeuvre are used as a conceptual frame in this chapter, and relate to Giroux's (2005) theory of border crossings. These crossings can be envisaged as a set of collective manoeuvres (a vehicle for positive transformation) within a longer journey where supervisors and students alike develop greater awareness of their own strengths. Going on manoeuvre is divided into visioning, planning, journeying, reflecting, and evaluating. Insights will be provided on the process of how the supervisor and student came to understand and use PLR and then scaffold the PhD accordingly. This chapter will also add some insight into a maturing relationship between the supervisor and student, for example, understanding and working with each other's limitations and strengths. The journey is only part way complete since the PhD is still in progress. Furthermore, the student began this PhD journey incarcerated in a women's Correctional Center.

LITERATURE ON CREATIVE PRACTICE RESEARCH SUPERVISION

Much of the literature on supervisor–student relations in creative writing PhDs is from the perspective of 'expert' supervisor and 'novice' student, exploring best practice, relationships, as well as supervisory challenges (Brien, 2004; Dibble & van Loon, 2004; Brien & Williamson, 2009; Kroll, 2009; Kroll & Finlayson, 2012). Brien and Williamson (2009) explore the notion of unclear and differing expectations in the supervisor–student relationship. Arnold (2008) provides a useful checklist for supervisors in PLR degrees. This chapter focuses on the novice perspective in

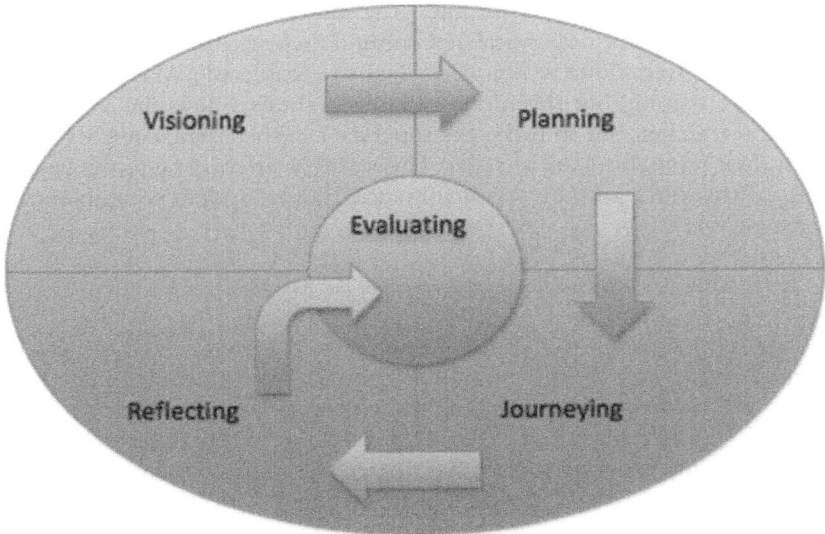

Fig. 11.1   Conceptualization of their collective manoeuvre

the supervisor–student relationship, using both voices, and helps make PLR more accessible by sampling their experience through a somewhat murky journey (Fig. 11.1).

VISIONING

Visioning is the first stage of their manoeuvre and refers to visualizing the whole and seeing the desired future state, which in this case is a successful PhD in creative writing. Visioning also includes conceptualizing the many questions that each of them raise in terms of how best to tackle the PhD project. For the supervisor, this shared PhD journey of a creative writing piece and accompanying exegesis was a first time encounter, and that was a sobering thought in itself with its element of risk taking. He had not supervised such a PhD style before, one that concerns the nature of research in an artistic discipline. There was consequently some trepidation on his part to prepare for such a shared journey. Considerable responsibility is rightly placed on a supervisor in normal circumstances, but in this PhD he felt this more so because of his lack of experience with this kind of

PhD. Moreover, the supervisor knew the student had limited knowledge of research practices and critical and cultural theory, although her creative writing skills were quite well honed. She had completed a Master's degree in creative writing, but this did not involve a thesis. She is the archetypal novice researcher, but so too is the supervisor in this particular PhD field. Both their reputations are at stake. This sense of foreboding at the beginning of this PhD journey was heightened by the student's comment to her supervisor:

Hello Mike, Boy you won the lottery when you got me. Ha.

The supervisor felt this comment could easily have been reciprocated. Though he is new to this methodology, he is not uncontaminated by previous knowledge of and experience with singular or multiple research methodological frameworks. Therefore, he came to this supervision with knowledge and experience of higher degree research generally, and can be envisaged as an 'expert' novice. With other higher degree research students, the supervisor commonly asks the student to define their research focus; to clarify the relevance of their research; and to develop an appropriate methodological thinking in order to select specific methods.

As a mature age student, Margaret knew she could draw on her life's experience as part of the methodology used in preparing the novel and exegesis. Her vision in starting this journey was underpinned by wanting to show fellow incarcerated women that study was possible, and particularly that reading historical romance novels was enjoyable and empowering. The power in the historical romance resides in its representation of the empowered heroines who subvert traditional expectations of women's roles in marriage and in society (Regis, 2003). There are limited research opportunities in prison and without the Internet the student had to rely on the research efforts of others to some extent. She found the research librarians at the university made her continuing study possible. Undertaking a PhD in custody is a lonely experience; one becomes isolated within the main body of the population. Although people are aware of what is being attempted and are supportive, there is little understanding of the complexities of the task.

Before embarking on the PhD, the student undertook a Master of Arts, also while incarcerated. However, the Master's did not assist her in regard to deploying a research methodology in the PhD because there was no research thesis as part of it, a condition of doing the degree from 'inside'.

The Master's however provided her with some skills to write her novel for the PhD. In a normal university setting, the Master's degree would set down the basic methods for research. The student did explore the writings of Jane Austen, Emily Brontë, Michel Faber, and Olive Schreiner in order to obtain some ideas for her novel. These authors criticized the traditional gender roles and promoted an assertive heroine who could shape her own life free from rigid societal conventions. Now free from incarceration the student has the opportunity to use the Internet, as well as converse with other students, and is able to put a more solid research structure in place for her PhD exegesis.

Part of the visioning stage was to also work out what the supervisor and student needed to know in terms of the whole methodological approach to the study. This was not just in relation to PLR but also in relation to the structure of this PhD, which includes a creative novel plus a research exegesis. It is worthwhile in the visioning stage to consider the wider question of what is the purpose of a PhD. A PhD has two main purposes according to Burnett (2015). One is contributing to the advancement of new knowledge, and part of this is the need to publish this new knowledge. The second purpose is that a PhD is a training program for future researchers so that they have the necessary research skills to tackle other problems. These two purposes then clarify the significance of the novel and exegesis as well as contextualize supervision. Another aspect of visioning is to understand the purpose of a research methodology, and part of this is to decide whether the project is qualitative or quantitative. This project is qualitative.

One of the first manoeuvres is to work out the most appropriate research methodology for the particular project. Since the mid-1990s, postgraduate research candidates in art, design, and media disciplines have pursued a model of PLR, submitting creative works along with an accompanying exegesis (Hamilton & Jaaniste, 2009). PLR is a form of research that aims to advance knowledge partly by means of practice, or as Green (2006, p. 177) puts it: 'new knowledge in the arts is created through practice-led research'. Moreover, the justification for PLR is that certain kinds of knowledge can be created only through practice (Green, 2006). Because it situates creative practice as both an outcome and driver of the research process, PLR is a unique research paradigm, and the exegesis is, necessarily, a new form of academic writing (Hamilton & Jaaniste, 2009). Furthermore, Candy (2006) distinguishes between two types of practice-related research: practice-based and practice-led. In this PhD, it is practice-led because the study is 'concerned with the nature of practice and leads to new knowledge that has operational significance for that practice. The primary focus of the research is to advance knowledge about practice or within practice. Such research includes practice as an integral part of its method and often falls within the general area of action research' (Candy, 2006, p. 3).

PLR in the field of art usually involves a study of the interplay between a researcher–practitioner and her artistic work in process (Nimkulrat, 2007). Even though the term 'practice-led research' encompasses various kinds of approaches, it requires equal partnership between artistic practice and research practice; the role of an artist/writer as a researcher investigating a research question; and thorough documentation of the creative production and the overall research process (Mäkelä et al., 2011, p. 7). It is a common model for a PhD in a number of artistic fields, including creative writing because it helps to guide one's knowledge production in the creative arts field. Arnold (2007) explains: The artifact production or practical research component of the PhD process, then, is part of producing a work that, in Scrivener's (2002) words, will in its own terms and genres 'stand up in the public domain. In writing, this means that peers/examiners would judge the work worthy of publication' (pp. 51–52). With the aforementioned justification, the supervisor advised that the PhD's overarching methodological framework be PLR.

PLANNING

Planning is the process of thinking about and organizing the activities required to achieve a desired goal, in this case a PhD. Once the supervisor and student justified why PLR was the best methodology for this PhD, they then need to plan how to learn more about it, and how to incorporate it as the methodological framework for the exegesis. First, both the supervisor and student need to understand the structure of this PhD. The artifact is straightforward in the sense that in this case it will be a historical romance novel, although one that should be worthy of publication in its own right. The exegesis, in many ways the more challenging part of this kind of PhD, can be quite varied so there is room to move in terms of what you include within it. The supervisor and student, however, have to fully understand what the exegesis should achieve and what it should include. Both the artifact and exegesis should inform each other. It is through an ongoing dialogue between the practice, concepts, precedents, and topic that the project unfolds in PLR (Hamilton & Jaaniste, 2009). So they need to go to the literature about exegeses. Literature on the structure of an exegesis indicates that there are multiple forms it can take, but it usually follows the basic structure of traditional research by encompassing a central research question, a defined methodology, and a substantive list of references (Mäkelä et al., 2011, p. 7).

According to Arnold (2005, 2008), the exegesis involves placing the artifact within a body of scholarly knowledge and hence acting to bring together theory and practice. Moreover, the exegesis provides an opportunity for the creative arts researcher to elucidate why and how processes specific to the arts discipline concerned (in this case creative writing) mutate to generate alternative models of understanding (Barrett, 2004). The exegesis also evolves into a more reflective and reflexive piece of writing in which the contribution to knowledge becomes insights into the individual creative process with reference to ideas in the relevant literature (Arnold, 2005; Nimkulrat, 2007; Bacon, 2014) and to the student's own central argument. Anything the supervisor learns about PLR and what goes into an exegesis is passed onto the student. The student has to then synthesize that information in her own way, after all, the supervisor should not write the thesis.

The next planning task is to unpack PLR. This is not made easy when Green (2007, pp. 1–2) claims 'Practice-led research is a notoriously difficult concept to define.' The supervisor's initial readings on PLR also led him to characterize the methodology as rather vague, so he had to be careful as to how he constructed the methodology in his own mind, and how he communicated that to the student. PLR works on the basis of the main research question, so the next move is to formulate a research question that is going to advance new knowledge about the practice, in this case the practice of writing historical romance novels. The research question is how can historical romance novels empower women.

McNamara (2012) advises students to incorporate into the exegesis analyses of practices or intellectual discussions that are at once removed from their own practice because this helps to avoid the conflation of the creative practice with the exegetical component. In other words, avoid making one's own creative practice the sole focus of the PLR exegesis.

> It is helpful instead to establish an independent research question from a context that consists of a rigorous literature review examining other practices, wider creative and cultural contexts, historical precedents, or shared

themes explored elsewhere in other practices—all of which permits a certain degree of critical distance from the remorseless consideration of one's own practice. (McNamara, 2012, p. 8)

To better understand what is expected in PLR, the student found the writings of Hecq (2008, p. 1) useful: 'the methods of research are both qualitative and quantifiable in which the writer must look into the methodologies that work in their specific type of writing'. For the student this means that she as the creative writer can research using different methods, such as narrative inquiry, historical method, and autoethnography, to produce a more accurate piece of writing, both academic or for pleasure. Milech and Schilo (2004) gave the student a further understanding of what was expected in producing the critical component of a research exegesis. In looking back at the genre in which she has chosen to write, popular historical romance embracing feminism, she became aware that as the text grew in both complexity of plots and the length of time many genres were crossed, each genre taking on a spirit of its own. A wormhole was opened up to another world. In the crossing of these boundaries, it became apparent that there was no defined border. In trying to work her exegesis around PLR, the student also looked at the writings of Vella (2005, p. 2), who opened up the methodology to a better understanding, when he discussed the term *exegetical perspective* and wrote 'artistic work has its own embedded knowledge'. The student sat squarely within the constraints of the Corrective System and as one who feels oppression, placed herself as part of the artifact and within the center of her PLR.

Having lived with other incarcerated women, the student observed the helplessness that they felt. Many of these women said they would appreciate female role models whom they could both relate to and be inspired by. Many of these women also had a poor understanding of literature or indeed reading. The student believed that by introducing the historical romance novel to these women, it would provide an easy read with a positive outcome on their self-esteem. The historical romantic novel can take a lonely isolated woman to a place where she can find companionship and beauty. So this premise was the basis for her research aims, and she could identify with PLR being useful to the unpacking of the power of the historical romance genre.

The independent research on PLR by the supervisor and student led them to some fundamentals, which are important to share with each other in the planning stage. Using PLR as the methodological structure for the exegesis has enabled the student to reflect on the creative method and allows her to enter into the scholarly debate that is pertinent in the writing of her novel. PLR is regarded largely as a qualitative research methodology and has only recently been accepted as a way of contributing to knowledge within the creative arts academy.

The core thread running through the exegesis is the student's main argument, which is a historical romance novel is not trivial, but rather is empowering to its female readers mainly through resonance with, and inspiration from, the lives of the heroines. So how does the student use PLR to show how writing the novel demonstrates female empowerment? What are the narrative strategies used by the student to achieve this? This research methodology opens up the practice of writing the novel to scrutiny, and allows the student to confront her practice in a focused way about what the genre can achieve. In this way, the student is advancing knowledge about the qualities and potentiality of the historical romance genre to empower women.

The planning stage has signaled the need to read the literature on PLR. There are lots of models and examples in the literature to look at on PLR, even where the art is not a novel, but rather photography or music. In this planning stage, the supervisor not only felt responsible for the need to be the 'expert' in the relationship but also encouraged the student to become an 'expert' too. He placed confidence in her to be able to do literature searches on PLR, but more importantly to come to know PLR intimately. This is a key aspect of her training as a researcher in this field.

JOURNEYING

Journeying is the act of traveling from one place to another, especially when involving a considerable distance. This is the stage when the supervisor and student both set off to learn how to apply what they have read about the exegesis and PLR (conceptually for the supervisor, and in practice for the student). They do this on their own and bring back their understandings during catch-ups, and through the supervisor reading drafts and giving feedback. An important element in this journey is for the student to acquire the ability to become a researcher, taking responsibility for her PhD.

According to Green (2007), while rigor is necessary to meet the full requirements of PLR, it is not sufficient. Validity is also required. Valid research in practice-led terms establishes itself as addressing an issue, which is of relevance to the artistic community for which the research is undertaken. This does not preclude new ideas and investigations, but it does mean that a new arena opened up for research has to be justified in terms of what has gone before and why this endeavor is relevant (notwithstanding the fact that it has not previously been pursued). This points to the inclusion of a thorough and pertinent literature review in the exegesis. In this PhD, the student needs to specifically show how the historical romance novel can empower female readers, and how her novel does that as well. In this way, the research follows established protocols from both scientific practice and the humanities that sees research as 'standing on the shoulders of history'—establishing the boundaries of what is known at the start of the project and demonstrating how more has been discovered and communicated by the end. As with all research, the practice-led paradigm creates new knowledge and successfully convinces examiners of this fact (Holbrook et al., 2008).

The student's journey into the practice of PLR initially went from euphoria to frustration. Her characters were talking to her but she did not have the knowledge or skills to narrate their story. Assistance came through the readings of Max van Manen (2002), who suggests that the writer in their research gains distance through the act of reflection. The student empathized with this view as it allowed her to stand outside the project and look in as a critical friend to her other role, the writer. The student gained strength from her reflective journal. The layers of isolation and negativity started to dissolve and *Sarah's Story*, the title of her novel, started to take form. Her reflective journal told her that the ideas that were being formed were constantly interrupted from the daily grind of incarceration. To overcome this, she started writing through the night when the quietness was rarely disturbed.

The issues that she felt emotionally about, upon reflection, often pushed her away from the goal of researching, editing, and producing a good piece of writing. By reflecting on positive thoughts, she hoped to overcome this. In reading Bundy's *Reflective Practice and the Playwright/Scholar* (2006), the student realized this problem is the one experienced by many writers. Although she tried to keep to the paradigm of PLR, the student found that the whole concept of this research was difficult to process for her as an artistic creator and also difficult to mold into a particular formula. The reflective journal formed the center of her research approach, linking the artifact and the exegesis. The journal was the repository of self-observational data of the present creative process and self-reflective data from the past.

Part of using PLR was to understand the period in time in which the student chose to write. Then it was to understand the methods used by other historical romance writers, as well as to research how feminism played an important part in showing the determination of their heroines. All the heroines were strong independent role models and this formed the foundation for her exegesis. The student recalled the details of her great-grandmother's diary, in which she had scripted her life as a nurse living in outback Australia. The student's family also told her the stories of their heritage, which she is able to recall, and this adds to her own form of methodology. Thus, the student is tapping into the autoethnographic tools of personal memory and external data to both write her novel and reflect on the creative process. The student's great-grandmother's strength and endurance form the basis for her heroine. The strategies she used were reinforced by referring to her journal and the research articles that she had collected, as well as with a fellowship that she had forged with other writers, including the late Colleen McCullough.

Reflecting

Reflecting is the process of critically thinking back on the journey and experience so far. Reflection in action is the ability to be self-aware, to analyze experiences, to evaluate their meaning, and to plan further action (dela Harpe & Radloff, 2003). The role of the reflection is also to tease out ideas, explore problems, and work out your position on a whole range of issues (Burr & Hanley, 2008). The main aspect is to reflect on how well PLR is being deployed in the exegesis. Reflecting involves the student's self-reflections and the supervisor reflecting on what the student writes in her drafts. Reflection can be guided by these questions: Does it make sense? Does it fulfill the aims and does it help to answer the research question? Does it contribute to new knowledge?

For the student the term reflection also refers to the way in which she remembers, self-reflects, and places herself as a part of the artifact. Critical reflection during the writing of this exegesis has been used to review the ideas embedded in the novel, and her theorized insight into creative writing and her emerging insight into exegesis writing. This is all informed by PLR.

Part of the reflection process involved the supervisor having to also better understand the student as a person, and vice versa. The supervisor came to realize that for the student, this PhD undertaking was a cathartic process, and very much about a journey to her own wellbeing from a position of incarceration. The student was also keen on establishing a mentoring role for other incarcerated women. When the supervisor and student came to understand and appreciate each other's backgrounds more, it assisted to fine-tune a more informed working relationship.

EVALUATING

Evaluating in this study involves determining the merit and significance of the applicability of PLR. How did the student find PLR in helping her to draw new knowledge about the writing of historical romance novels? PLR encouraged the student to be critical of how the genre works and provided insights about the nature of change over time when confronting gender inequalities. For example, the student reached a deeper understanding of the difficulties experienced by women in colonial Australia. As her novel developed around the obstacles that her characters experienced, she came to realize that some aspects regarding gender inequality have not changed much over time. The following is an extract from the student's reflective journal showing how PLR encouraged self-examination of the creative process:

> I realised that I didn't start to reflect on my writing until I started thinking about the people that I had based my characters in *Sarah's Story* on. After this I was able to focus on the plot and settle down to research the story lines. My writing started to improve in historical input and I was able to bring a more human feel to the story. Over time, I can see how I have developed as a writer.

The good practice that the student has learnt so far is to trust her supervisors, to give over to them her ideas, and to entrust them with her novel, which can sometimes be difficult because of the ownership one forges with a creative piece. The student's research journey so far has also been difficult and lonely because there are very few research articles from other women who are doing similar studies from a position of incarceration.

LESSONS LEARNED

This set of collective manoeuvres is conceptually helpful in breaking down the various tasks, and in a logical order, for getting started on a creative writing PhD. Each manoeuvre challenges both the supervisor and student to confront their respective strengths and weaknesses, to share them, and to use them positively. These manoeuvres also help to humanize the process; that for both the supervisor and student there will be struggles with understanding PLR, and that this is normal. The supervisor came to understand what motivates the student and this is an important revelation in the PhD journey because one can turn to that motivation when frustration inevitably sets in.

The supervisor and student are building up a shared literature on PLR and are teasing out of it the elements that make most sense. As the manoeuvres continued there became a necessary focus on understanding the role and layout of the exegesis. Literature was explored around the exegesis and its relationship to the artifact. Again the trick is to draw on elements of an exegesis that make most sense and use those elements as scaffolding. PLR is intrinsically related to the main research question and the focus becomes how PLR can be used to answer that question (Milech & Schilo, 2004). The research question is important because answers to it advance new knowledge through the practice and for the practice.

Further manoeuvring highlighted the importance of the student keeping a reflective journal on her writing practice. Her journal has to encapsulate thoughts on the practice and then links the practice to the exegesis around the research question. Eventually, the supervisor should see evidence of the student becoming a researcher. The binary opposites encoded in this case study are novice versus experienced researcher, and student versus supervisor. The discussion in this chapter has revealed that these binaries have been disrupted because the supervisor and student both began the collective manoeuvres as novices in unfamiliar terrains. The supervisor and student have learnt from each other in terms of the PLR methodology, and this is a legitimate form of learning.

References

Arnold, J. (2005). The PhD in writing accompanied by an exegesis. Journal of University Teaching and Learning Practice, 2(1). Retrieved from http://ro.uow.edu.au/jutlp/vol2/iss1/5

Arnold, J. (2007). *Practice led research: A dynamic way to knowledge*. Camberwell, VIC: Rockview Press.

Arnold, J. (2008). Supervising PhD candidates in Practice Led Research degrees, Proceedings of the Paris International Conference on Education, Economy and Society, Paris, France, 17–19 July 2008.

Bacon, E. (2014). Journaling—A path to exegesis in creative research, TEXT, 18 (2). Retrieved from http://www.textjournal.com.au/oct14/bacon.htm

Barrett, E. (2004). What does it meme? The exegesis as valorisation and validation of creative arts, Text Special Issue No 3.

Brien, D. L. (2004). The problem of where to start: A foundation question for creative writing higher degree candidates and supervisors. In J. Fletcher & A. Mann (Eds.), *TEXT Special Issue Website Series: 'Illuminating the Exegesis'* (April).

Brien, D. L., & Williamson, R. (2009). Supervising the creative arts research higher degree: Towards best practice. In D. L. Brien & R. Williamson (Eds.), Introduction to *TEXT Special Issue Website Series No 6: Supervising the Creative Arts Research Higher Degree* (October).

Bundy, P. (2006). Reflective practice and the playwright/scholar. *NJ Drama Australia Journal, 30*, 51–60.

Burnett, P. (2015). Australian research training landscape: Quality assurance. Paper presented to Research Higher Degree Supervisor Training Event, CQUniversity.

Burr, S., & Hanley, P. (2008). TEXT review Josie Arnold, practice led research, TEXT, 12 (2). Retrieved from http://www.textjournal.com.au/oct08/burr_hanley_rev.htm

Candy, L. (2006). *Practice based research: A guide, Creativity & Cognition Studios.* Sydney: University of Technology.

de la Harpe, B., & Radloff, A. (2003). From practice to theory in developing generic skills. In C. Rust (Ed.), *Improving student learning: Theory and practice - 10 years on.* Oxford: OCTD, Oxford Brookes University.

Dibble, B., & van Loon, J. (2004). The higher degree research journey as a three-legged race. *TEXT, 8*(2), 1–15.

Frayling, C., Stead, V., Archer, B., Cook, N., Powell, J., Scrivener, S., et al. (1997). *Practice-based doctorates in the creative and performing arts and design. UK Council for Graduate Education.* Staffordshire: Lichfield.

Giroux, H. A. (2005). *Border crossings: Cultural workers and the politics of education.* New York: Routledge.

Green, L. R. (2006). Creative writing as practice-led research. *Australian Journal of Communication, 33*(2,3), 175–188.

Green, L.R. (2007). Recognising practice-led research ... at last! Paper presented at the Hatched 2007 Arts Research Symposium, Perth.

Hamilton, J. G., & Jaaniste, L. O. (2009). *Content, structure and orientations of the practice-led exegesis.* Art Media Design: Writing Intersections, Swinburne University, Melbourne.

Hecq, D. (2008). Writing the unconscious: Psychoanalysis for the creative writer. *TEXT, 12*(2).

Holbrook, A., Bourke, S., Lovat, T., & Fairbairn, H. (2008). Consistency and inconsistency in PhD thesis examination. *Australian Journal of Education, 52*, 36–48.

Kroll, J. (2009). The supervisor as practice-led coach and trainer: Getting creative writing doctoral candidates across the finish line. In D. L. Brien & R. Williamson

(Eds.), *TEXT Special Issue Website Series No 6: Supervising the Creative Arts Research Higher Degree* (October).

Kroll, J., & Finlayson, K. (2012). Transforming creative writing postgraduate and Supervisor identities: Ways of becoming professional. *TEXT, 16*(2).

Leech, B. (2002). Asking questions: A technique for semi-structured interviews. *Political Science and Politics, 35*, 665–668.

Mäkelä, M., Nimkulrat, N., Dash, D. P., & Nsenga, F.-X. (2011). On reflecting and making in artistic research. Journal of Research Practice, 7(1). Retrieved from http://ezproxy.cqu.edu.au/login?url=http://search.ebscohost.com/login.aspx?direct=true&db=a9h&AN=79542643&site=eds-live&scope=site

McNamara, A. (2012). Six rules for practice-led research, TEXT, Issue 14, Queensland University of Technology. http://www.textjournal.com.au/speciss/issue14/McNamara.pdf

Midgley, W., Tyler, M. A., Danaher, P. A., & Mander, A. (Eds.), (2011). Beyond binaries in education research (Routledge research in education vol. 59). New York: Routledge.

Milech B., & Schilo A. (2004). 'Exit Jesus': Relating the Exegesis and Creative/Production Components of a Research Thesis. TEXT Special Issue No 3. Retrieved from http://www.textjournal.com.au/speciss/issue3/milechschilo.htm

Nimkulrat, N. (2007). The role of documentation in practice-led research. Journal of Research Practice, 3(1). Retrieved from http://jrp.icaap.org/index.php/jrp/article/view/58/83

Regis, P. (2003). *A natural history of the romance novel.* Penn Press: University of Pennsylvania.

Scrivener, S. (2002). Characterising creative-production doctoral projects in art and design. *International Journal of Design Sciences and Technology, 10*(2), 25–44.

Smith, H., & Dean, R. T. (Eds.) (2009). *Practice-led research, research-led practice in the creative arts.* Edinburgh: Edinburgh University Press.

van Manen, M. (2002). *Writing in the dark: Phenomenological studies in interpretive Inquiry.* London: Althouse Press.

Vella, R. (2005). Keeping the degree creative. Real time: Australia's critical guide to International contemporary arts, 68: 2. Retrieved from; http://www.realtimearts.net/article/issue68/7916

Methodological and Other Research Strategies to Manoeuvre from Single to Multi- and Interdisciplinary Project Partnerships

Donna Lee Brien and Margaret McAllister

INTRODUCTION

It makes intuitive sense that important social and cultural problems may be best interrogated, tackled, and resolved, if disciplines collaborate, enabling groups of researchers to train a multidimensional lens on situations and thus illuminate complexity, and reveal possible new solutions to difficult issues. Such collaboration is advocated at the highest policy levels, for example, by organisations such as the World Health Organisation (2010) but, in practice, working collaboration between disciplines is difficult

D.L. Brien (✉)
School of Education and the Arts, CQUniversity Australia, Noosaville, QLD, Australia

M. McAllister
School of Nursing and Midwifery, CQUniversity Australia, Noosaville, QLD, Australia

© The Author(s) 2016

171

B. Harreveld et al. (eds.), *Constructing Methodology for Qualitative Research*, DOI 10.1057/978-1-137-59943-8_12

to establish and sustain (Brien & Brady, 2003). Commentators have attempted to provide explanations for this tension between policy and practice. Giroux (2014) suggests that disciplines have steadily grown apart from each other in the past few decades because of their quests for professionalism and to create their own unique cultures, languages, and knowledge domains. D'Amour et al. (2005) add that a routine and mechanical approach to collaboration tends to occur when it is insisted upon, a more delicate and nuanced handling is required. Ironically, despite the academy's diversity, its different disciplines rarely interact either in formal or informal ways that are likely to engender rigorous and sustained ways of working together (Cameron, 2011).

DEFINITIONS OF TERMS

This chapter shares the authors' experiences of working collaboratively as academic researchers who each hail from different disciplines (creative arts and nursing). Foundational definitions are important because, as the European Union Research Advisory Board has stated, such definitions are not only "many, varied, vague, and conflicting" but also "often simply absent" (2004, p. 2) from such discussions. Using personal experience and approaches, the below also draws on the findings of Lau and Pasquini who note not only the "profound degree to which researchers' assumptions, expectations and attitudes … influence the very notion of interdisciplinarity, and what it involves and consists of" (2008, p. 552), but that these personal factors are also "often neither noted nor appreciated" (p. 552).

In this, the authors, as reflective researchers, understand a single disciplinary research approach as one where a problem is approached by drawing on one main disciplinary base, using research methodologies, instruments for data collection, and analytic approaches familiar to that discipline. This might well involve a number of methodologies, including a mixed-methods approach. It is useful to note that the term "mixed methods" is often incorrectly used to refer to research involving a number of research disciplines, but it has a singular and more specific meaning: as Creswell states, it involves the "collection of both qualitative (open-ended) and quantitative (closed-ended) data" (2014, p. 217). For example, one of the authors of this chapter, McAllister, recently led a nursing project (McAllister et al., 2012) that utilised a mixed-methods approach to examine the changes affecting nursing. The first phase involved a narrative review of the literature to identify pertinent issues shaping nursing. The second phase involved in-depth qualitative interviews exploring key informants' views of the changes and their likely impact. The third phase was a statewide survey examining how ordinary nurses reacted to these views. The study produced not only a picture of how nursing is changing, but also commentary on both how nurses feel about those changes and how prepared they are for them (McAllister, Madsen, & Holmes, 2013).

In a multidisciplinary project, investigators from at least two disciplines work on a single project, working relatively independently on separate tasks (Klein, 2010). In a recent project that involved introducing student group curatorial activity into a multi-arts postgraduate programme, the other author of this chapter, Brien, worked with researchers from both creative arts and education to run and evaluate a pilot programme in this area (Sturm, Beckton, & Brien, 2015). In this project, each individual brought her own knowledge, experience, and approach to the task at hand, but did not step out of this area to any extent—the input of the various disciplines "additive" but not "integrative" (Weech, 2007, p. 2).

Interdisciplinary projects are different from multidisciplinary undertakings in that such disciplinary integration is enacted throughout the research process. Interdisciplinary researchers, for instance, consider the problem together, and then design a study that blends aspects of the underpinning understandings, approaches, methodologies, and tools available in each of their disciplines. The aim is to design an approach that explores the issue by utilising relevant methodologies in order to achieve a holistic understanding of the matter at hand. Brooks and Thistlethwaite note that interdisciplinarity moves beyond disciplines working together to the "linking, blending and integration" of specialised knowledge fields (2012, p. 404). The authors have purposefully and wilfully worked to foster progression to multidisciplinarity and then interdisciplinarity in their joint projects.

SINGLE DISCIPLINARY ORIGINS

Brien, the researcher in the creative arts, works in, and from, the discipline of creative writing, working with a range of methodological tools and approaches accepted in creative writing research (Kroll & Harper, 2013), but where the overarching methodological umbrella is usually practice-led research (Brien et al., 2011). Practice-led research is a qualitative methodology that focuses on the production of work and its consideration in context (in terms of practice) (Webb & Brien, 2012). Practice-led research mobilises a range of qualitative approaches, including autoethnography, case study, and narrative, discourse, and textual analysis. It can include quantitative analysis of such factors as readerships and sales figures, but it is extremely rare for this kind of research to form a major part of the process. Such methodological sampling is particularly useful for practice-led creative writing researchers, many of whom utilise a "bowerbird" (Brady, 2000) or bricolage (Kincheloe, 2001) approach, whereby they pick and choose the research methodologies, approaches, tools, and content that are useful to the particular project, and the creative work that lies at its core.

The other researcher—McAllister—comes from a very different field. Competent nurses today need to enact the principle of evidence-based practice—that is, a qualified health care professional needs to be able to provide interventions that are proven to be safe, effective, and world's best practice (Jirojwong, Johnson, & Welch, 2011). Issues needing attention are complex, and choosing a fitting research methodology to investigate a particular problem will depend on the nature of that problem and its end goal, and nursing researchers are trained in a worldview that envisions and values both qualitative and quantitative methods (Powers & Knapp, 2010), including mixed methods. In her own work, McAllister is most interested in the problems impacting these fields at a cultural level, asking such questions as why stigma, fear, and misunderstanding about mental disorder is still so common (Drew et al., 2011) and, why, when nurses have had well over two centuries to finesse the art of compassionate care, patient neglect, and dehumanisation continue within health systems. Such complex questions certainly cannot be approached solely by survey or other quantitative tool.

Culturally embedded problems are, by their nature, based in quotidian practices (Smith, 1989), and certain culturally based problems—such as oppressed group behaviour in nursing or why women's writing is undervalued in comparison to men's—have often become so deeply entrenched that they have become naturalised and almost unnoticed (Matheson & Bobay, 2007). In this environment, the close examination of everyday practice and deconstruction of its elements—be they linguistic, non-verbal, action-based, interpersonal, tacit, or attitudinal—helps to uncover and destabilise the hegemonic forces that reinforce the status quo and prevent change (Crotty, 1998). In these inquiries, methods that move beyond understanding towards those that facilitate change are important, and these are located within critical social science methodology, and include participatory action research, narrative inquiry, and critical ethnography.

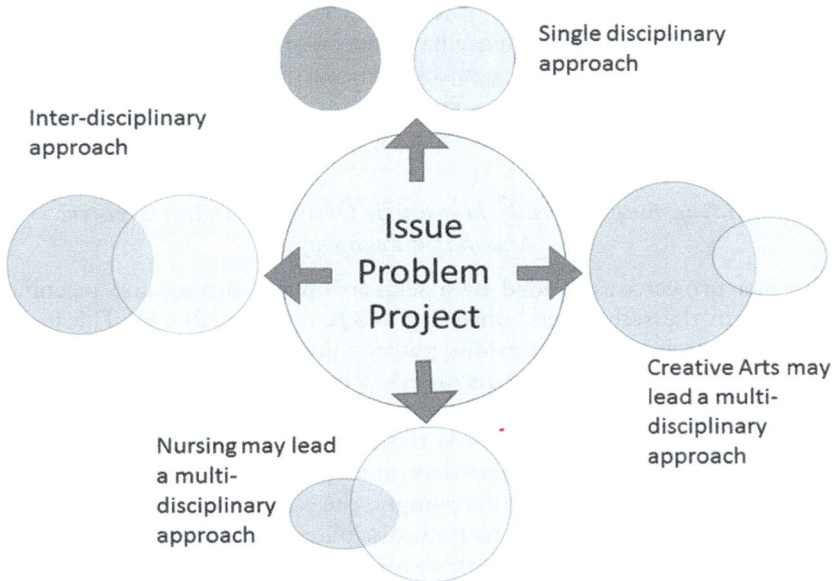

Fig. 12.1   Flexible collaborative approaches

PROCESSES AND PRODUCTS OF COLLABORATION

From late 2012, the authors developed and analysed an approach to research problems that seemed to require input from multiple fields and perspectives, and have increasingly sought to enact an interdisciplinary (blended) methodological approach to these projects (see Fig. 12.1). One commonality across this joint work has been, as mentioned above, around disrupting routines of practice that have become embedded into culture, and therefore ritualised. With such routines relegated to the everyday landscape of thinking and behaviour, they are often overlooked in terms of being worthy of inquiry and/or research. In working together to find ways to understand and, thereby, explore such social and culturally embedded problems, habits, and practices, these researchers often began with discussion of puzzling problems. In retrospect, this act of dialogue and reflexive critique aided the research analysis of each researcher's pursuits and, once its value was recognised, has now become a characteristic of the shared collaborative practice. Other ways of working have similarly evolved as familiarity with each other's research and thinking processes has developed, and shared experience have increased.

Profiling two collaborative projects demonstrates how research was initially conducted in a multidisciplinary (joint) way, and then in a more interdisciplinary (blended) manner.

Building Empathy and Therapeutic Optimism Using Creative Arts-Based Pedagogy

The first project was funded by a scholarship of learning and teaching grant from the researchers' university (CQUniversity, 2013). The focus of this research built on previous joint enquiry into the possible use of the life experiences of illness recorded in popular published memoirs as teaching resources in the nursing classroom (McAllister et al., 2014). The extension of this work aimed to test the impact of engaging with such creative narratives about eating disorders on mental health students' empathy and therapeutic optimism. Interestingly, the subject matter of empathy is a concept of deep interest to both disciplines and, in essence, became the bridge to connect them in this project. Whilst empathy is a foundational concept in mental health practice (See Rogers, 1961), the health disciplines are increasingly aware of the tendency of medical training to decrease health care practitioners' propensity to empathise with patients (Halpern, 2001) and are, thus, interested in innovative approaches which will encourage engagement with patients' lived experiences (Wasson, 2015). Within the creative arts, audiences need to engage with a work of art in order to appreciate it (Leder et al., 2014). While literary theory works to unpick and unpack the possible meanings of a work, creative arts research seeks to investigate the relationships between the art work and both its creator and consumers, and empathy is an important component of this investigation (Oremland, 2014).

This multidisciplinary project sought to investigate whether, and how much, empathy could be built via engagement with the creative arts. It aimed to explore the viability of using what are often undervalued creative writing products—those which are regularly dismissed as "misery memoirs"—in order to attempt to raise mental health students' awareness of the complex personal experience of living with a particular disorder. To contain the scope of the investigation, the illness was narrowed to that of eating disorder. Brien brought to this project her knowledge of these memoirs and how they can be read (see Brien, 2011, 2013, 2014).

McAllister brought her knowledge that nursing students, because of their exposure to clinical procedures such as diagnosis, monitoring, and treatment, are usually well versed in the objective signs of illness and disorder, but not in its subjective experience (Fukui et al., 2010). The project was driven by the hypothesis that these students, although technically competent and able to deliver medically evidenced interventions, may well not be competent or confident in the deep listening, suspending judgement, and responding empathically and compassionately to consumers that are the basis of empathic care (Adame & Hornstein, 2006). A further hypothesis was that there was a possibility that this reading and discussion would lead to increased feelings of empathy and therapeutic optimism. The researchers also knew that these students might well not be avid readers and thus careful choice of not only pertinent, but highly engaging, texts was essential.

This project was conducted in a multidisciplinary manner. Sometimes one researcher would take the lead, depending on the expertise needed, and sometimes the other would. Brien's creative writing-based knowledge about book-length memoirs of eating disorders (Brien, 2013) and what makes a text compelling was drawn upon in order to select a number of well written, engaging books from the hundreds in circulation. In this, Brien utilised what Watters and Biernacki call "targeted sampling" (1989), working from the large number of memoirs she had collected in the course of her research. Then, McAllister's mental health nursing knowledge was mobilised in order to identify the ways in which people with eating disorders struggle through the illness and recovery periods (Bulik, 2011). The two researchers then came together to select short excerpts from the selected memoirs that would foreground, and thus illuminate for students, the various critical points that patients experience in their illness journey. Using these resources—and each drawing on her own teaching experience—the researchers then jointly designed a learning experience. This involved guided reading of memoir excerpts (using a classic textual analysis model as used in literary studies and creative writing), which was modelled, and led, by Brien. After this, the learning experience then passed to McAllister's leadership when she drew on evidence-based quantitative methodology (Crotty, 1998; Long, 2010) to design and deliver a mixed-method pre-post test quasi-experiment that would examine participants' levels of empathy and therapeutic optimism, and any changes in this arising from their learning experience.

The study revealed numerous benefits from the workshop. Quantitative data revealed improvements in therapeutic optimism and empathy in a majority of the participants. Qualitative data, obtained from open-ended questions posed in the evaluation survey, revealed that participants were able to both empathise with the characters' struggles in the memoirs and articulate a range of new ways to respond should they meet similar patients in their future practice, indicating what Stanghellini and Rosfort (2013) describe as second-level empathy. These authors explain that a first level of empathy, one that is predominantly felt by health care workers, is a pre-reflective mobilisation of empathy, involving a feeling for the other as a human being. This was apparent in participants' responses early in the experience, in that all appreciated the memoir subjects as people, not just patients. A second level of empathy, a rarer skill but one of deep importance for mental health workers, is reflective empathy, whereby individuals are able to discern the barriers faced by another that cause them to stagnate or be unable to change. This too, became apparent as participants shared the new insights they said they gained from the inquiry. Using guided reading, learners developed the kind of empathy that is more conducive for the collaborative, non-judgemental stance required in the recovery approach. This is when, even though a client may engage in behaviours that are off-putting to others, the clinician must remain open, engaged, and optimistic about the potential for change. The participant evaluation of the workshop also produced affirming responses and that illustrated its impact.

Although this project was focused on the area of nursing education and training, there were a number of unexpected findings in relation to the creative arts, including that, despite the obvious focus, the learnings from such research can flow to both disciplines. This awareness validates the hypothesis that continued interaction, exploration and collaboration between the creative arts and health disciplines has benefit and indeed may yield new insights that could perhaps cast new light on entrenched problems and challenges facing both disciplines.

This project culminated in the production of two conference papers written collaboratively but delivered in a single disciplinary context (McAllister & Brien, 2014a, 2014b), as well as a number of co-written journal articles, which were published in single discipline-based journals (Brien & McAllister, 2013; McAllister et al., 2014) to report the outcomes of this research. These presentations and articles elaborated on a range of matters of relevance for each discipline: the significance of learning experiences that can awaken fitting values for practice in students; the potential of memoir use for health care workers, students, and patients; and on new ways of conceptualising the memoir for writers, publishers, and readers.

Reviewing the Asylum Through a Gothic Lens

The second project is an example of how this research work became more interdisciplinary as this collaborative practice continued. In the second project to be profiled here, almost two years later, Brien became aware of a forthcoming conference calling for innovative applications of Gothic theory in contemporary research. Discussion about how images of mental instability recur within Gothic literature led to a joint realisation that there was an opportunity to raise scholarly discussion around the idea that mental health is—to use a key concept in Gothic theory—"haunted" by unhelpful images of madness. These images are negative in contemporary mental health care and training because, as stereotypes, they exacerbate stigma. As Thornicroft (2006) and other researchers (Corrigan et al., 2006) have repeatedly shown, negative attitudes towards people affected by mental health problems lead to discrimination and social rejection, which in turn exacerbates illness. It also impedes the general population from taking early and preventative action in maintaining their own mental health because individuals are fearful of treatment (Power, 2010). Yet, despite research on this issue in the mental health discipline, the findings have not translated into general understanding or behaviour. A literature review further proved that although mental instability is a trope of Gothic literature (McGrath & Morrow, 1993, xiv), looking at this in relation to mental health history, care, and training is a relatively untheorised area. The researchers surmised that, thus, the Gothic that could be explored as a potential way to deepen mental health practitioners' understandings of the illness, the way clients understand what is happening to them, and to challenge public stereotypes. At the same time, such a consideration could also contribute to what is known as "contemporary Gothic" studies (see Piatti-Farnell & Brien, 2015).

This collaborative inquiry took a concept developed and used within literary studies and popular culture research—the Gothic—and used it to critique both the idea of the "mental asylum" as tourist attraction and the ways health service users may or may not be influenced by stereotypes of madness and its treatment. This work combined joint knowledge developed by both researchers about what happens in health systems when human values are overlooked. This project, based on mutually active questioning, hypothesising, and knowledge development, drew upon the two core disciplines, but then moved this project beyond these findings into a new and productive area of enquiry.

A critical reading of recent media publicity for the Annual Royal Perth Show (in Australia)—which was about to open a new one-million-dollar "family entertainment" attraction: a haunted house based on the horrors of a seventeenth-century asylum, complete with actors pretending to be inmates (Hiatt, 2014)—critiqued this attraction in two stages. The first was as a text, using semiotics and exploring its signs and signifiers, while the second was to determine how these operated as a source of mental illness stereotyping that could result in negative health outcomes (Cheng, Hawton, Lee, & Chen, 2007). An interdisciplinary approach led to the development of a hypothesis that would lead to new knowledge: that mental health practitioners may benefit from learning about the Gothic in order to understand how Gothic ideas and language are so entrenched in contemporary understanding that they operate at a subliminal level to influence peoples' behaviour and attitudes in a negative way. This includes not only prospective patients, but also members of the public who may have deeply embedded prejudices and fears reignited and/or reinforced by such experiences. Investigating this hypothesis of an underexplored issue not only led to the consideration of this subject matter primarily through the scholarly curiosity and developing shared interests of the researchers, but also brought their joint analytical skills, as well as individual disciplinary expertise and knowledge, to develop a project to interrogate and theorise this issue.

This project produced a well-received co-authored refereed paper in the Gothic Studies stream of a popular culture conference (McAllister & Brien, 2015b), with comments from the audience that the disciplinary blending provided a novel dimension to Gothic discourse. This led to an invited journal article (McAllister & Brien, 2015a) and an invitation to edit a themed issue of a Gothic Studies journal as well as new scholarly networks to draw upon. This work provided the inspiration for a larger project based around exploring how the Gothic intersects with, informs, and (possibly) illuminates aspects of health care that remain hidden to both clinicians and society.

Insights from This Research Practice

Knowing that collaborative practice is important, yet difficult to sustain (Cameron, 2011), a reflective evaluation of these joint and blended approaches was undertaken in order to share practical insights (Brien & McAllister, 2015). This led to the identification of a series of benefits and challenges, as well as greater awareness of the significance of, and potential for, collaborative practice within the academy.

The benefits of this collaboration have been multiple. The researchers found that working in such multi- and interdisciplinary projects is interesting, exciting, meaningful, and productive. The new interdisciplinary methodologies and processes have built on, and consolidated, these researchers' already eclectic practice of utilising a range of research methodologies, and has allowed for a deeper interrogation of the methodological approaches that can otherwise tend to be seen as "sacrosanct" in a single discipline. This has led to the two authors having deeper knowledge of their individual disciplines, as it is necessary to discuss and articulate information about each respective discipline, and interrogate the methodological and other gaps and limits in those fields.

As, at the moment, their approach is a relatively novel, even newsworthy, initiative, it has led to enhanced dissemination opportunities and, therefore, helped increase the impact of the research conducted. These dissemination opportunities have had a "multiplier effect", leading to new projects with their own attendant dissemination opportunities. On a personal level, the approach has generated an economy of scale for both researchers, which has included the opportunity to share a number of other research-related tasks, including research-grounded teaching and course development tasks in postgraduate coursework programmes, and the training of higher degree students of research and other emerging researchers— the latter endeavour which has been positively recognised by the institution involved (CQUniversity, 2015). Finally, the joint projects are driven by not only need, but by the intense personal interest of each of the researchers, which is highly motivating. This methodological approach has, indeed, opened up a wider range of professional research opportunities than those provided by each respective discipline alone. It has opened up rich fields of inquiry, research, and dissemination, offering both researchers new journals to publish in and new readers for the work thus produced.

There are also challenges involved in working in such a collaboration. The interdisciplinary effort discussed herein is personally driven. If one of the pairs driving this collaboration was to drop out of these joint projects, the activities would immediately become unsustainable, and single disciplinary pursuits would re-emerge. Furthermore, the knowledge domain within which this research is being undertaken—the medical humanities, or narrative medical, area—is an emerging field and, in times of economic austerity, unlikely to be an area engendering plentiful grant opportunities anytime soon. In the contemporary university environment, frequent reorganisations tend to create "vertical" mega-schools that are usually led by a cognate disciplines. As Pelan (2013) argues, a horizontal model is necessary to allow cross-disciplinary engagement. Finally, the Australian Federal Government's research quality evaluation mechanism (Australian Research Council, 2014) is currently discipline-based, and does not possess a reporting category for multidisciplinary work. Whilst these challenges are significant, the above evidences however that such practice is possible and worthwhile.

Conclusion

This reflective exploration has demonstrated how identifying and applying insights in conducting multi- and interdisciplinary research can enrich and benefit the researchers and disciplines involved. The chapter has, moreover, emphasised the benefits of seeking deeper and more holistic approaches to important social and cultural issues. Such approaches have the potential to make a significant contribution to the cultivation of skills fitting for the twenty-first century, a time calling for empathic connection, shared decision making, empowerment, and sustainability in many areas of life including, but also beyond, research and its associated knowledge work. Certainly, a knowledge of the porosity of discipline boundaries and accepted methodologies in the two disciplines represented in this collaboration—and a recognition of the limitations of those boundaries—has led to the identification of projects that have allowed the collaborating researchers to find more commonalities than initially envisaged. This has led to the recognition of more subtle points of intersection and investigation, and the identification of a rich vein of material and questions for future collaboration.

REFERENCES

Adame, A., & Hornstein, G. (2006). Representing madness: How are subjective experiences of emotional distress presented in first person accounts? *The Humanistic Psychologist, 34*(2), 135–158.

Australian Research Council. (2014). *ERA 2015. Excellence in research for Australia. 2015 Submission Guidelines.* Canberra: Commonwealth of Australia.

Brady, T. (2000). A question of genre: De-mystifying the exegesis. *TEXT: Journal of Writing and Writing Courses, 4*(1). Retrieved from http://www.textjournal. com.au

Brien, D. L. (2011). Pathways into an "elaborate ecosystem": Ways of categorising the food memoir. *TEXT: Journal of Writers and Writing Courses, 15*(2). Retrieved from http://www.textjournal.com.au.

Brien, D. L. (2013). Starving, bingeing and writing: Memoirs of eating disorder as food writing. *TEXT: Journal of Writers and Writing Courses,* Special Issue no 18: Nonfiction now. Retrieved from http://www.textt.com.au/.

Brien, D. L. (2014). In the best of taste: Contemporary food writing as literature. *TEXT: Journal of Writers and Writing Courses.* Special issue no 26: Taste and, and in, writing and publishing. Retrieved from http://www.textjournal.com.au

Brien, D. L., & Brady, T. (2003). Collaborative practice: Categorising forms of collaboration for practitioners. *TEXT: The Journal of the Australian Association of Writing Programs, 7*(2), Retrieved from http://www.textt.com.au/.

Brien, D. L., Freiman, M., Kroll, J., & Webb, J. (2011). The Australasian Association of Writing Programs 1996–2011. *New Writing, 8*(3), 238–263.

Brien, D. L., & McAllister, M. (2013). Off the shelf and into practice: Creatively repackaging popular memoirs as educational resources in health disciplines. *TEXT: Journal of Writers and Writing Courses,* Special Issue no 23. Retrieved from http://www.text.com.au/.

Brien, D. L., & McAllister, M. (2015). Revisioning research in social and cultural practice: Multidisciplinary/interdisciplinary research methodologies. Paper presented at the *Revisioning Space(s), Time and Bodies Conference Proceedings.* Sydney, April 2015.

Brooks, V., & Thistlethwaite, J. (2012). Working and learning across professional boundaries. *British Journal of Educational Studies, 60*(4), 403–420.

Bulik, C. (2011). *The woman in the mirror: How to stop confusing what you look like with who you are.* New York: Walker and Company.

Cameron, A. (2011). Impermeable boundaries?: Developments in professional and interprofessional practice. *Journal of Interprofessional Care, 25,* 53–58.

CQUniversity. (2013). Using narrative pedagogy to facilitate learner engagement in the recovery approach in mental health. Scholarship of Learning and Teaching Grant.

CQUniversity. (2015). Vice-chancellor's award for good practice in learning and teaching. Retrieved from http://www.cqu.edu.au/

Cheng, A., Hawton, K., Lee, C., & Chen, T. (2007). The influence of media reporting of the suicide of a celebrity on suicide rates: A population-based study. *International Journal of Epidemiology, 36*(6), 1229–1234.

Corrigan, P. W., Larson, J. E., Watson, A. C., Boyle, M., & Barr, L. (2006). Solutions to discrimination in work and housing identified by people with mental illness. *Journal of Nervous and Mental Disease, 194*(10), 716–718.

Creswell, J. (2014). *Research design: Qualitative, quantitative and mixed methods approaches* (4th ed.). Thousand Oaks: Sage.

Crotty, M. (1998). *The foundations of social research.* St Leonards: Allen & Unwin.

D'Amour, D., Farrada-Videla, M., San Martin Rodriguez, L., & Beauliey, M. (2005). The conceptual basis for inter-professional collaboration: Core concepts and theoretical frameworks. *Journal of Interprofessional Care, 19*(1), 116–131.

Drew, N., Funk, M., Tang, S., Lamichhane, J., & Chavez, E. (2011). Human rights violations of people with mental and psychosocial disabilities: An unresolved global crisis. *The Lancet, 36*(11), 1664–1675.

(EURAB) European Union Research Advisory Board. (2004). *Interdisciplinarity in research.* Retrieved from http://europa.eu.int/comm/research/eurab/pdf/eurab_04_009_interdisciplinarity_research_final.pdf/

Fukui, S., Davidson, L., Holter, M., & Rapp, C. (2010). Pathways to recovery (PTR): Impact of peer-led group participation on mental health recovery outcomes. *Psychiatric Rehabilitation, 34*(1), 42–48.

Giroux, H. (2014). Public intellectualism today. *Arena Magazine, 128*, 42–45.

Grenville, K. (1990). *The writing book.* St Leonards: Allen & Unwin.

Halpern, J. (2001). *From detached concern to empathy: Humanising medical practice.* Oxford: Oxford University Press.

Hiatt, B. (2014, September 24). Show house riles mental health lobby. *The West Australian.* Retrieved from https://au.news.yahoo.com/thewest/a/25091931/show-house-riles-mental-health-lobby/

Jirojwong, S., Johnson, M., & Welch, A. (2011). *Research methods in nursing and midwifery: Pathways to evidence based practice.* Sydney: Oxford University Press.

Kincheloe, J. (2001). The bricolage: Conceptualizing a new rigor in qualitative research. *Qualitative Inquiry, 7*(6), 679–692.

Klein, J. (2010). A taxonomy of interdisciplinarity. In R. Frodeman, J. T. Klein, & C. Mitcham (Eds.), *The Oxford handbook of Interdisciplinarity* (pp. 15–30). London: Oxford University Press.

Kroll, J., & Harper, G. (2013). *Research methods in creative writing.* Basingstoke: Palgrave Macmillan.

Lau, L., & Pasquini, M. (2008). "Jack of all trades?": The negotiation of interdisciplinarity within geography. *Geoforum, 39*(2), 552–560.

Leder, H., Gerger, G., Brieber, D., & Schwart, N. (2014). What makes an art expert?: Emotion and evaluation in art appreciation. *Cognition and Emotion, 28*(6), 1137–1147.

Long, R. (2010). Using bibliotherapy as a tool for counselling students. *Journal of Research in Innovative Teaching, 3*(1), 77–83.

Madsen, W. (2007). *Nursing history: Foundations of a profession.* Frenchs Forest: Pearson Education Australia.

Matheson, L., & Bobay, K. (2007). Validation of oppressed group behaviors in nursing. *Journal of Professional Nursing, 23*(4), 226–234.

McAllister, M., & Brien, D. L. (2014a). Shaping the future: Interdisciplinary, innovative approaches to enhance therapeutic engagement with the person experiencing disordered eating. Paper presented at the *40th Annual Conference of the ACMHN*, Melbourne, October 2014.

McAllister, M., & Brien, D. L. (2014b). Investigating the educative potential of eating disorder memoirs. Paper presented at the *Eating Disorders and Obesity Conference*, Gold Coast, May 26–27, 2014.

McAllister, M., & Brien, D. L. (2015a). Haunted: Exploring representations of mental health through the lens of the gothic. *Aeternum: The Journal of Contemporary Gothic Studies, 2*(1), 72–90.

McAllister, M., & Brien, D. L. (2015b). Haunted: Teaching mental health nurses about the Gothic to help promote understandings of mental health and ill-health. Paper presented at the *Gothic Association of New Zealand and Australia*. Sydney, January 21–23, 2014.

McAllister, M., Brien, D. L., Flynn, T., & Alexander, J. (2014). Things you can learn from books: Exploring the therapeutic potential of eating disorder memoirs. *International Journal of Mental Health Nursing, 23*, 553–560.

McAllister, M., Madsen, W., & Holmes, C. (2013). Newton's cradle: A metaphor to consider the flexibility, resistance and direction of nursing's future. *Nursing Inquiry, 21*(2), 130–139.

McAllister, M., Madsen, W., Holmes, C., & Morrissey, S. (2012). *2020 vision: The view from Queensland stakeholders on the changes affecting nursing.* Maroochydore: University of the Sunshine Coast.

McAllister, M., Oprescu, F., & Jones, C. (2014). N²E: Envisioning a process to support transition from nurse to educator. *Contemporary Nurse, 4*(2), 246–252.

McGrath, P., & Morrow, B. (1993). Introduction. In P. McGrath & B. Morrow (Eds.), *The Picador book of the new gothic* (pp. xi–xiv). London and New York: Picador.

Oremland, J. D. (2014). Empathy and its relation to the appreciation of art. In J. D. Lichtenberg, M. Bornstein, & D. Silver, *Empathy I* (pp. 239–265), Hove: Routledge. (1st pub. 1984).

Pelan, R. (2013). Practising disobedience: Feminist politics in the academy. *Hecate, 38*(1/2), 210–222.

Piatti-Farnell, L., & Brien, D. L. (Eds.) (2015). *The gothic compass: New directions in scholarship and inquiry*. Abingdon: Routledge.

Power, A. (2010). Transforming the nation's health: Next steps in mental health promotion. *American Journal of Public Health, 100*(12), 2343–2346.

Powers, B., & Knapp, T. (2010). *Dictionary of nursing theory and research* (4th ed.). New York: Springer.

Rogers, C. (1961). *On becoming a person: A therapist's view of psychotherapy*. London: Constable.

Smith, D. (1989). *The everyday world as problematic: A feminist sociology*. Boston: Northeastern University Press.

Stanghellini, G., & Rosfort, R. (2013). Empathy as a sense of autonomy. *Psychopathology, 46*(5), 337–344.

Sturm, U., Beckton, D., & Brien, D. L. (2015). Curation on campus: An exhibition curatorial experiment for creative industries students. *MC Journal, 18*(4), Retrieved from http://www.journal.media-culture.org.au/

Thornicroft, G. (2006). *Shunned: Discrimination against people with mental illness*. Oxford: Oxford University Press.

Wasson, S. (2015). Useful darkness: Intersections between medical humanities and gothic studies. *Gothic Studies, 17*(1), 1–12.

Watters, J. K., & Biernacki, P. (1989). Targeted sampling: Options for the study of hidden populations. *Social Problems, 36*(4), 416–430.

Webb, J., & Brien, D. L. (2012). Addressing the "ancient quarrel": Creative writing as research. In M. Biggs & H. Karlsson (Eds.), *The Routledge companion to research in the arts* (pp. 186–204). Abingdon: Routledge.

Weech, Terry L. (2007). Multidisciplinarity in education for digital librarianship. In *Proceedings of the 2007 Informing Science and IT Education Joint Conference*, University of Illinois at Urbana-Champaign, IL: Graduate School of Library and Information Science. Retrieved from http://www.proceedings.informing-science.org/InSITE2007/InSITE07p011-021Weec285.pdf/

World Health Organisation. (2010). *Framework for action on interprofessional education and collaborative practice*. Geneva: World Health Organisation Press.

CHAPTER 13

Contested Concepts: Negotiating Debates About Qualitative Research Methods Such as Grounded Theory and Autoethnography

Steven Pace

INTRODUCTION

I considered using the grounded theory method for my study, but my
supervisor warned me that it has a bad reputation.

I'm basically using grounded theory as my research method, but I'm not
going to call it that. I'm going to refer to it as "qualitative data analysis" to
avoid getting into any debates about the right way to do grounded theory.

I'm feeling apprehensive about using autoethnography for my project.
What happens if the examiners feel that I haven't used it the right way?

These are some of the comments I have heard from research higher
degree students expressing their apprehension at the prospect of using
particular qualitative research methods. Learning how to use a qualitative
research method is a challenging task that is often made more difficult

S. Pace (✉)
School of Education and the Arts, CQUniversity Australia,
Mackay, QLD, Australia

© The Author(s) 2016   187
B. Harreveld et al. (eds.), *Constructing Methodology for
Qualitative Research*, DOI 10.1057/978-1-137-59943-8_13

by contested definitions and descriptions of the method in question. Novice researchers, who typically want clarity and reassurance about the procedures they will follow, are often confronted with controversies and debates within the research community that they look to for guidance. Statements made by the originators of a particular research method may co-exist with contradictory statements about variations of the method developed by others. Adherents to particular versions of the method may criticise other perspectives as being inferior or invalid. Misconceptions about the contested research method may be presented in the literature as fact. Well-meaning supervisors who have limited understanding of the issues at stake may encourage their students to adopt alternative methods as a safer option. How should novice researchers deal with these issues when attempting to employ a contested qualitative research method for their own study? This chapter explores this question using two well-known contested research methods as examples: grounded theory and autoethnography. This discussion may be of particular interest to researchers who are currently grappling with these specific research methods or variations of them.

GROUNDED THEORY—A CONTESTED CONCEPT

Grounded theory is a research method for building a theory from data (Charmaz, 2014; Creswell, 2013; Dey, 1999). The method was developed and established more than 40 years ago by Glaser and Strauss (1967) in their seminal work *The Discovery of Grounded Theory*. A theory that results from the application of the grounded theory method is typically a general explanation of a "process, action or interaction shaped by the views of a large number of participants" (Creswell, 2013, p. 83). The data from which the theory is derived commonly consists of interviews, observations, or documents, but it may be broader than that, even encompassing quantitative data, which has been described as a rich medium for discovering theory (Glaser & Strauss, 1967, p. 185). Although the grounded theory method can be used with any kind of data, it is widely regarded to be a qualitative research method. Charmaz (2014, p. 10) describes grounded theory as a major force in the growth of qualitative research during the latter part of the twentieth century. Thomas and James (2006, p. 767) describe grounded theory as "a major—perhaps the major—contributor to the acceptance of the legitimacy of qualitative methods in applied social research". Grounded theory differs sharply from quantitative research methods in the sense that its aim is to build theory, not to

Table 13.1 Grounded theory as a contested concept

Characteristics of a contested concept (Gallie, 1956)	Characteristics of a contested concept, as applied to grounded theory (Bryant & Charmaz, 2007)
The concept is appraisive in the sense that is significant and valuable.	Grounded theory is widely recognised as a valid research method.
The achievement has an internally complex character.	Grounded theory redefined the character of qualitative research and of social research methods in general.
The complexity of praiseworthy achievement leads to a variety of descriptions.	Grounded theory is known for its variety of descriptions.
The achievement is open in the sense that there has been considerable modification in the light of changing circumstances.	Grounded theory has undergone considerable modification, as evidenced by the paths taken by its proponents since 1967.
The concept is used aggressively and defensively by parties who recognise that their use is contested by other parties.	The grounded theory literature contains many examples of researchers taking either Glaser's position or Strauss' position.
There is an original exemplar whose authority is acknowledged by all users of the concept.	The original exemplar of grounded theory is the method described in the seminal book *The Discovery of Grounded Theory* (Glaser & Strauss, 1967).
Continuous competition for acknowledgement enables the original exemplar's achievement to be sustained and/or developed in optimum fashion.	Ongoing debate and adaptation of the grounded theory method sustains and develops the original exemplar.

test theory. Grounded theories are suggested, not proven (Glaser, 1978, p. 134). A researcher who uses this primarily inductive research method does not deduce testable hypotheses from existing literature. Instead, the researcher begins with a question and a general field of study, and allows a theory to emerge from the data.

Bryant and Charmaz (2007, p. 3) describe grounded theory as a "contested concept"—an expression that was first introduced by Gallie (1956) to refer to concepts that have a variety of interpretations within the domains of aesthetics, political philosophy, philosophy of history, and philosophy of religion. Gallie proposed a set of seven conditions for the existence of an essentially contested concept. Bryant and Charmaz (2007) applied these conditions to grounded theory, demonstrating that it qualifies as a contested concept. Table 13.1 summarises Gallie's characteristics of a contested concept alongside Bryant and Charmaz's application of those characteristics to grounded theory.

To fully understand why grounded theory has been characterised as a contested concept, it is necessary to understand the details of the method and the disagreements that surround it. The grounded theory method consists of a collection of flexible guidelines for systematically gathering and analysing data with the aim of formulating a theory. The following phases are common features of many interpretations of the method.

1. *Open coding* is the process of breaking the data down into significant concepts (Dey, 1999; Strauss & Corbin, 1998; Urquhart, 2013). Incidents in the data (objects, events, actions, ideas, etc.) are closely examined and compared for similarities and differences. Incidents that the researcher identifies as being significant are assigned labels known as codes. Codes identify concepts or abstractions of incidents in the data. Charmaz (2014, p. 109) refers to this phase as "initial coding" rather than open coding.

2. *Theoretical coding* is the process of taking the concepts that emerged during open coding and reassembling them with propositions about the relationships between those concepts (Charmaz, 2014; Dey, 1999; Urquhart, 2013). Like the concepts, the relationships are grounded in the data. Glaser (1978) discusses 18 theoretical coding families that can help researchers conceptualise how concepts may relate to each other. For example, the Six Cs coding family encourages researchers to look for causes, contexts, contingencies, consequences, co-variances, and conditions in the data.

3. *Selective coding* is the process of delimiting coding to only those concepts that relate to a core explanatory concept (Dey, 1999; Strauss & Corbin, 1998; Urquhart, 2013). The core concept reflects the main theme of the study; it sums up the substance of what is going on in the data (Glaser, 1978, p. 61). Charmaz (2014, p. 138) refers to this phase as "focused coding" rather than selective coding.

Although these coding activities are described here as distinct phases, distinguishing between them is not so clear in practice. Different coding activities may proceed quite naturally together. For example, theoretical coding requires that the researcher has some concepts to work with, but often a sense of how concepts relate to each other emerges during open coding. Furthermore, not all grounded theory researchers would agree on this description of the method. Dey (1999, p. 2) observes that "some critics dispute the claims of other researchers to have used grounded theory—not unlike, it may seem to an outsider, the way exponents of various cults bicker over the right interpretation of a religion". These differences of opinion began in the 1990s with a public dispute between Glaser and Strauss, the original founders of the grounded theory method. As mentioned earlier, Glaser and Strauss first articulated their strategies for developing grounded theory in the 1967 book *The Discovery of Grounded Theory*. Glaser took these ideas further in his lesser-known 1978 book *Theoretical Sensitivity*; however, "the abstract terms and dense writing Glaser employed rendered the book inaccessible to many readers" (Charmaz, 2000, p. 512). Grounded theory gained a larger following when Strauss and Corbin released the book *Basics of Qualitative Research* in 1990. It became "the standard introduction to grounded theory in place of the original text" (Dey, 1999, pp. 13–14), but Glaser (1992, p. 2) rejected this publication, claiming that it "distorts and misconceives grounded theory, while engaging in a gross neglect of 90% of its important ideas". Glaser objected to the book so strongly that he asked Strauss to withdraw it from publication, pending a rewrite. When Strauss refused to comply, Glaser wrote a seemingly angry correctional rejoinder entitled *Basics of Grounded Theory Analysis* in 1992. His intention was to write a "cogent, clear correction to set researchers using grounded theory on a correct path to discovery and theory generation" (Glaser, 1992, p. 3). Despite this controversy, Strauss and Corbin released a second edition of *Basics of Qualitative Research* in 1998.

Glaser's primary objection to Strauss and Corbin's version of the grounded theory method is that it forces data into preconceived concepts rather than allowing the theory to emerge naturally through the constant comparison of incidents in the data. The result, he states, is "a forced, preconceived, full conceptual description", but not grounded theory (Glaser, 1992, p. 3). The problem centres on the theoretical coding phase that was described earlier—the phase in which researchers try to ascertain the relationships that exist between the concepts that have emerged from the data. In the book *Theoretical Sensitivity*, Glaser (1978) discussed 18 theoretical coding families that can help researchers conceptualise those relationships. Strauss and Corbin's version of grounded theory focuses on only one coding family, which they refer to as a "coding paradigm". Using an alternative technique named "axial coding", Strauss and Corbin (1998, pp. 127–128) suggest that researchers should look for conditions, actions/interactions, and consequences as a guide to establishing relationships between concepts. Glaser (1992, p. 62) argues that this focus on a single coding paradigm "is clearly the beginning of forcing the theory and derailing its grounded character". Dey (1999, p. 14) concurs that "as this paradigm seems to impose a conceptual framework in advance of data analysis, it does not sit easily with the inductive emphasis in grounded theory".

Around the time of this debate, Charmaz (1990) began to advocate the notion of taking a constructivist approach to grounded theory, rather than accepting the positivistic assumptions that she perceived in the work of Glaser and Strauss. Constructivist grounded theory adopts the flexible, open-ended strategies of Glaser and Strauss' original approach and avoids prescriptive formulaic applications of it (Charmaz, 2014). Rather than accept the positivistic assumption of an external reality than can be described, analysed, explained, and predicted, constructivist grounded theory assumes that people create and maintain their own realities by seeking understanding of the world in which they live and by developing subjective meanings of their experiences (Charmaz, 2000). By extension, researchers who develop constructivist grounded theory can only claim to have interpreted *a* reality, dependent on their own experience and their study participants' portrayals of their experiences, rather than a universal, external reality. A constructivist grounded theory does not claim to be a lasting, generalisable truth, but constitutes a set of concepts and hypotheses that other researchers can consider in similar research problems. It is not entirely objective, but reflects the bias of the researcher. It tells a story about people, social processes, and situations that has been composed by the researcher. Thomas and James (2006, p. 770) describe Charmaz's offerings as "helpful developments in the move to open qualitative inquiry, faithful to the thinking which gave rise to it and continues to inspire it".

Grounded theory clearly fits the description of a contested concept. This discussion highlights some of the challenges faced by novice researchers who wish to employ this method for their own studies. Before they can even begin to apply a contested research method, they must first negotiate these controversies and debates within the research literature. Grounded theory researchers are not alone in this regard. Students who wish to undertake an autoethnographic study face similar challenges.

AUTOETHNOGRAPHY: A CONTESTED CONCEPT

Autoethnography is a qualitative research method that combines characteristics of autobiography and ethnography. Autoethnographers reflect upon and interpret their personal experiences and their interactions with others as a way of achieving wider cultural, political, or social understanding. The output of an autoethnographic study commonly takes the form of a narrative written in the first-person style such as a short story or novel (Bartleet, 2009; Ellis, 2004), but it may also include graphic, audio-visual, or performative components (Miller, 2010; Saldana, 2008; Scott-Hoy, 2002). The term "autoethnography" has been used by many researchers going back as far as Hayano (1979), but today it is commonly associated with the research method championed by Ellis and Bochner (2000, p. 739) who define autoethnography as "an autobiographical genre of writing and research that displays multiple layers of consciousness, connecting the personal to the cultural". Chang (2008, p. 43) observes that autoethnography can be distinguished from other genres of self-narrative, such as memoir and autobiography, by the way it "transcends mere narration of self to engage in cultural analysis and interpretation".

Ellis (2004) identifies several distinguishing characteristics of autoethnographic projects. She notes that the text of an autoethnographic study is typically presented as an autobiographical story with a narrator, characters, and plot, and it is often evocative in the sense that it highlights emotional experiences or discloses private details. Relationships are presented as connected episodes that unfold over time rather than as snapshots, and the researcher's life is explored together with the lives of other participants in a reflexive manner. The accessibility of this writing style helps readers to feel like involved participants in the dialogue, rather than as passive receivers. Ellis, Adams, and Bochner (2011) suggest that by producing accessible texts, researchers may be able to reach wider and more diverse audiences than those touched by traditional research. Greater reach may, in turn, make personal and social change possible for more people.

Although autoethnography has gained a large following, it has also been criticised for its rejection of traditional analytic goals such as abstraction and generalisation (Anderson, 2006). Atkinson (2006), for example, laments that "the goals of analysis and theorizing are too often lost to sight in contemporary fashions for subjective and evocative ethnographic work". Ellis (2004, pp. 195–196) argue that autoethnographic studies do incorporate analysis in the sense that "when people tell stories, they employ analytic techniques to interpret their worlds". The generalisability of a story is constantly being tested by readers as they decide whether a story speaks to them about their experience or the lives of others they know. This nontraditional view of analysis and generalisation does not sit comfortably with researchers who employ a realist or analytic approach. Ellis and Bochner (2006, p. 440) acknowledge that point, but note that "If you turn a story told into a story analyzed ... you sacrifice the story at the altar of traditional sociological rigor. You transform the story into another language, the language of generalisation and analysis, and thus you lose the very qualities that make a story a story." Autoethnographers do not privilege traditional analysis and generalisation over story.

Anderson (2006, p. 374) has expressed concerns about the autoethnographic method championed by Ellis and Bochner (2000), claiming that "'evocative or emotional autoethnography' may have the unintended consequence of eclipsing other visions of what autoethnography can be and of obscuring the ways in which it may fit productively in other traditions of social inquiry". Specifically, he has expressed dissatisfaction with the limitations that so-called evocative autoethnography places on researchers who want to practise autoethnography within a realist or analytic tradition. To redress this situation, Anderson (2006) proposed an alternative autoethnographic research method that is committed to an analytic tradition, which he labels "analytic autoethnography". "The purpose of analytic ethnography is not simply to document personal experience, to provide an 'insider's perspective', or to evoke emotional resonance with the reader", Anderson (2006, p. 386) writes. "Rather, the defining characteristic of analytic social science is to use empirical data to gain insight into some broader set of social phenomena than those provided by the data themselves" (Anderson, 2006, p. 387). While some researchers such as Atkinson (2006), Charmaz (2006), and Vryan (2006) have written positively about Anderson's proposal, others such as Ellis and Bochner (2006) and Denzin (2006) have opposed it on the grounds that it could dilute the current meaning of the term "autoethnography". Denzin (2006, p. 421) describes analytic autoethnography as a return "to traditional symbolic interactionist assumptions" of the past. Ellis and Bochner (2006) express concern that if analytic autoethnography became mainstream, it could reduce publishing opportunities for researchers who practise evocative autoethnography.

What is the point of unpacking these disagreements about the nature and practice of autoethnography? Familiarity with these issues is vital to

Table 13.2 Autoethnography as a contested concept

Characteristics of a contested concept (Gallie, 1956)	Characteristics of a contested concept, as applied to autoethnography
The concept is appraisive in the sense that is significant and valuable.	Autoethnography is widely recognised as a valid research method.
The achievement has an internally complex character.	Autoethnography challenged the realist conventions of an objective observer in contemporary ethnography.
The complexity of praiseworthy achievement leads to a variety of descriptions.	Autoethnography has a variety of descriptions such as Anderson's (2006) distinction between evocative and analytic autoethnography.
The achievement is open in the sense that there has been considerable modification in the light of changing circumstances.	Autoethnography has undergone modification, as evidenced by the paths taken by Ellis and Bochner (2006) and Anderson (2006).
The concept is used aggressively and defensively by parties who recognise that their use is contested by other parties.	A special thematic issue of the *Journal of Contemporary Ethnography* contains examples of researchers taking either Ellis and Bochner's (2006) position or Anderson's (2006) position.
There is an original exemplar whose authority is acknowledged by all users of the concept.	The term "autoethnography" is commonly associated with the research method championed by Ellis and Bochner (2000)
Continuous competition for acknowledgement enables the original exemplar's achievement to be sustained and/or developed in optimum fashion.	Ongoing debate and adaptation of autoethnography sustains and develops the original exemplar.

understanding the challenges faced by novice researchers who wish to employ this method for their own studies. Like grounded theory, autoethnography can clearly be characterised as a contested concept. Just as Bryant and Charmaz (2007) applied Gallie's seven conditions for the existence of a contested concept to grounded theory, Table 13.2 summarises and applies those same conditions to autoethnography.

NEGOTIATING DEBATES ABOUT CONTESTED RESEARCH METHODS

The previous sections have explained why grounded theory and autoethnography qualify as contested concepts. This status does not detract from their value as research methods, but it adds to the challenges faced by novice researchers who wish to employ these research methods for their own studies. How should research higher degree students negotiate these disagreements and debates? The following suggestions have been drawn from the experiences of supervisors and candidates.

1. Do not shy away from using a research method merely because of controversy. Some researchers claim that contested research methods should be avoided because of the difficult questions that surround them. Dey (1999), on the other hand, suggests that these questions are of considerable merit because they force researchers to confront some fundamental and difficult issues about the nature of social research. "If we accept the elementary (but awkward) principle that to do research requires reflection on what we are doing and how we do it, at the very least we should try to confront and clarify these issues", he writes (Dey, 1999, p. 24).

2. Learn about research paradigms and related concepts such as ontology, epistemology, methodology, and axiology because these topics are often pertinent to disagreements and debates about research methods (Guba & Lincoln, 2005). All research is guided by a basic set of beliefs about the world and how it should be understood and studied. This basic set of beliefs has been termed a "paradigm" (Kuhn, 1970). Paradigms are human constructions and can never be established in terms of their ultimate truthfulness. They are not open to proof in any conventional sense. The basic beliefs that define a paradigm can be summarised by the responses that proponents of that paradigm give to four fundamental, interconnected questions (Guba & Lincoln, 1994, 2005; Heron & Reason, 1997). The question of ontology asks: What is the form and nature of reality, and therefore, what can be known about it? The question of epistemology asks: What is the relationship between the researcher and what can be known? The question of methodology asks: How can the researcher gain knowledge about whatever he or she believes can be known? The question of axiology asks: What kind of knowledge is intrinsically valuable to the researcher?

3. Become sufficiently acquainted with the details of the contested research method, its history, and its controversies. This foundation knowledge is needed to make an informed decision about your position on the disputed aspects of the method.

4. Adopt a "bowerbird" approach—drawing together ideas from different interpretations of the contested research method if necessary. A bowerbird is an Australian bird that is known for its courtship behaviour. The male of the species attempts to attract a mate by building a structure called a bower out of sticks and brightly coloured objects he has collected. Brady (2000) uses the bowerbird as a metaphor to describe her behaviour as a researcher. Just as a bowerbird might collect blue objects and disregard other colours, Brady needed to acquire a working knowledge in a range of fields and disciplines to progress her study, isolating the essence of what she needed rather than becoming a specialist in every area. Webb and Brien (2011, p. 199) suggest that this eclectic approach to research can lead to "a fresh way of understanding ... points of connection and their wider implications and applications".

5. Explain the approach that you are taking to the research method in any publications arising from your research. This is especially important if your approach is an adaptation of well-established procedures. Failing to adequately explain your approach or your adaptation could lead to criticism or rejection from reviewers, editors, or examiners.

6. Study examples of research projects that employ the same approach that you are taking. Trauth (2001, p. 2) observes that "throughout ... my research career what I most often sought were examples to help show me the way". Reviewing studies that demonstrate how others have engaged with research issues like yours can clarify particulars around the choice of research method, data collection, analysis, evaluation, and more. Where appropriate, reference studies that are similar to yours in your research output to help justify the approach that you have taken.

7. Be aware of the target audience of any publications arising from your research, particularly if that audience includes readers who will disagree with the approach that you have taken. Certain topics in your article may need to be explained in greater detail than others to cater for the views and prejudices of your target audience.

Adopting a contested research method, executing it well, and communicating it clearly can be a rewarding experience. It may even make a valuable contribution to scholarly debates about the method in question.

Since this chapter commenced with comments from three research higher degree students who feared the risks of working with contested research methods, consider the following comments that were made by three examiners in response to dissertations submitted by students who applied the suggestions above.

> The significance of this piece of research cannot be overstated; there is simply nothing quite like this study in the research literature. The study manages to move forward the field of autoethnography ...
>
> The treatment of the research method is as close to exhaustive as I have ever seen in a PhD thesis. It embeds Grounded Theory into the wider context of qualitative research per se and gives a thorough overview of the actual research activities.
>
> Not only does the researcher know herself and her own journey well, she shows a strong knowledge of the approaches for turning this self-knowledge into research ... The thesis, in many ways, can serve as a model for this type of study.

The final piece of advice about negotiating contested research methods could appropriately come from Miles and Huberman (1994, p. 5) who believe that "research is actually more a craft than a slavish adherence to methodological rules". They remind readers that "no study conforms exactly to a standard methodology; each one calls for the researcher to bend the methodology to the peculiarities of the setting". Reflecting on these words brings some perspective to scholarly debates about contested research methods, and highlights the importance of contributing to those debates by continuing to apply contested methods in meaningful ways.

References

Anderson, L. (2006). Analytic autoethnography. *Journal of Contemporary Ethnography, 35*(4), 373–395.

Atkinson, P. (2006). Rescuing autoethnography. *Journal of Contemporary Ethnography, 35*(4), 400–404.

Bartleet, B. L. (2009). Behind the baton: Exploring autoethnographic writing in a musical context. *Journal of Contemporary Ethnography, 38*(6), 713–733.

Brady, T. (2000). A question of genre: De-mystifying the exegesis. TEXT, 4(1). Retrieved from http://www.textjournal.com.au/april00/brady.htm

Bryant, A., & Charmaz, K. (2007). Introduction. Grounded theory research: Methods and practices. In A. Bryant & K. Charmaz (Eds.), *The SAGE handbook of grounded theory* (pp. 1–28). Thousand Oaks, CA: Sage.

Chang, H. (2008). *Autoethnography as method*. Walnut Creek, CA: Left Coast Press.

Charmaz, K. (1990). 'Discovering' chronic illness: Using grounded theory. *Social Science and Medicine, 30*(11), 1161–1172.

Charmaz, K. (2000). Grounded theory: Objectivist and constructivist methods. In N. K. Denzin & Y. S. Lincoln (Eds.), *Handbook of Qualitative Research* (2nd ed., pp. 509–535). Thousand Oaks, CA: Sage.

Charmaz, K. (2006). The power of names. *Journal of Contemporary Ethnography, 35*(4), 396–399.

Charmaz, K. (2014). *Constructing grounded theory* (2nd ed.). Thousand Oaks, CA: Sage.

Creswell, J. W. (2013). *Qualitative inquiry and research design: choosing among five approaches* (3rd ed.). Thousand Oaks, CA: Sage.

Denzin, N. (2006). Analytic autoethnography, or déjà vu all over again. *Journal of Contemporary Ethnography, 35*(4), 419–428.

Dey, I. (1999). *Grounding grounded theory: guidelines for qualitative inquiry*. San Diego, CA: Academic Press.

Ellis, C. (2004). *The ethnographic I: a methodological novel about autoethnography*. Walnut Creek, CA: AltaMira Press.

Ellis, C., Adams, T. E., & Bochner, A. P. (2011). Autoethnography: An overview. *Historical Social Research, 36*(4), 273–290.

Ellis, C., & Bochner, A. P. (2000). Autoethnography, personal narrative, reflexivity: researcher as subject. In N. K. Denzin & Y. S. Lincoln (Eds.), *Handbook of qualitative research* (2nd ed., pp. 733–768). Thousand Oaks, CA: Sage.

Ellis, C., & Bochner, A. P. (2006). Analyzing analytic autoethnography: An autopsy. *Journal of Contemporary Ethnography, 35*(4), 429–449.

Gallie, W. B. (1956). Essentially contested concepts. *Proceedings of the Aristotelian Society*, 167–198.

Glaser, B. G. (1978). *Theoretical sensitivity: Advances in the methodology of grounded theory*. Mill Valley, CA: Sociology Press.

Glaser, B. G. (1992). *Basics of grounded theory analysis: Emergence vs forcing*. Mill Valley, CA: Sociology Press.

Glaser, B. G., & Strauss, A. L. (1967). *The discovery of grounded theory: Strategies for qualitative research*. New York: Aldine De Gruyer.

Guba, E. G., & Lincoln, Y. S. (1994). Competing paradigms in qualitative research. In N. K. Denzin & Y. S. Lincoln (Eds.), *Handbook of qualitative research* (1st ed., pp. 105–117). Thousand Oaks, CA: Sage.

Guba, E. G., & Lincoln, Y. S. (2005). Paradigmatic controversies, contradictions, and emerging confluences. In N. K. Denzin & Y. S. Lincoln (Eds.), *Handbook of qualitative research* (3rd ed., pp. 191–215). Thousand Oaks, CA: Sage.

Hayano, D. (1979). Auto-ethnography: Paradigms, problems, and prospects. *Human Organization, 38*(1), 99–104.

Heron, J., & Reason, P. (1997). A participatory inquiry paradigm. *Qualitative Inquiry, 3*(3), 274–294.

Kuhn, T. S. (1970). *The structure of scientific revolutions* (2nd ed.). Chicago: University of Chicago Press.

Miles, M. B., & Huberman, A. M. (1994). *Qualitative data analysis: an expanded sourcebook* (2nd ed.). Thousand Oaks, CA: Sage.

Miller, A. (2010). Grunge blotto. TEXT, 14(2). Retrieved from http://www. textjournal.com.au/oct10/miller.htm

Saldana, J. (2008). Second chair: An autoethnodrama. *Research Studies in Music Education, 30*(2), 177–191.

Scott-Hoy, J. (2002). The visitor: juggling life in the grip of the text. In A. P. Bochner & C. Ellis (Eds.), *Ethnographically speaking: Autoethnography, literature and aesthetics* (pp. 274–294). Walnut Creek, CA: AltaMira Press.

Strauss, A., & Corbin, J. (1998). *Basics of qualitative research: Techniques and procedures for developing grounded theory* (2nd ed.). Thousand Oaks, CA: Sage.

Thomas, G., & James, D. (2006). Reinventing grounded theory: Some questions about theory, ground and discovery. *British Educational Research Journal, 32*(6), 767–795.

Trauth, E. (2001). The choice of qualitative methods in IS research. In E. M. Trauth (Ed.), *Qualitative research in IS: Issues and trends* (pp. 1–19). Hershey, PA: Idea Group Publishing.

Urquhart, C. (2013). *Grounded theory for qualitative research: A practical guide*. Thousand Oaks, CA: Sage.

Vryan, K. D. (2006). Expanding autoethnography and enhancing its potential. *Journal of Contemporary Ethnography, 35*(4), 405–409.

Webb, J., & Brien, D. L. (2011). Addressing the 'ancient quarrel': Creative writing as research. In M. Biggs & H. Karlsson (Eds.), *The Routledge companion to research in the arts* (pp. 186–203). Abingdon, Oxon: Routledge.

Discursive Manoeuvring in the Borderlands of Career Transition: From Trade to Teacher

Bill Blayney and Bobby Harreveld

INTRODUCTION

Methodological frameworks are constantly evolving as qualitative research-ers manoeuvre through contexts, concepts, paradigms, and methods. This chapter offers a distinctive view of the relationship between methodology and method from an interpretive constructivist paradigm (Creswell, 2013; Punch, 2014). In the context of investigating the career transitions of trade-qualified workers to secondary school teachers, this chapter explores three interrelated discourses of methodological manoeuvring: conceptual, methodological, and analytical. This work extends from the doctoral study of the first-named author that focused on tradespeople transition through a career change to become secondary school teachers in their techni-cal vocational areas. The extension occurs as we articulate and examine critically the discursive manoeuvring encountered in the borderlands of research design when being and becoming qualitative researchers.

B. Blayney (✉) • B. Harreveld
School of Education and the Arts, CQUniversity Australia,
Rockhampton, QLD, Australia

© The Author(s) 2016
B. Harreveld et al. (eds.), *Constructing Methodology for Qualitative Research*, DOI 10.1057/978-1-137-59943-8_14

201

The chapter begins with a brief overview of the doctoral study that investigated the borderland discourses of 16 participants who graduated from an initial pre-service teacher education degree through distance education, between 1999 and 2007. At the intersection "of multiple worlds and multiple ways of knowing" (Alsup, 2006, p. 15), the research participants were themselves manoeuvring through changing personal epistemologies and ontologies of becoming and being a teacher. The phases of discursive manoeuvring in these borderlands and their inductive development are outlined in this first section. Here, the seminal works of Anzaldúa (1987) and Gee (2005) guided our conceptual thinking in a manner similar to that of Alsup (2006).

Methodological insights are then provided by the rich debates interrogating case study as methodology and/or method (Merriam, 2009; Stake, 1995; Stenhouse, 1984; Yin, 2009). The ensuing analytic manoeuvring from themes to discourses provides insights into the dilemmas encountered when seeking to investigate career transitions in the borderlands.

Manoeuvring Conceptually: Discourses of Transition

Discourses of transition are well represented in the literature from the UK to the USA and Australia as *career changers*, having mobilised discourses such as helping, making a positive difference in young people's lives, and repaying society for earlier opportunities in life (Barmby, 2007; Castro & Bauml, 2009; Manuel & Hughes, 2006; Richardson & Watt, 2005). Another cadre of discourses is evident as career changers broker the borderlands of transition when combining formal university education with teaching practicums in schools while maintaining personal life commitments. Discourses of vulnerability, insecurity, and uncertainty emerge in these contexts (Ewing & Manuel, 2005; McCormack, Gore, & Thomas, 2006). Yet people continue to change careers into new geographies of teaching requiring learning and earning at the education–training–work interface (Harreveld & Singh, 2009; Singh & Harreveld, 2014).

Since the late 1990s (Green, 2006, 2009; Harreveld, 2010), Australian universities have delivered teacher education programmes specifically designed to target tradespersons wishing to undertake a career transition to become secondary school teachers specialising in Vocational Education and Training (VET). However, there is limited data concerning graduates of these particular teacher education programmes, their achievements following graduation, and the roles they undertook subsequently within secondary schools (Blayney, 2013). Accordingly, the underpinning/related doctoral study here aimed to identify why a cohort of 16 trades-people decided to undertake a career transition from *Trade to Teacher*, how they achieved such a transition, and what kind of teacher identity they constructed. The investigation was concerned with the discourses of transition as the two worlds of trade and school were merged and technology teacher identities were created.

Research questions were generated on the basis of a review of both contextual and conceptual literature. Firstly, the disorienting events (Cranton, 2006) that motivated the career change were identified: what are the disorienting events that motivate a tradesperson to become a technology teacher in secondary schools? Secondly, the support mechanisms assembled to affect their transitions emerged in response to the question: what support mechanisms does a tradesperson require to transition from trade to teacher?

Fifteen of the 16 participants were still teaching up to ten years after graduation when the questions were asked. Responses to these retrospective questions provided them an opportunity for critical reflection and analysis of their times in the borderlands of transition. Findings were theorised through the conceptualising lens of the third research question: what are the borderland discourses that characterise a career transition from trade to teacher? Thus, our first major manoeuvre after the review of the contextual literature about career change teachers was an investigation of the concept of borderland discourses that may inform understandings of this transition phenomenon.

IN THE BORDERLANDS

Discourses are ways of conceptualising the world so as to understand it. People construct discourses through narrative, metaphor, and philosophical statements about the way they perceive the world to be or as they think it should be (Alsup, 2006; Anzaldúa, 1987; Gee, 2011; Lakoff & Johnson, 2003). In particular, Anzaldúa's (1987) conceptualisation of the borderlands and discourse construction in and through the borderlands resonated with our study. Her semi-autobiographical work, *Borderlands/La Frontera: The New Mestiza*, theorised the social and cultural marginalisation experienced as a woman of mixed racial ancestry and sexual orientation from the borderlands of Mexico and Texas (USA). Theoretically, such *new mestiza* constructed their own discourses through metaphorical narratives in prose and poetry in which:

> A borderland is a vague and undetermined place created by the emotional residue of an unnatural boundary. It is in a constant state of transition. The prohibited and forbidden are its inhabitants. (Anzaldúa, 1987, p. 25)

The power of metaphors such as border and transition when expressed through narrative requires a paradigmatic stance robust enough to contest culturally determined roles, and the collective unconsciousness of both linguistic and visual orientations (Aigner-Varoz, 2000). Thus, essentially, "the borderland is the discourse of people who live in-between different worlds" (Elenes, 2001, p. 359).

The language constructed in and through the borderlands is central to the discourse. Language has the power to exclude those who are not part of the in-between worlds, and include those who are recognised as also being in-between. For instance, Blackburn (2005) examined the language of queer black youth in a community centre in Ohio. She identified a learned language and culture which involved the construction of a discourse she coined *gaybonics* (italics in original, Blackburn, 2005). This hybrid term was originally described by Smith (1998) as derived from the term ebonics; meaning African grammar with English words. It was later defined by Smitherman (1998) to mean black sounds. Blackburn (2005) asserted that the *gaybonics* discourse constituted, first, a protection from the homophobia these youth experienced. Second, it created an identity kit that came complete with costume (dress code) and a guide (gestures, mannerisms) on how to talk and act in order to take on an identity that others recognised (Gee, 2011).

A key feature of borderland discourses is that while they are perhaps equally powerful when viewed from within, they may not be represented equally in society because some discourses are considered more powerful than others (Gee, 2011). Earlier studies (Anzaldúa, 1987; Barrett, 1999; Blackburn, 2005) grappled with similar tensions and contradictions. Discursively, the "borders are set up to divide the places that are safe and unsafe, to distinguish us from them" (Anzaldúa, 1987, p. 25). At the same time, borderland discourses share symbols and rituals to create belonging and identification within a particular community (Jenkins, 2008). This gives rise to the transformative power of borderland discourse. For instance, Alsup (2006) found primary teacher education graduates constructed a borderland discourse that integrated both "personal and professional subjectivities while creating a professional identity and personal pedagogy" (p. 192). Their borderland discourse was powerful enough to ensure successful transition into teaching roles.

Investigating the social practices of career change transitions requires careful consideration of methodological options. To undertake this task, we embarked on manoeuvres, specifically methodological manoeuvres.

Manoeuvring Methodologically: A Case for Case

Methodological manoeuvres began with establishing ontological and epistemological perspectives consistent with the study's aim and research questions within a world view or paradigm that was congruent with our values and beliefs as to what counts as research, how it is conducted and reported. This was a pragmatic decision because it resonated with our experiences as teacher educators in these discursive borderlands of career transition from trade-qualified worker to secondary school teacher. It was also a strategic decision because as demonstrated in the previous section, there was fruitful work to be done in building on the conceptual work of Anzaldúa (1987), Gee (2011), and Alsup (2006) about the meanings these participants brought to their transitions and the ways in which they made sense of their changing worlds (Punch, 2014).

Methodologically, the commitment to a constructivist ontology meant that we recognised those who volunteered to be interviewed as participants in the study, and ourselves, as holding multiple and relativist views of the transitions from trade to teacher (Guba & Lincoln, 2005). Thus, the knowledge to be produced would be subjective, particular to the interpretations of both participants and researchers as explanations, analyses, and critiques of these lived transitions into, through, and beyond the borderlands were articulated (Guba & Lincoln, 2005; Schlossberg, 1984). The choice of case study as both methodology and method was consistent with these ontological and epistemological perspectives (Stake, 2005; Yin, 2009).

The Case for Case

The case for case was determined by the boundedness (Merriam, 2009; Punch, 2014; Stake, 2005) of the study; that is, the context, the ontological and epistemological beliefs, and methodological design choices were consistent with the study's aim and research questions previously considered. Indeed, Stake (1995) argues that "case study is not a methodological choice, but a choice of what is to be studied" (p. 443). From the three types of case study offered by Stake (1995, 1998)—instrumental, intrinsic, and collective—it was the collective case type that articulated most appropriately the study's purpose to explore "a number of cases in order to investigate a phenomenon, population, or general condition" (Stake, 1995, p. 437). In contrast, Yin (2003, 2009) sets conditions for the effective development of case study designs that reflect a positivist orientation somewhat at odds with our interpretivist stance here. However, both Yin (2009) and Merriam (2009) shared the view that the importance of articulating the unit of analysis is a distinguishing feature of case study research. Further, a commonality among all views is that case provides in-depth study of a complex phenomenon, in real-life settings, and is in and of itself valued as a unit for analysis (Saldana, 2011).

Ongoing debates continue as to whether case study is a methodological choice or choice of method/s (Tight, 2010). This may be because case is perhaps best known for its inclusiveness of a variety of data collection methods (Simons, 2009); as well as different processes for data analysis, known as "analytical eclecticism" (Thomas, 2013, p. 592). Such methods optimise understanding of each case's uniquely complex contexts and the social, economic, political, cultural influences in those contexts (Punch, 2014; Stake, 2005). On the other hand, Denscombe (2010) warns that critics disparage the knowledge produced because it is perceived to be developed from "*soft data* ... lacking the degree of rigour expected of social science research" (italics in original, p. 63).

Aware of these debates, our methodological choice was both interpretive and descriptive as we articulated the contextualised choices of what would count as data, the methods by which it would be generated and analysed and the outcomes represented. The case construction process is reminiscent of the four phases of case production proposed by Stenhouse (1978, 1984) in his seminal work conceptualising qualitative case through: (1) gathering initial raw product as case data, (2) editing that data into a case record, (3) producing the case and interpreting across cases, and (4) constructing new meaning through surveying the case study thus produced.

In this case of transition, the generation of case data involved the collection of the initial raw data such as interview transcripts, archival student records, and documents from the teacher education programme. Ethical clearance for the collection of the case study data was obtained via the University's Human Research Ethics Committee (Approval H11/05–078). Anonymity of participants and confidentiality of the information provided was assured under these ethical guidelines. A case record for each participant was the first edited product of the data and in the second phase, case summaries of the data sources were created to improve manageability and cross-referencing potential. The third phase involved the case study data analysis and interpretation to create narrative representations of the actual participants' lived experiences through their career transitions. The final phase involved surveying across the cases looking for emergent themes.

In summary, this process afforded the opportunity to undertake a study that was particularistic, as it elicited the decision-making processes of the 16 participants to leave their trade, and their lived experiences over time as they undertook a career transition through an initial teacher education degree to become secondary school technology teachers; teachers also qualified to deliver VET in schools programmes. The case was bounded by the following criteria:

- Cases were drawn from graduates of an initial trade entry teacher education programme that was offered via distance education;
- Graduates were from the first intake of students into the degree in 1998, to the final student intake in 2005[1];
- Of the over 100 possible participants, 16 agreed to be interviewed.

A case study approach was chosen for this research because:

- It offered the opportunity for participants to describe and explain what happened throughout the career transition.
- It enabled an in-depth study of process and relationships as experienced by participants completing the transition.
- It allowed the researchers to reveal "the subtleties and intricacies of the complex situations" experienced by the participants as they transitioned from trade to teacher (Denscombe, 2010, p. 62).

Thus, each case was heuristic (interpretative) and descriptive as it offered the opportunity to richly describe the case participants' journeys as they transitioned from trade to teacher and interpret the data in depth. Each participant constituted a case that acted as a unit of analysis for the single *case of transition*, which was also particularistic, interpretative, and descriptive. The final phase of case production presented the greatest analytical challenge and the manoeuvring that ensued is now examined.

MANOEUVRING ANALYTICALLY: FROM THEMES TO DISCOURSES

The third type of manoeuvring that we undertook involved analytical manoeuvring. This is where thematic analysis was used to generate meaning from the interview transcripts initially, thus improving manageability. The analytic manoeuvring used to collect and analyse the data followed Stenhouse's (1978) phases of case construction as previously noted. The four phases of case construction provided a rigorous foundation for analytic manoeuvring to occur with the research question always in mind: *What are the borderland discourses that characterise a career transition from trade to teacher?* The following section unpacks the four phases of case construction and highlights the benefits of this rigorous method in yielding themes from which to derive discourses.

Phase One: Case Data (The First Cut)

The initial case data phase included interview transcripts and archival student records. The *first cut* of the data was derived by reading and listening to the first four transcripts consisting of two males and two females, to determine common themes arising from their conversations and responses. Hatch (2002) referred to this process as "organising and interrogating data in ways that allow researchers to see patterns, develop explanations and make interpretations" (p. 148). All 16 transcripts were then read and reread multiple times in a search for common themes and related characteristics (Merriam, 2009). Further analysis was possible by repeatedly listening to the recordings of the interviews. This followed Silverman's (1993) recommendation, thus revealing previous "un-noted recurring features of the organisation of talk" (p. 17).

An example of this was the previously "un-noted reoccurring feature" of swearing by some participants throughout the interviews (Silverman, 1993, p. 17). Swearing emerged as an identity indicator from one participant's past career, forming a significant part of his "tradie" culture that considered the use of swearing as part of normal expression. For example:

I had to learn to bite my tongue and not swear, and I tell you it was hard. Because, even now, occasionally the kids will come in and I'll say, "Mate, that's shit." They say, "Sir, you just swore." I say, "Mate, that's not swearing. There's a few other colourful words I could have used to describe it." [Pat]

Therefore, it was decided to include the swearing in transcript extracts to provide an insight into a part of his previous identity that was difficult to leave behind as part of his new secondary school teacher identity.

Phase Two: Case Record (Emergent Themes)

Case record was the first edited product of initial data analysis. This phase consisted of creating a list of emergent themes from the first cut of the 16 transcripts. During this phase, the original recordings of the interviews were revisited while rereading the transcripts looking for pauses, or silences and diversions from the actual interview questions; or, if the participants took hold of the conversation when they felt they wanted to express strong opinions concerning particular issues. This data analysis phase was also where the following linguistic features were identified and highlighted in the transcripts.

- **Repetition**: Repeated use of words, phrases, and shifts in content throughout the interview (Agar & Hobbs, 1985).
- **Transitions**: The way in which participant's speech pauses occurred, often punctuated changes in tone to indicate sarcasm, seriousness, or joking to make a point. The ways in which participants may change the direction of the conversation because they had left something out previously and wanted to make a point of it, or by interrupting to the normal flow of speech (Bernard & Ryan, 2010).
- **Similarities and differences**: Looking for these within the transcript of an individual participant and then across all participants' transcripts. For example, noting the similarities and differences between all the participants' reasons for transitioning from trade to teacher (Bernard & Ryan, 2010).
- **Metaphors**: How the participants represented their thoughts, actions, and experiences using a metaphor or analogy (Bernard & Ryan, 2010).

Table 14.1   Themes of career transition from trade to teacher

Themes	1. Flexible study	2. Trade pride	3. Culture clash
4. Mentoring	5. Tough women	6. Reward and recognition	7. Trade disillusionment
8. Delivered training	9. Student connection	10. Lack of confidence	11. Support mechanisms

Phase Three: Case Study (Creating a Narrative)

This phase involved the creation of the case study where data sources were analysed and interpreted to create a narrative representation of each participants' lived experiences through a career transition; hence, drawing on the strength of each theme as it emerged through reanalysis of the primary and secondary data sources (Bryman, 2012). The final component of this phase was to collect key quotations from each interview transcript and to place them into the appropriate themes through a *cutting and sorting* process, and then revisiting the archival data to complement the case constructions. The process of creating a narrative for each theme was to provide an account of the transitional journeys undertaken by the participants while utilising all the available data, yet being necessarily selective in its appropriateness for each theme. It also provided insights for the analysis of "what actually happened, how people made sense of what happened and to what effect?" (Bryman, 2012, p. 582). This approach was consistent with Guest, McQueen, and Namey's (2012) proposition that the researcher's choice of a thematic analysis approach "is the most useful in capturing the complexities of meaning within textual data" (p. 11).

Eleven themes were constructed with descriptive and explanatory text inclusive of direct quotations from the total data set. Table 14.1 sets out the themes.

These themes addressed the first two research questions. For all participants, Themes 6 (reward and recognition) and 7 (trade disillusionment) were common and addressed the first research question of the doctoral study: *What are the disorienting events that motivated a tradesperson to become a technology teacher in secondary schools?* Participants were disillusioned with their trade work, experiencing a lack of reward and recognition that was not necessarily financial but primarily social and personal. Theme 5 (tough women) was significant for the four female participants. They had overcome the physically and mentally tough work of nursing,

hairdressing and hospitality; combined study and work while raising families; and post-graduation experienced variable in-school supportive mentoring. The second research question asked, *What support mechanisms does
a tradesperson require to transition from a trade to a teacher?* Themes 1,
4, 6, 8, 9, and 11 addressed this research question. Flexible study via the
distance education delivery of the teacher education programme (Theme
1) was essential as was the mentoring (Theme 2) available from fellow
teachers or school administrators (or not available in some cases) in their
career transitions. Reward and recognition (Theme 6) came through again
in relation to their academic results as well as their sometimes swift promotion in schools as their teaching capabilities and previous life experiences were valued. These career changers connected easily with students
whom they taught (Theme 9) as their prior experiences delivering vocational training (Theme 8) in workplaces with apprentices, and in some
instances technical colleges, were valued by students and fellow teachers.
All experienced some form of culture clash (Theme 3) as they encountered the worlds of university teaching and learning and that of secondary
schooling while seeing themselves initially as a practical, hands-on tradesperson. The culture clash continued into their teaching careers as they
negotiated cultures of various schools, students, and local communities.
Theme 11 was named "support mechanisms" to capture other ways in
which participants were supported in their transition that were not necessarily consistent across all cases. In the following section, the third research
question is addressed as the theorised relationships between these themes
are represented in the borderland discourses.

Phase Four: Case Survey (Cross-Case Analysis)

The fourth phase of data analysis was to "combine themes into conceptual
models and theories to explain and predict social phenomena" (Bernard
& Ryan, 2010, p. 292). This final phase, defined as case survey, drew
from the work of Bryman (2012), Bernard and Ryan (2003, 2010), and
Symons (2009). While the case construction (Phase 3) provided the foundation from which to develop the themes from all 16 participants, the
cross-case analysis process (Phase 4) developed the borderland discourses,
which played a significant role in conceptualising the sense-making processes of transition. Figure 14.1 displays this relationship as it addresses
the third research question: "*What are the borderland discourses that characterise a career transition from trade to teacher?*"

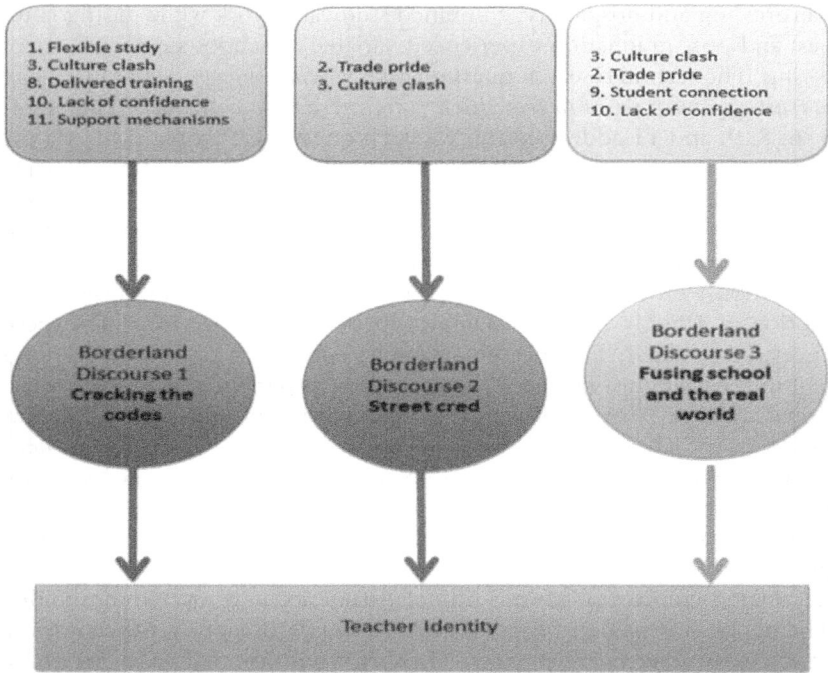

Fig. 14.1 From themes to discourses

Three borderland discourses were constructed: cracking the codes; street cred (i.e., street credibility); and fusing the school and the real world. The themes from which they were constructed are indicated and from the previous section's explanation of each theme, their relationship to the naming of the discourses is provided. Of the 16 participants in the study, two chose not to take up careers as secondary school teachers; however, they still encountered the first two of the three borderland discourses listed in Fig. 14.1. All had to crack the codes of school teaching and university learning. They all had to construct credibility as teachers, learners, and colleagues, that is, street cred. For those 14 who managed to overcome the perhaps inevitable culture clashes, crises of confidence, pride in their trade background, which connected with their students, the fusion of school and the real world of trade work (its knowledge and skills) was a positive experience.

The significance of these discursive borderlands characterised in the career transition from trade to teacher is that although the original theory from Anzaldúa's (1987) is based upon sexuality, cultural dividers, and race borders with their attendant conflicting ideologies, it also has the power to translate into the borderlands that divide the worlds of the trades and schools. "Borders are set up to divide the places that are safe and unsafe, to distinguish us from them" (Anzaldúa, 1987, p. 25). These were the discursive borderlands that the participants in the study experienced through their transitional journey. Like previous studies, (Barrett, 1999; Blackburn, 2005), this study grappled with similar tensions and contradictions of how the research participants developed their own identities.

These borderland discourses experienced by the participants were acquired over time, manoeuvring through boundaries, cracking codes, acquiring knowledge and skills along the way. Participants drew upon knowledge and experiences from their past, sought direction from others and teamed up with similar minded travellers on the same journey as they manoeuvred through the borderlands. They eventually emerged from the borderlands, focused on a different future, but having to leave some of their past behind. They were now tied to both worlds where the journey became more than the destination, creating a future from which a new identity could emerge. Although some returned across the borderlands to former identities as industry trainers, the journey left a lasting impression as to who they were at the time of interview for this study, and what they were capable of achieving since first embarking on a transition from trade to teacher.

CONCLUSION

This chapter has articulated a unique relationship between methodology and method used in qualitative research. It has offered an insight into three types of manoeuvring, conceptual, methodological, and analytical, undertaken by the authors when constructing and investigating the career transitions of trade-qualified workers to become secondary school teachers. Furthermore, it has provided some useful lessons in tackling a research problem and bringing it to life. By utilising various manoeuvres through the methodological maze, the relationship between methodology and method became evident.

The chapter also makes a contribution to knowledge about methodological manoeuvring and the consequences of decision-making in search of a "fit for purpose." Finally, the chapter has extended the knowledge pertaining to the processes of articulating and critically examining the discursive manoeuvring encountered in the borderlands of research design when being and becoming qualitative researchers.

NOTE

1. Although the final intake of this particular program ceased in 2005, it was replaced with an alternative program in 2006 that merged two degrees, the trade entry pathway and the mainstream secondary pathway into one degree. As a result a number of the distinctive features of the trade entry pathway degree were removed to accommodate a mainstream secondary cohort of students.

REFERENCES

Agar, M., & Hobbs, J. (1985). How to grow schemata out of interviews. In J. W. D. Dougherty (Ed.), *Directions in cognitive anthropology* (pp. 413–431). Urbana: University of Illinois Press.

Aigner-Varoz, E. (2000). Metaphors of a mestizo consciousness: Anzaldúa's Borderlands/La Frontera. *Oxford University Press*, on behalf of *The Society for the Study of the Multi-Ethnic Literature of the United States* (MELUS), 25, 47–62.

Alsup, J. (2006). *Teacher identity discourse: Negotiating personal and professional spaces*. Mahwah, NJ: Lawrence Erlbaum Associates.

Anzaldúa, G. (1987). *Borderlands: La Frontera—The New Mestiza*. San Francisco, CA: Aunt Lute Book Company.

Barmby, P. (2007). Improving teacher recruitment and retention: The importance of workload and pupil behaviour. *Educational Research, 48*(3), 247–265.

Barrett, R. (1999). Indexing polyphonous identity in the speech of African American drag queens. In M. Bucholtz, A. C. Liang, & L. A. Sutton (Eds.), *Reinventing identities: The gendered self in discourse* (pp. 313–331). New York: Oxford University Press.

Bernard, R. H., & Ryan, G. W. (2003). Data management and analysis methods. In N. K. Denzin & Y. S. Lincoln (Eds.), *Collecting and interpreting qualitative materials* (2nd ed., pp. 259–319). Thousand Oaks, CA: Sage.

Bernard, H. R., & Ryan, G. W. (2010). *Analyzing qualitative data: Systematic approaches*. Thousand Oaks, CA: Sage

Blackburn, M. V. (2005). Agency in borderland discourses: Examining language use in a community centre with queer black youth. *Teachers College Record, 107*(1), 89–113.

Blayney, W. R. (2013). *A case of career transitioning: From trade to teacher.* Doctor of Education thesis, Central Queensland University, Rockhampton.

Bryman, A. (2012). *Social research methods.* Oxford: Oxford University Press.

Castro, A. J., & Bauml, M. (2009). Why now? Factors associated with choosing teaching as a second career and their implications for teacher education programs. *Teacher Education Quarterly, 36*(3), 113–126.

Cranton, P. (2006). *Understanding and promoting transformative learning. A guide for educators of adults* (2nd ed.). San Francisco, CA: Jossey-Bass.

Creswell, J. W. (2013). *Qualitative inquiry and research design: Choosing among five approaches.* Los Angeles: SAGE.

Denscombe, M. (2010). *The Good Research Guide* (4th ed.). New York, USA: Open University Press.

Elenes, C. A. (2001). Transformando fronteras: Chicana feminist transformative pedagogies. *Qualitative Studies in Education, 14*(5), 689–702.

Ewing, R., & Manuel, J. (2005). Retaining quality early career teachers in the profession: New teacher narratives. *Change: Transformations in Education, 8*(1), 1–16.

Gee, J. P. (2005). *An introduction to discourse analysis: Theory and method.* New York: Routledge.

Gee, J. P. (2011). *An introduction to discourse analysis: Theory and method* (3rd ed.). New York: Routledge.

Green, A. (2006). Following through: Longitudinal research into new VET in schools teachers with an industry background. *Proceedings of the 9th Australian Vocational Education and Training Research Association (AVETRA) Conference: Global VET: Challenges at the Global, National and Local Levels.* Wollongong. Australia.

Green, A. (2009).Teachers from industry: From work to school. *Proceedings of the 12th Annual Australian Vocational and Training Research Association (AVETRA) Conference: Aligning Participants, Policy and Pedagogy: Traction and Tensions in VET Research.* Sydney. Australia.

Guba, E. G., & Lincoln, Y. S. (2005). Paradigmatic controversies, contradictions, and emerging confluences. In N. Denzin & Y. Lincoln (Eds.), *The Sage handbook of qualitative research* (3rd ed., pp. 191–215). Thousand Oaks, CA: Sage.

Guest, G., McQueen, M., & Namey, E. E. (2012). *Applied thematic analysis.* Sage.

Harreveld, B. (2010). A capability approach to open and distance learning for in-service teacher education. In A. Umar & P. Danaher (Eds.), *Perspectives on teacher education through open and distance learning* (pp. 47–60). Vancouver, Canada: Commonwealth of Learning.

Harreveld, B., & Singh, M. J. (2009). Contextualising learning at the education-training-work interface. *Education + Training, 51*(2), 92–107.

Hatch, J. A. (2002). *Doing qualitative research in educational settings*. Albany: State University of New York Press.

Jenkins, R. (2008). *Social identity* (3rd ed.). London: Routledge.

Lakoff, G., & Johnson, M. (2003). *Metaphors we live by*. Chicago: University of Chicago Press.

Manuel, J., & Hughes, J. (2006). It has always been my dream: Exploring pre-service teachers' motivations for choosing to teach. *Teacher Development, 10*(1), 5–24.

McCormack, A., Gore, J., & Thomas, K. (2006). Early career teacher professional learning. *Asia-Pacific Journal of Teacher Education, 34*(1), 95–113.

Merriam, S. B. (2009). *Qualitative research: A guide to design and implementation. Revised and expanded from qualitative research and case study applications in education*. San Francisco, CA: Wiley.

Plank, G. (1994). What silence means for educators of American Indian children. *Journal of American Indian Education, 34*(1), 1–11.

Punch, K. F. (2014). *Introduction to social research: Qualitative and quantitative approaches* (3rd ed.). Thousand Oaks, CA: Sage.

Richardson, P. W., & Watt, H. M. G. (2005). I've decided to become a teacher: Influences on career change. *Teaching and Teacher Education, 21*, 475–489.

Saldana, J. (2011). *Fundamentals of qualitative research: Understanding qualitative research*. Oxford: New York.

Schlossberg, N. K. (1984). *Counselling adults in transition: Linking practice with theory*. New York: Springer.

Silverman, D. (1993). *Beginning research. Interpreting qualitative data*. London: Sage.

Singh, M., & Harreveld, B. (2014). *Deschooling l'earning: Young adults and the new spirit of capitalism*. Basingstoke: Palgrave Macmillan.

Smith, E. (1998). What is Black English? What is Ebonics? In T. Perry & L. Delpit (Eds.), *The real Ebonics debate: Power, language, and the education of African American children* (pp. 49–58). Boston: Beacon Press.

Smitherman, G. (1998). Black English/Ebonics: What it be like? In T. Perry & L. Delpit (Eds.), *The real Ebonics debate: Power language, and the education of African American children* (pp. 29–37). Boston: Beacon Press.

Stake, R. (1998). Case studies. In N. K. Denzin & Y. S. Lincoln (Eds.), *Strategies of qualitative inquiry*. Thousand Oaks, CA: Sage.

Stake, R. E. (1995). *The art of case study research*. Thousand Oaks, CA: Sage.

Stake, R. E. (2005). Qualitative case studies. In N. K. Denzin & Y. S. Lincoln (Eds.), *The Sage handbook of qualitative research* (3rd ed., pp. 443–466). Thousand Oaks, CA: Sage.

Stenhouse, L. (1978). Case study and case records: Towards a contemporary history of education. *British Educational Research Journal, 4*(2), 21–39.

Stenhouse, L. (1984). The research process in educational settings: Ten case studies. In R. G. Burgess (Ed.), *An autobiographical account* (pp. 211–234). London: Falmer.

Simons, H. (2009). *Case study research in practice*. London: Sage.

Thomas, G. (2013). From question to inquiry: Operationalising the case study for research in teaching. *Journal of Education for Teaching: International Research and Pedagogy, 39*(5), 590–601.

Tight, M. (2010). The curious case of case study: A viewpoint. *International Journal of Social Research Methodology, 13*(4), 329–339.

Yin, R. K. (2003). *Applications of case study research* (2nd ed.). Thousand Oaks, CA: Sage.

Yin, R. K. (2009). *Case study research: Design and methods* (4th ed.). Los Angeles, CA: Sage.

Yin, R. K. (2013). Validity and generalization in future case study evaluations. *Evaluation, 19*(3), 321–332.

CHAPTER 15

Understanding and Influencing Research with Children

Alison L. Black and Gillian Busch

INTRODUCTION

Research 'with' children is becoming increasingly valued and accepted and there are many research projects where children are directly involved in research processes as researchers in their own right. Yet, even with changing views, children largely remain a silenced and invisible group—their faces typically absent or blurred in research, their voices usually missing from community decisions and forums.

Views about research relationships with children and their status and location in research must continue to be topics of discussion, particularly in relation to ethical considerations and children's visibility in research and broader society. We use this chapter to consider how our researcher values

A.L. Black (✉)
School of Education, University of the Sunshine Coast, Maroochydore, QLD, Australia

G. Busch
School of Education and the Arts, CQUniversity Australia, Rockhampton, QLD, Australia

B. Harreveld et al. (eds.), *Constructing Methodology for Qualitative Research*, DOI 10.1057/978-1-137-59943-8_15

and ethical commitments position children, determine their visibility and influence wider cultures of listening to children. We also explore the challenges of attending to and negotiating these.

INITIATING A DIALOGUE

Across the chapter, we seek to pay attention to views and alliances about researching with children, to the values and motivations that inform our research work, and to how we manoeuvre through boundaries and markers that currently control research. Using interlacing storylines and winding threads of meaning-making, we frequently interrupt the main text to discuss our experiences.

Valuing narrative inquiry, we are interested in capturing our thinking, questions and experiences of researching with children (Clandinin, Pushor, & Orr, 2007). We are interested in examining the dissonant qualities and challenging characteristics. And we seek to reflect on recognised and long-standing boundaries and indicators for ethical research, with a view to seeing or suggesting alternatives (Black, 2014; Cumming, Sumsion, & Wong, 2013).

This collection of narratively assembled research encounters relate to research infrastructures, the integrity of research projects and the connecting of researchers to their motivations and ethical commitments. More than capturing the tensions of researching with children, our chapter seeks to open channels for dialogue so that questions and perspectives about research with children continue to circulate.

The challenge of ethics requirements and the hypervigilance of ethics committees approving research are real (Bessant, 2006; Skelton, 2008); the boundaries and territories surrounding researching and working with children numerous and changing (Cumming et al., 2013). Authors engaged in contemporary writing about researching with children have many suggestions for ways forward (Clark, 2011; Waller & Bitou, 2011). But, new dilemmas and concerns are continually emerging, making this kind of research daunting (Spyrou, 2011).

Bessant (2006, p. 54) outlines that anecdotal evidence suggests many researchers are deciding not to research with children *at all* 'because the ethics requirements create too much work'. Those researchers that do continue researching with children are deciding 'to avoid any methods that involve interviewing, surveying or talking with children or young people in any way' (Bessant, 2006, p. 54). Valid representations of children's views and voices are hardly possible if the most valuable sources of the perspectives of children—children themselves—are not active participants in research.

> Threads of meaning-making: Will it only be the 'confident and experienced researcher' who can make sense of the concerns, respond to their own guiding values and ethical commitments, and negotiate their 'potentially eager hopes to listen to children'? How is the novice researcher affected by the myriad of warnings and discourses that surround researching with children—issues of ethics, consent, relations of power, subjectivities and authenticity?
>
> Given this backdrop, perhaps it is not surprising that we find ourselves feeling hesitant, wondering about binaries, dominant theories, sanctioned ways of thinking, new and emerging cautions. How do we situate ourselves as researchers researching with children? There are so many concerns, protocols and recommendations. We too could be easily discouraged from researching with children and from pursuing children's perspectives. Just writing this chapter has engendered a sense of timidity.

When researchers hope to influence, understand and change what is happening in educational and wider worlds, they need to interrogate motivations and meanings (Black, 2014). This may involve attending to uneasy experiences, interrupting everyday ways of thinking or parting with typical ways of thinking and seeing to see 'what else' might matter. This meaning-making space is where we seek to dwell. It is where we invite others to dwell.

THINKING ABOUT CHILDREN AND RESEARCH

Historically, children have been a researched group with few rights. Popular constructions of childhood characterise this time as a period of vulnerability and powerlessness. Research relationships with children, their status in research and their representation in the research process are topics of ongoing discussion (Christensen & James, 2008). Research with children is still considered a risky enterprise requiring protective governance and the protective responsibility of researchers (Danby & Farrell, 2004).

Binaries of safe/unsafe or respectful/disrespectful research practices often demarcate sanctioned practices for research of/with children, making 'research with children' an intimidating and formidable space in which to work (McNamara, 2013). Research involving children commonly seeks to generate knowledge about children and their childhoods (Kellett, 2011) with increasing importance being given to children's accounts and views. Yet, a long-held belief is that disrespectful research methods include 'not hiding the names and identities of people involved in research' (Rhedding-Jones, 2005).

> Threads of meaning-making: In our research work with children we want to listen to and understand their perspectives, to see through their eyes, to see more than our adult lenses allow. Could it be that respectful research actually acknowledges and makes children visible and that ethics is about ensuring proper representation, recognition and power?
>
> Asking this question shows how we have been influenced by contemporary sociological understandings of children as competent in life and in research.

Theoretical perspectives of the capable and competent child and movements focused on the rights of the child have influenced shifts in the valuing of children's views and opinions in research (Danby & Farrell, 2004). Yet, before we can celebrate the views of children coming from these perspectives, new concerns are being raised about the 'pro voice climate' and the tendency of researchers to 'overly stress the agency and capability of children' (Spyrou, 2011).

> Threads of meaning-making: It is clear that every research choice communicates a view about children. But the concerns are unsettling. We welcome the move from children 'as subjects of research' to children 'as social actors in research'. But, now researchers are being asked to consider if what is represented is the 'authentic' voice of the child.
>
> While heeding the warning to take care, we want to invite children's voices into research. But in our desire to listen we do not want to propagate the idea that children and their voices are out there 'waiting to be captured and documented by us'.
>
> What is the danger if we DO fall victim to the fear. What if, instead of choosing to lean toward our values and desired methodologies for researching with children, we decide it is all too hard? We do not want to join those researchers who stop researching with children altogether. We like what Spyrou (2011, p. 162) is suggesting—that we need to 'accept the messiness and ambiguity, the non-factuality and multi-layered nature' of meaning in the stories that we (and children) tell and represent. Listening to children's perspectives expand our understandings.

Researchers are experimenting with ways to listen to and promote children's views. Interested in the standpoints of children, Theobald (2012) uses video-stimulated accounts, a research method that reflects a changing view of children, that is, as experts in accounting for their own lives, and as active participants in research. Yet, Theobald (2012) takes great pains to define what her research is and is not, and does and does not claim to do. In collaborating with children to examine their accounts of a dispute that occurred during a play session, Theobald (2012) positions young children as competent and her research reveals the complexity of children's social worlds, what 'children consider important' in their peer relationships, and how 'they' account for their interactions in front of others (p. 46).

> Threads of meaning-making: In everything we do we are guided by our ethics and values for children and research. We are committed to research ethics, to relationships, and to children's rights—within and beyond research practice. We respect children's competencies and agency, and feel strongly about children making informed decisions.
>
> There is no doubt that we have been influenced by philosophical and theoretical perspectives about the rights of the child and the competent child. When writing our ethics proposal for our recent published research (Black, Busch, & Hayes, 2015) linked to our research project, we actively sought to position children as competent in the research. We valued relationships with children and we wanted to be responsive throughout the research process. We brought to the research ideals and ethics about how the process would involve the building of relationships and offer children invitations to share their thinking. Not only did we value their thinking and want to listen closely to their views, but we felt as researchers we had 'a duty to consult them' about their perspectives (Christensen & Prout, 2002, p. 80). But more than duty, we wanted the research to be flexible, iterative and responsive to children.

VALUING COMMUNAL RESEARCH PROCESSES

Our experiences with research have shown us that producing knowledge is a cooperative venture. Whilst researchers often seek to control the script and deliver desired project outcomes, it is those with whom we research who provide the most crucial part of the conversation (Black, 2014). To undertake research with others, and with children, is to enter into ethical relationships with them—ethics of justice, and ethics of care and caring (Noddings, 2012).

As researchers, we can without realising it bring with us 'taken-for-granted' attitudes and approaches. Whilst our true intent may well be to listen to children and value their voices, our actions and decisions always warrant further reflection (Harcourt & Einarsdottir, 2011). We can always ask questions like 'how are we positioning knowledge and who holds it?' 'How is our valuing of "relationship" evidenced in our research methods?'

For us, research with children, and research with others, is often an organic, social and intellectual coming together; involving cycles of reflection and meaning-making. While our roles in the projects and our contributions may not look the same, we are co-inquirers involved in storytelling, listening, reflection and representation. When researching with young children we may not know the end point, but we have a willingness to find the way as we go. We seek to listen to children, to be guided by children, by their silences and their inquiry interests (Black et al., 2015).

In our research work, and that of others', opportunities to interact with a range of people interested in children—be it in protecting them, listening to them, understanding them or engaging them—have supported relational knowledge construction and a relational ethics (Black et al., 2015).

Threads of meaning-making: It is interesting how we are often 'forced' to consider research positions and partiality. Concerns about protecting children informed our university ethics committee's requests for more information about our research project. Exploitation of children is a genuine concern that researchers need to consider very carefully. But, for us, the committee's expectations with regard to 'protecting children' actually challenged our efforts to listen to and share children's contributions.

We wanted to explain the research to children and offer them ways of asking questions about the research in order for them to give consent or otherwise. We wanted to listen to their perspectives and silences in responsive and authentic ways. The committee wanted additional information about this process. They were not certain that children would be capable enough to identify whether they wanted to participate or not, or to withdraw consent.

In the end, we agreed that 'parent' approval and consent would determine whether data would be included or not. We also decided that if a 'child' communicated they didn't want to participate in particular experiences we would not include any data related to them in any publication. Given we value children's views, we found ourselves asking 'how often in the research process should young children be asked for consent?' and 'how often should we watch for their silences as well as their contributions?'

Ben-Ari and Enosh (2013, p. 425) remind us 'Interactions within the research process are essentially ongoing occurrences of potential misunderstandings. Hence we should perceive research not necessarily as shared and agreed-upon meaning-making endeavours, but rather as ambiguously complex processes with multiple levels of "differences interrupting differences".' So this notion of differences interrupting differences is important to our thinking about communal research processes and interactions, and how we make meaning in research.

> Threads of meaning-making: It is interesting to consider different viewpoints about how knowledge is positioned and who holds it. We have found that our interactions with research infrastructures and mechanisms have highlighted assumptions about expert knowledge and researcher roles that we hadn't even perceived would be areas for misunderstanding. Ethical clearance for our project was not granted initially as the ethics committee wanted to see written approval from our partnering child care centre to participate in the research as well as details of interactions with staff, information about the personnel to be involved and how centre data would be made available to researchers.
>
> In particular, the committee wanted specific information about our relationship and interactions with the Director, who we had identified as both educator and co-researcher in our application form. The committee were uncomfortable with the duality of the researcher/participant role. We had not foreseen that this relationship would be considered problematic or an example of uneven power relations. Our intent was to value the Director as a co-researcher with us and we were a little surprised that the committee required clarification. We wondered whether this was linked to research traditions where educators have more typically been the 'subjects' of research.

CRITIQUING ETHICAL MOTIVATIONS AND ASSUMPTIONS

Many of the questions surrounding researching with children ask us to think about relationships and to think about ethics. When we think of 'ethics', we consider responsibility, respect, integrity, morals, values, accountability and regard. Ethics is an important part of any research project that involves people.

Researchers' chosen approaches to research and inquiry are closely linked to their ethical desires as researchers. Researchers conducting research with children emphasise the ongoing complexity of ethical considerations and highlight that to research with children is to be engaged in 'continual examination and exploration of dilemmas', much more than merely 'adhering to rules of research conduct' (Powell, Fitzgerald, Taylor, & Graham, 2012).

Early childhood researchers locate their work within codes of ethics and care and the rights of children (United Nations, 1989). The ethical issue of protecting children from harm is not straightforward when the aims of research are to move from anonymity towards visibility, from vulnerability to capability. Views about protecting children from harm in research can increase barriers to children's participation in research, and stop them from benefiting from the results (Hood et al., 1996).

> Threads of meaning-making: Our ethical commitments provide an anchor for our practice and we use our guiding values to work sensitively and reflexively in changing research circumstances and relationships. At the heart of our research is a desire for research that values and projects the lives of children and their ways of knowing and being in the societies in which they live.
>
> We understand that ethical mechanisms are there to ensure ethical standards are met in research and submitting an ethics application to the Human Research Ethics Committees (HRECs) is an important process. But we experienced a disproportionate emphasis to certain features of the research process which served to block those aspects that sought to be child-centric. The requests from the university ethics committee are reflective of a traditional research paradigm and old views about children in research. Our views were of research as an ongoing social practice and children as active agents in our research.
>
> Many issues required clarification. Some of these related to photographing children and retaining samples of their work. Explanation was required with regard to our focus on collecting data in identifiable formats. Why did we want this data? (Images of children, their comments, their art work). How would we use it? How would it be analysed?
>
> Connecting to our researcher motivations, we wanted data to be identifiable because we wanted visibility for children. We wanted their ways of knowing and their contributions to be seen and acknowledged. The ethics committee were not familiar with such motivations. Typically, researcher requests for data to be identifiable are made in instances where

a group of participants 'are to be compared with another' or 'to support the aggregation of data'.

It is clear that the benefits and costs of research practices have to be explored beyond rules and binaries. Additionally, researchers have to become better at communicating their ethical commitments and motivations (to children and to others) and at challenging the othering of children in research (Powell et al., 2012). It is also clear that ethical codes and practices need to be iterative and responsive to those being researched and to research processes and contexts. We may not always know in advance what will happen or how it will be managed and so our ethical practice needs to be negotiated and situated (Ebrahim, 2010).

Threads of meaning-making: We were required to confirm our compliance in terms of ensuring all raw data would be de-identified and not made public. Assurance was required that no child would be named or recognisable in the dissemination of research results.

The ethics committee wanted children's faces blurred as a matter of course, not just if parents or children requested it. They wanted to remove the visibility of children from storying, data collection and reporting.

We experienced real tension. We wanted children's contributions to be made visible and public, and their role as thinkers and community members recognised. What is lost when children do not appear alongside their meaning-making attempts? (Fig. 15.1).

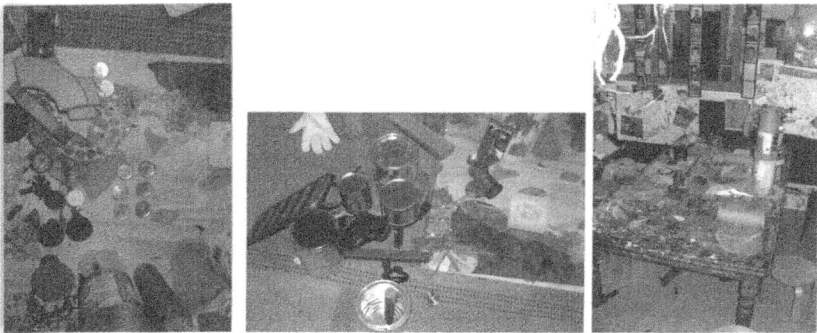

Fig. 15.1 We can photograph how children have used materials, but if children are missing from the images we take, can we see what matters to them? Can we see and understand the meaning they are making? What is visible/invisible?

We need to become better at communicating our ethical commitments. Ethics committees often have a strong protectionist discourse and this can serve to gate-keep children out of research processes, and particularly out of research reporting (Skelton, 2008). We found there were limited avenues to talk with the committee about research perspectives. Time was of the essence and we needed ethics approval to go forward. So, we agreed we would blur children's faces for publication in book chapters and journal articles so that the research project could 'commence'. So for us, having opportunities for dialogue with ethics committees is a potential place for change.

> Threads of meaning-making: What is the impact of our willingness to comply? How can new ways of thinking occur if researchers give up on their motivations? How can children and their ways of knowing be made visible in these 'protective' spaces? What is in the 'best interests' of children? Does our taken-for-granted view that documentation of children's stories and meaning-making (and making photographs of children public) is a 'valuable early childhood practice' fully appreciate the ethical dilemmas that might surround this practice? What else might we need to consider in relation to our own agendas and ways of seeing?

The process of 'getting research projects approved' often feels like a top-down driven guessing game, filled with hoop jumping and obstacles to negotiate and little room for conversation and debate. Fostering dialogue about 'ethical research with children' is important so that mechanisms are responsive to the nature of researching with children and to new developments and understandings about methodologies and ethics. We need to work together to create support structures for critical colleagueship and dialogue (Pasque, Carducci, Gildersleeve, & Kuntz, 2011).

> Threads of meaning-making: We also think about the impact that our efforts to research with children have had and are having on us, on our identities as 'researchers researching with children'. Across a range of projects we have repeatedly found that ethics committees and their decisions are contextualised within a discourse of children's vulnerability. Invariably the committee sees its role as protecting and defending vulnerable children, viewing us and our research as risk factors and potential threats. It has been incredibly disheartening and disempowering for us as researchers and educators who follow codes of conduct, live by codes of ethics, and value children, to have our ideas and approaches questioned and rejected multiple times by these ethic mechanisms.

Technology is also bringing developments in methodologies and further increases the need to foster dialogue regarding ethics. Public images of children and families abound within the contemporary world. They appear in the media, on the internet, in advertising, on YouTube clips and in photos uploaded by families to social networking sites. Such images are publically available, potentially providing rich data that may be accessed by researchers.

Threads of meaning-making: It is interesting to think about the contemporary world and the differences in approaches to sharing knowledge and experiences about children. Alongside our research project, the child care centre we were working with engaged with community groups (such as local industry and the art gallery) in a pedagogical project that explored children's understandings of their local community including local industry. The centre engaged a local artist in an extended 'artist-in-residence' program as part of this project. To broaden children's understandings about industry, children toured an industry site and staff from industry visited the centre. The industry group, so impressed with the learning and knowledge being generated by children, documented these visits and included children's stories, conversations and images in their regular employee newsletter. (See Fig. 15.2)

The artist in residence planned an exhibition of sculptural pieces and the creation of an interactive arts-based installation for children as part of an exhibition at the local gallery. The aim of the installation was to engage children from the wider community with the exhibition and with opportunities to make meaning about local industries and environments. Photos and stories about the projects and art-making that children at the child care centre had engaged with featured prominently in the gallery's exhibition brochure and booklet, as well as throughout the gallery's interactive installation space (see Figs. 15.3–15.5). The pedagogical project at the child care centre had influenced and informed the gallery installation. The images around the walls of the gallery documented how children at the child care centre had used and played with materials and ideas. These images in turn influenced how children attending the exhibition interacted with the display materials and activities.

In contrast with these public displays of children and their learning, the ethics mechanisms in place for us as researchers meant that children had to be completely 'de-identified' in anything we produced or made public. Engaging with the various visual sources below it can be seen that these were valuable opportunities to expand community awareness of children and their thinking and learning. There are many benefits for children as others begin to see children's capabilities and knowledge, and recognise the importance of their voice in society.

Childs Play

In issue seven of Aluminews we mentioned local artist Margaret Worthington has been working with QAL as part of her Master of Contemporary Art project, 'Industry sited within the Environment'.

Other than the work for her Masters, including the sculptures featured in issue seven, Margaret has been working alongside Coordinators from Rainbow Valley Kindergarten; Paul and Marion. They have been developing a unique educational program with the kindy kids teaching them about the industrial giant that they see every day.

They have been talking about aerial photographs of QAL and relating them to road maps. they have also talked about machinery and bright safety clothing QAL workers wear. QAL have donated some of the safety gear; shirts, hard hats, ear muffs and mono-goggles to the Kindergarten for the children to play dress-ups.

Recently some of the students from Rainbow Valley came to QAL on an excursion. The children each remembered snippets of their journey so they compiled their memories and have recreated sections of QAL back at the Kindergarten. Complete with Raw Materials and the big bauxite stockpile

Paul said the children are really enjoying the experience and love playing in the 'mock up' sections of QAL.

"Now that the children have seen QAL we should be able to represent it with more detail. It seems lots of children took different snippets from the trip. The areas at the fore front of the children's mind when they came back from the tour were; the ships, water, pipes, mud and the big mounds of "red dirt" (bauxite)," Paul said.

"The total concept of bauxite to alumina then into aluminium might still be beyond a lot of the children, but at least an awareness has been generated."

This is what some of the children had to say about their tour of QAL when they got back to the kindergarten;

"We went on the bus and we stopped on the seats while the bus drove around QAL. Crystal from QAL was our guide and she showed us around and told us what is done in each section"

"What are chemicals?" (Mason), when Crystal mentioned the caustic soda chemical

"I could see the island where my Mum worked on." (Kelsey)

"I liked the pipes because steam goes through it and I saw steam coming out of it." (Oliva)

When Brynn saw all the steam at ground level he said, "it was like the sand pit at Rainbow Valley"

"I saw water and the mud that was coming out of the big pipes." (Riley) in reference to the red mud

The green shower lights were a big hit. Crystal said they are green because it's the best colour you see before you go blind. There was green lights everywhere and we wore our name tags on the bus." (Montannah)

"The pipe was like the hot water inside the darkness." (Abbie)

"I saw a rocket like fire." (Ryder)

"I really like this world." (Ben)

"I liked the tanks because they were so hot and there was dirt and bauxite." (Sam)

"I saw three chimney pots and smoke (steam) was coming out of it." (Hannah)

"The spinning wheels were great." (Cohen)

"I know where QAL is." (Ella)

Kelsey takes Crystal on a guided tour of the Kindergarten and shows off their version of the Raw Materials bauxite stockpile.

Sam, Hunter and Kelsey enjoy dressing-up in the QAL safety gear.

Hunter talks through their own version of an aerial look at QAL.

Fig. 15.2 This Queensland Alumina Limited (QAL) industry staff newsletter includes photos of children and transcripts of their conversations. Staff and others can see what children know and understand. Ethic mechanisms prohibited us from producing identifiable material

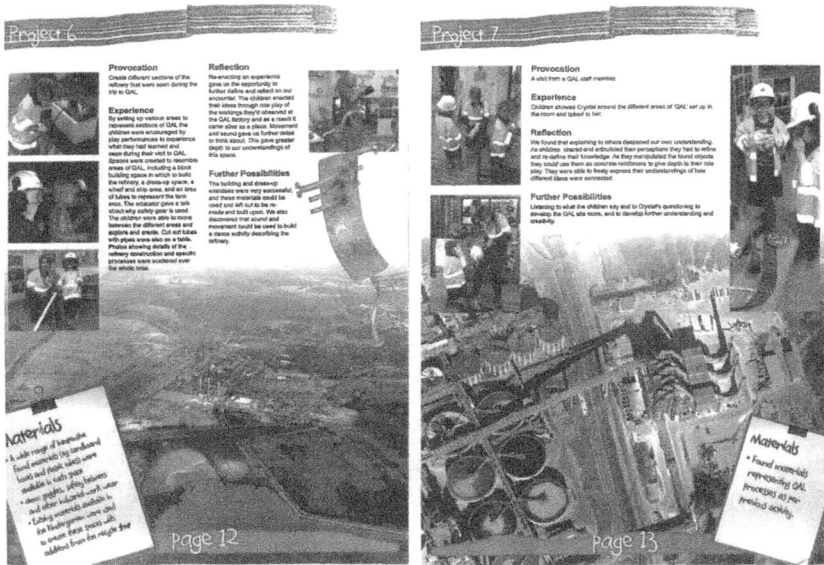

Fig. 15.3   The Art Gallery brochure that accompanies the exhibition has images of children, their play and creations. Ethic mechanisms prohibited us from producing identifiable material

CREATING SPACES FOR ONGOING DIALOGUE

With this chapter, we have sought to create a range of spaces to ask questions and to ponder the challenges and fruitfulness of researching with children. We think there needs to be more of these safe spaces; spaces where reflection is encouraged and valued as a resource that researchers can use to consider their motivations and methodologies for researching with children.

A viable educational research community in the future will need to look within and it will need to look beyond. It will need to consider the contemporary world and the twenty-first-century child. It will need to consider its diverse purposes and possibly rethink what constitutes the boundaries of educational research, of research with children.

Threads of meaning-making: We have encountered a range of dilemmas connected to research infrastructures and the integrity of research projects. We

Fig. 15.4 This child attended the art gallery exhibition and children's installation. She was photographed by the artist who wanted to show how children were responding to her work and exploring materials and ideas. Ethic mechanisms prohibited us from producing identifiable material

have experienced first-hand that research mechanisms can potentially remove us from our critical stance and the core values behind our research. We have found that responses from internal and external stakeholders in research highlight big differences in terms of how children and ethics are viewed.

Many questions emerge for us around researching with children: Are we listening to children? Are children central? Where are our blind spots? What assumptions do we bring? Self-awareness on the part of the researcher is critical. And so is awareness of diverse and alternative views and practices in relation to visibility, consent, and ethical commitments. How might we advocate for, rather than reduce, what we see as the 'integrity' of our research? What might 'equal partnerships' in research look like when children are involved? How might we create support structures for critical colleagueship and dialogue for all the stakeholders in research? Can we move beyond questions of who has the most and least power? How might we manage the range of research dilemmas and concerns to produce meaning,

Fig. 15.5 Is there reduced understanding if children are not visible? What happens when children are removed or anonymised? Ethic mechanisms prohibited us from producing identifiable material

reciprocity and understanding? How are responsive, reflexive relationships created in research? How might we support each other to process and work through the many warnings, perspectives and discourses so that we do not decide to 'not research with children at all'?

Research, and meaning-making, is not a simple and precise process; rather, it involves 'ongoing occurrences of potential misunderstandings' and 'ambiguously complex processes' (Ben-Ari & Enosh, 2013). Embracing internal and relational entanglements and the disruption of everyday ways of thinking about things is therefore important; it is here we learn and imagine possibilities (Giugni, 2011). Mutually disquieting conversations that 'stir things up' between researchers/researched/other stakeholders are crucial for responsive and improved education research that makes a difference. Disquiet, dissonance and difference can stimulate fresh ways of seeing and thinking and interrupt old patterns, perceptions and assumptions.

Guidance also comes as we look within to core values and ethics of care. These opportunities for reflection, self-awareness and knowledge generation are best served not in isolation but in relationship and ongoing dialogue with others (Ben-Ari & Enosh, 2013; Lawrence, 2005). We need to work together to create critical colleagueship. The generation of fresh knowledge is possible when we experiment together, when we question and unsettle each other's rhetoric and when we reflect deeply. With these commitments, we can consider and circulate new ways of understanding and influencing research with children.

REFERENCES

Ben-Ari, A., & Enosh, G. (2013). Power relations and reciprocity: Dialectics of knowledge construction. *Qualitative Health Research, 23*(3), 422–429. doi:10.1177/1049732312470030.

Bessant, J. (2006). The fixed age rule: Young people, consent and research ethics. *Youth Studies Australia, 25*, 50–57.

Black, A. L. (2014). Reconceptualising meaning-making and embracing disruptive inquiry. In J. K. Jones (Ed.), *Weaving words: Personal and professional transformation through writing as research.* UK: Cambridge Scholars Publishing.

Black, A. L., Busch, G., & Hayes, M. (2015). Reducing the marginalization of children: Relational knowledge production and the power of collaboration. In K. Trimmer, A. L. Black, & S. Riddle (Eds.), *Mainstreams, margins and the spaces in-between: New possibilities for education research.* London: Routledge.

Christensen, P., & James, A. (2008). *Research with children: Perspectives and practices.* Oxon: Routledge.

Christensen, P., & Prout, A. (2002). Working with ethical symmetry in social research with children. *Childhood, 9*(4), 477–497.

Clandinin, D. J., Pushor, D., & Orr, A. M. (2007). Navigating sites for narrative inquiry. *Journal of Teacher Education, 58*(1), 21–35.

Clark, A. (2011). Breaking methodological boundaries? Exploring visual, participatory methods with adults and young children. *European Early Childhood Education Research Journal, 19*(3), 321–330. doi:10.1080/1350293X.2011.597964.

Cumming, T., Sumsion, J., & Wong, S. (2013). Reading between the lines: An interpretative meta-analysis of ways early childhood educators negotiate discourses and subjectivities informing practice. *Contemporary Issues in Early Childhood, 14*(3), 223–240.

Danby, S., & Farrell, A. (2004). Accounting for young children's competence in educational research: New perspectives on research ethics. *Australian Educational Researcher, 31*(3), 35–50.

Ebrahim, H. (2010). Situated ethics: Possibilities for young children as research participants in the South African context. *Early Child Development & Care, 180*, 289–298.

Giugni, M. (2011). "Becoming worldly with": An encounter with the early years learning framework. *Contemporary Issues in Early Childhood, 12*(1), 11–27.

Harcourt, D., & Einarsdottir, J. (2011). Introducing children's perspectives and participation in research. *European Early Childhood Education Research Journal, 19*(3), 301.

Hood, S., Kelley, P., & Mayall, B. (1996). Children as research subjects: A risky enterprise. *Children & Society, 10*(2), 117–128.

Kellett, M. (2011). Researching with and for children and young people *Centre for Children and Young People: Background Briefing Series* (Vol. 5). Lismore: Centre for Children and Young People, Southern Cross University.

Lawrence, R. L. (2005). Knowledge construction as contested terrain: Adult learning through artistic expression. *New Directions for Adult and Continuing Education, 107*, 3–11.

McNamara, P. M. (2013). Giving voice to children and young people in research: Applying rights-based frameworks to meet ethical challenges. *Developing Practice: The Child, Youth and Family Work Journal, 37*, 55.

Noddings, N. (2012). The caring relation in teaching. *Oxford Review of Education, 38*(6), 771–781. doi:10.1080/03054985.2012.745047.

Pasque, P. A., Carducci, R., Gildersleeve, R. E., & Kuntz, A. M. (2011). Disrupting the ethical imperatives of "junior" critical qualitative scholars in the era of conservative modernization. *Qualitative Inquiry, 17*(7), 571–588.

Powell, M. A., Fitzgerald, R., Taylor, N. J., & Graham, A. (2012). International literature review: Ethical issues in undertaking research with children and young people, for the Childwatch International Research Network. Lismore: Southern Cross University; and Dunedin, New Zealand: University of Otago, Centre for Research on Children and Families.

Rhedding-Jones, J. (2005). *What is research? Methodological practices and new approaches.* Oslo: Universitetsforlaget.

Skelton, T. (2008). Research with children and young people: Exploring the tensions between ethics, competence and participation. *Children's Geographies, 6*(1), 21.

Spyrou, S. (2011). The limits of children's voices: From authenticity to critical, reflexive representation. *Childhood: A Global Journal of Child Research, 18*(2), 151–165.

Theobald, M. (2012). Video-stimulated accounts: Young children accounting for interactional matters in front of peers. *Journal of Early Childhood Research, 10*(1), 32–50.

United Nations (1989). *United Nations Convention on the Rights of the Child.* New York: United Nations.

Waller, T., & Bitou, A. (2011). Research with children: Three challenges for participatory research in early childhood. *European Early Childhood Education Research Journal, 19*(1), 5–20. doi:10.1080/1350293X.2011.548964.

CHAPTER 16

From Fledgling Manoeuvres to Methodological Confidence: Conversations Between a Doctoral Student and Supervisor on Ethnomethodology and Conversation Analysis to Explore the Everyday Worlds of Children and Families

Gillian Busch and Susan Danby

INTRODUCTION

This chapter discusses the methodological journey, from the candidate's first thinking about undertaking a doctorate to enrolling, considering, and undertaking data collection and analysis, and to writing

G. Busch (✉)
School of Education and the Arts, CQUniversity Australia,
Rockhampton, QLD, Australia

S. Danby
School of Early Childhood, Faculty of Education, Queensland
University of Technology, Brisbane, QLD, Australia

© The Author(s) 2016
B. Harreveld et al. (eds.), *Constructing Methodology for Qualitative Research*, DOI 10.1057/978-1-137-59943-8_16

237

a thesis. In addition to exploring some milestone events of a doctorate, the chapter highlights aspects of undertaking a doctorate that are rarely found in texts about undertaking postgraduate studies, that is, the methodological manoeuvres. Personal, professional, and academic aspects are integral to a successful completion of a doctorate, but rarely shared by a candidate and her supervisor. Using second stories (Sacks, 1995), the journey explored in this chapter includes the stories of the fledgling researcher and her supervisor. Features of second story include links back to matters discussed in the first story, demonstrations of understanding of the first story, the proffering of parallel experiences, and new perspectives that were invited by the first story (Arminen, 2004; Sacks, 1995).

First Manoeuvres

Gillian: Initially, my focus was with the practical issues of choosing a topic and a supervisor with similar research interest/s and who was prepared to accept a doctoral student. I was interested in researching children in the their everyday lives, in either family settings or educational sites. After considerable reflection and guidance, I decided that I was most interested in studying children in family settings.

Susan: My first contact with Gillian was when she called me to discuss the possibility of doing a PhD. Her research interests were similar to mine, investigating aspects of children's everyday lives. I recall that we had many conversations about possible topics; although the one constant focus was that the project would explore some aspect of young children's everyday lives. I suggested that Gillian read some of the new work coming out the sociology of childhood paradigm (James, Jenks, & Prout, 1998) and some of the early sociology of childhood work by early ethnomethodologists, including Speier (1971). Following extensive reading around the sociology of childhood, Gillian decided on the topic of family mealtimes, which was of interest to me too.

While discussing possible topics, we talked about how to approach undertaking the study. I provided readings to provide an overview of the research that investigated children's everyday worlds. We also talked about the doctoral journey milestones and expectations of how a student and supervisor could work together (Danby, 2005).

Methodological Manoeuvres

Susan: An early task for a fledgling researcher is to grapple with explorations of methodological approaches and their use in investigating the selected topic. This methodological exploration involves examining the concepts relevant for that methodology, often requiring a new theoretical language to be mastered.

Gillian: The approach for my study was drawn from ethnomethodology and conversation analysis (CA). I selected these methodologies only after extensive exploration of how studies of family mealtimes had been examined previously, and after reading studies that had drawn on these methodologies to show how everyday practices can be examined in detail to reveal previous unnoticed or invisible features of everyday interaction.

Overview of Ethnomethodology and Conversation Analysis

Ethnomethodology is the study of how participants participate in everyday social practices (Garfinkel, 1967), such as eating a family meal. It examines how "ordinary members of society make sense of, find their way about in, and act on the circumstances in which they find themselves" (Heritage, 1984b, p. 4) on a moment-by-moment basis (Lynch & Peyrot, 1992). An ethnomethodological approach remains focused on "explication, not explanation" (Baker, 1997, p. 44); that is, it does not posit *why* something occurs, but rather considers "*how*" action is accomplished. Adopting an ethnomethodological approach that focuses on "how practices are accomplished" has implications for the kinds of research questions that can be addressed.

At the center of ethnomethodology is the assumption that social order is present because members "put it there, accountably, for anyone to see as being always-already there" (McHoul, 2008, p. 825) and, as such, it is the members' achievement. "Putting it there" is "ongoingly achieved ... through the behaviour which members produce" (Payne, 1976, p. 33). Talk is one way in which social order is accomplished routinely by members (Baker, 1997) and is central to social life. An ethnomethodological interest in talk is with "what people do with words, how and when participants use language to accomplish social action" (Baker, 1997, p. 44). Accompanying talk are also gestures and other embodied actions.

CA has its origins in ethnomethodology (Francis & Hester, 2004), and is considered a "prominent form of ethnomethodology work" (Heritage, 1984b, p. 233). Harvey Sacks, recognized as the founder of CA, embraced Garfinkel's interest in how social activities are constructed (Francis & Hester, 2004, p. 21), bringing this interest to the study of naturally occurring conversation. CA describes talk-in-interaction, focusing on the procedures by which speakers produce their own behavior, and interpret and deal with the behavior of others in situ (Heritage, 1984b; Pomerantz & Fehr, 1997). The data are of naturally occurring everyday interaction, and the core analytic object is to uncover how members produce and understand actions (Pomerantz & Fehr, 1997, p. 65) "by virtue of their placement and participation within sequences of actions" (Heritage, 1984b, p. 245). Actions that may be accomplished in interaction include answering, requesting, offering.

Gillian: My initial research question, "how do social interactions contribute to the social orders of mealtime and family interaction?", reflected an ethnomethodological focus. Acquiring and applying the skills and knowledge required for an ethnomethodological approach led to a number of challenges that involved data collection, transcription, and data analysis.

Susan: Undertaking a study that uses ethnomethodology and CA is a serious undertaking, as these approaches are complex and multifaceted. Gillian decided to undertake the study using these methodologies because they offered a focused way for her to address her research questions. There was a strong alignment between her research questions and how these approaches could support her to investigate these questions. While building the knowledge base was daunting, there were also moments of elation. I can distinctly remember Gillian calling me to say that she had just reread an article that made sense to her this time. This is a usual experience for doctoral candidates, as it takes persistence to grapple with new concepts and languages of theoretical and methodological approaches.

DATA COLLECTION MANOEUVRES: TRIALING METHODS AND PRACTICES

Ethnomethodology's concern with studying how ordinary folk produce and organize their everyday lives requires data to be naturally occurring. Collecting naturally occurring data of family mealtime interactions required careful planning at a practical logistic level and thinking about how best to capture both verbal and non-verbal interactions (e.g. gestures, eating).

Video recording was selected because it captured audio and visual data simultaneously (Heath et al., 2010), thus allowing analysis of the family's verbal interaction, its paralinguistic features, and the visual components, such as how participants used cutlery in mealtimes. Video recordings enable the researcher to revisit the data many times, and this provides a check for the accuracy of the data analysis and also a way to discover "subtle nuances" (McLarty & Gibson, 2000, p. 140). The capacities afforded through video recording data align with the fine-grained analysis of CA that uncovers "complex interactional phenomena" (Psathas, 1990, p. 5).

Deciding to use video recordings to collect data meant I needed to consider the selection of an appropriate video recorder, how I would use the video, and whether I would be present. As part of trialing the data collection method with the first family in the study, I chose to place the camera on a tripod, a strategy that is designed to "create as little disturbance as possible" (Sparrman, 2005, p. 249). Piloting the use of the video camera raised a number of challenges when using video recordings to collect naturally occurring data. First, finding times to join the family for a meal required considerable negotiation. Second, balancing the role of unobtrusive researcher and responding to the family members' initiation of talk with me was challenging. The mother in the pilot study suggested that she video record the family's interactions, as this meant that she could record at times that suited the family. Handing over the responsibility for videoing was certainly an unexpected outcome from the trial, which had additional implications for data collection. The family assumed greater responsibility for when recordings occurred, where the camera would be positioned, which participants were in view or out of view, and the length of time of the video recording. While the family managed the video recordings for data collection, I felt some tension in handing over responsibility for data collection to the family, experiencing a sense of separation from the study to which I was so committed. Handing over responsibility required the development of a protocol for the families including an overview of how to use the camera and the tripod, and the preparation of a kit of materials (e.g. long-life batteries).

Susan: I remember these discussions regarding the fieldwork phase of the study, related to how to undertake the video recording of family mealtimes. There were many aspects to consider as researching with families in their homes requires sensitivity, listening carefully to family members, and being flexible in approaching this. Having a pilot study is important for trialing aspects of data collection, and this led to exploring new approaches to video recording. The success of families video recording their own mealtime practices without a researcher present was a practice that consequently I used in research projects involving families.

Transcription Manoeuvres: An Interpretative and Representational Process

The first step in data analysis is the transcription of the recorded interactions using transcription conventions used in CA (Jefferson, 2004). Transcription systems are not "neutral" (Psathas & Anderson, 1990) with the organization of the system reflecting the "concerns and analytic stance" of the researcher (Psathas & Anderson, 1990, p. 76). While Jefferson's transcription notation system (2004) provides guidance in terms of how to transcribe the interaction, including features of talk such as intonation, pauses, sound stretches, and emphasis, a number of issues are evident in transcription (Baker, 1998). Practical issues include "matters of description, matters of format and layout, and matters of depiction" (Baker, 1998, p. 113). The transcription system "marks out the analytic concerns which conversation analysts bring to the data" (Hutchby & Wooffitt, 1998, p. 76). Thus, the transcript includes the "dynamics of turn taking" and the "characteristics of speech delivery" (Hutchby & Wooffitt, 1998, p. 76); both features used by conversation analysts as part of analysis.

Conversation analysts define transcription as a "situated practice" (Mondada, 2007, p. 810) that provides an account of the "social, political or moral order" (Baker, 1998, p. 110) of the interaction. The transcription process involves attention to two interrelated features of the process: "transcription as an interpretive process and transcription as a representational process" (Bucholtz, 2000, p. 1441). Thus, issues of interpretation and representation involve attention to *what* is transcribed and *how* the interaction will be transcribed by the transcriber (Bucholtz, 2000).

The interpretative act of transcribing what is said is a complex act. The transcriber makes decisions about utterance attribution, the content of what was said, and the intelligibility of what was said (Bucholtz, 2000). Thus, the transcript provides a selective representation of the interaction because not everything that happens in the interaction is recorded (Davidson, 2010). This process requires repeated listening to, and viewing of, the recordings, which facilitate an "intimate familiarity" with the words, with the prosodic shape of utterances and with the "temporal flow" of sequences (Psathas & Anderson, 1990, p. 77). Furthermore, the transcription process accomplishes a slowing down of the talk helping to focus the "researchers' interpretative eye" (Lapadat, 2000, p. 215). Repeated listenings contribute to the endless checking of the evolving transcript that is "settled on" for the purposes of specific analysis (Mondada, 2007).

Given the assumptions that a transcriber brings to the transcription process and their knowledge of the purpose for the transcript, transcription is not an objective or neutral process but rather it involves "interpretive choices" (Bucholtz, 2000, p. 1444), and thus it is a political process. In this way, the interpretative choices informed both tacitly and explicitly by theoretical and personal beliefs and assumptions lead to the construction of a transcript that reflects this authorship (Bucholtz, 2000).

Gillian: While my study was completed several years ago, I can still recall particular phrases and prosody used by the participants in the study. The acquisition of such an intimate familiarity was accomplished through constantly replaying the data. As a researcher, I was aware of how my knowledge, as a teacher and as someone who knew the children, influenced my initial transcription of the talk among the children in one family. When excited, one child spoke quickly and with a smiley voice and, even with repeated listening, was difficult to hear and thus transcribe accurately. While repeatedly listening, I consciously asked myself what could he be saying that could be so funny from his perspective, that is, from the perspective of a six-year-old boy. In so doing, I was listening for something that I might expect to hear, rather than what the child was actually saying.

In developing transcripts, four practical challenges emerged. The first challenge was how much detail to include in the transcript. Video data provides an overwhelming amount of detail and decisions about what to record and how to record this detail is ongoing. As a transcriber, I struggled with balancing the desire to provide enough detail about the gestures, expressions, and the physical activities that members were involved with as part of eating a meal with the need to keep the transcript easy to read. While the inclusion of information about members' physical actions enriches the transcript (Mondada, 2007) and provides details about the "interplay between the verbal and the visual depiction", Baker's (1998) reminder about what is important to participants helped settle some tensions related to transcription.

Pruso Patterns of stress & intonation in a language

Deciding to include descriptive information has implications for the layout of the transcript (Mondada, 2007; Ochs, 1979). Options include placing it in a separate line to the talk, placing it after the talk, placing it before the talk, placing it within the talk, or using symbols. Goodwin's analysis of children playing hopscotch shows how integral embodied actions are in interaction and how these may be recorded (Goodwin, 1995). Recognizing the importance of including details about embodied actions, I placed descriptions of actions within the transcript and included screen grabs to show particular actions or sequences of actions, which were difficult to describe. The following section of transcript provides an example of where descriptions of action have been used (see the section in the double brackets).

Extract

```
22   Emily     >What do you mean the cherry boots¿ < =((E looks
23             back at her food and rolls spaghetti onto her
             fork))
```

The second challenge that I experienced was how to identify speakers in the interaction. Danby (1998), in her study of social order in a preschool classroom, also grappled with this challenge. She noted how "whatever term or convention I used would provide a description of the participants that was not neutral but theoretically driven" (p. 82). She elected to use membership categorization terms (teacher/child) as the classroom participants oriented to these terms. My solution was to use the speakers' given names, rather than a membership category term such as mum or dad.

The third challenge was grappling with learning the transcription notation. With continued practice, I became more familiar with the notations. Also supporting my proficiency with transcription was feedback on my transcripts from more proficient transcribers and engaging with the transcripts in publications. Engaging with the transcripts of other analysts provided strategies for improving presentation, including, for example, the screengrabs or diagrams to help the reader. On occasions, the feedback providers would alert me to missing overlaps, prosody, gaps, and so on. As previously noted, sharing transcripts in data sessions are a common practice in CA including those who are very experienced and proficient.

A fourth challenge was developing a detailed transcript that included such details of the talk as overlaps, silences, and prosody, which requires "hearing" these features in the recordings. Accessing Audacity (free software) to support transcription offered the tools to time silences, listen more closely for overlaps, hear quietly spoken words, loop sections, and so on. With improved confidence, I moved to having two sources of data open on the computer working between Audacity that contained the extracted sound wave and iMovie. As I embraced the available technology, the detail in my transcripts improved significantly, which of course supported improved analysis. While technology supported the development of refined transcripts, collaboration with other researchers who "listen" to help make sense of difficult recordings is often adopted within the practices of CA (Bucholtz, 2000). Embracing this practice contributed to my refining the transcripts.

Susan: In CA, learning to use the transcription notation requires an orientation to careful listening and accessing support from relevant technologies. To give some idea of the length of time it takes to transcribe, I remember telling Gillian that it would take me 30–60 hours of transcription work to transcribe approximately 5 minutes of video interaction in a classroom. This is quite a typical time frame for this level of transcription that involved multiple participants and their multimodal actions.

ANALYTIC MANOEUVRES

Within the analytic approach of CA, the five-step process identified by Pomerantz (1997) was used:

1. The first step is "unmotivated looking" (Psathas, 1995a, p. 45), which requires selecting a sequence that was of interest (Pomerantz & Fehr, 1997).
2. The second step requires the characterizing of "actions in the sequence" (Pomerantz & Fehr, 1997, p. 72), as requests, questions, invitations, and so on. "Characterisations are provisional" (Pomerantz & Fehr, 1997, p. 72) and are reconsidered throughout the analytic process.
3. The next step is to consider the way in which speakers "package ... form up and deliver actions" (Pomerantz & Fehr, 1997, p. 73) from a range of alternatives. This involved consideration of the ways in which speakers referred "to persons, objects, places, activities etc." (Pomerantz & Fehr, 1997, p. 73). As part of this step, Pomerantz and Fehr (1997) suggest a number of questions that may help identify both the packaging of the action and the consequentiality of that action.
4. The fourth step requires the consideration of the "timing and taking" (Pomerantz & Fehr, 1997, p. 73) of turns which requires regard for

Table 16.1   Example of a transcript

116	Margot	(Do/did) you have cherry	Question—to her mother about
117		°(b's)/(bits)° ((M looks deliberately at E and proceeds to ask the question))	the—suggests a yes/no response
118	Emily	You love the cherries don't you ((E's gaze is on her food))	Offers some knowledge about M— asks M to confirm the knowledge Question suggests a yes/no response

"how the speaker obtained the turn, the timing of the initiation of the turn, the termination of the turn and whether the speaker selected a next speaker" (Pomerantz & Fehr, 1997, p. 73).

5. The final step considers the way in which "actions implicated certain identities, roles and or relationships for the interactions" (Pomerantz & Fehr, 1997, p. 74).

Gillian: While the five steps suggested by Pomerantz and Fehr (1997) provided a guide to begin analysis, analysis remained an ongoing challenge and an iterative process, one that required constant refinement to accomplish thorough analysis. This five-step process was not achieved quickly. Rather, it required constantly revisiting the video recordings in tandem with the transcript.

Following selecting the particular sequence, transcription of that mealtime recording occurred and boundaries indicating the beginning and conclusion of a sequence were identified. The first draft, a less refined transcript, was used in conjunction with the video recording to select a sequence. Once a sequence was selected for analysis, a more detailed transcript was developed.

My first attempt with analysis presented more as a telling or description, rather than as an explication of how the social activity was accomplished. Recognizing the importance of characterizing the actions was important in moving the analysis forward. I therefore resorted to recording each social action, and was constantly asking myself "what action is occurring here" and "what is the resulting relevant next turn", referred to as "sequential implicativeness" (Schegloff & Sacks, 1973, p. 296).

Below is one of my early attempts to produce a transcript and identify the action accomplished (Table 16.1).

Choosing to look at extended sequences within an episode of interaction (Psathas, 1995b) was selected because it enabled the examination of how everyday social life (family life) was constructed and organized. This meant that for each episode selected, I needed to examine significant literature on that topic. For example, in one sequence, and revealed following initial analysis, I focused on multiparty talk within the family. This required an examination of the literature on multiparty talk and the ways in which talk is accomplished in multiparty settings.

Susan: As Gillian began to explore in detail the transcript and video recordings, I suggested that she read widely in the CA literature and engage with Harvey Sacks' lectures, collated within "Lectures in Conversation" (Sacks, 1995), recognized as one of the most influential texts in CA. This resource was one that I had returned to many times throughout my analysis of data for my PhD.

Gillian: As a beginning researcher, I found that data transcription and analysis were slow processes, as I had no previous experience with CA. I know that I had many false starts when searching for the relevant references to support analysis of the sequence.

MANOEUVRES WITHIN THE RESEARCH COMMUNITY

Gillian: Making sense of the methodology was an ongoing process, with my supervisors providing many opportunities to support my skill development. This included supervisor meetings, participating in and sharing data at data sessions at the Brisbane Transcript Analysis Group (TAG) (Harris et al., 2012), connecting with the local postgraduate student research community, attending conferences and workshops.

False assumptions of research as a "private" activity were interrupted as I was invited to participate in supervisory sessions that involved showing fragments from the video recordings, transcripts, and drafts of analysis. While the environment was one of support and collaboration, there was a sense that I was putting beginning skills and competency up for scrutiny. These supervisory meetings, however, proved to be critical in developing my expertise as a researcher.

Another invaluable forum was participating in data sessions at the TAG meetings, which included highly skilled analysts, and sometimes international experts, as well as novice members. During data sessions, members work together to discuss noticings, that is, aspects of the interaction that is interesting (Harris et al., 2012). I recognized the value of data sessions as I listened to highly skilled analysts engaging in analysis and heard the language I was engaging with in the literature used to discuss the data. Also observed was how experienced analysts may have differing perspectives about what action was accomplished and how the particular actions were evidenced in the talk, which gave me more confidence to talk about analysis at such forums. Both the supervisory meetings and TAG sessions provided expert modeling of analysis, and thus both venues proved an important mechanism for becoming a more proficient researcher. Similarly, attending conferences continued my immersion in the language and practices of CA and enabled me to talk with researchers whose work I was using.

While apprehensive, I was encouraged to present some PhD data at TAG, which required sharing my transcript and proffering my emerging analysis. These sessions were invaluable for extending my understandings of what was occurring in my data and supporting me to identify relevant literature to use in the written analysis and grow my confidence with analysis.

My principal supervisor encouraged her cohort of students to connect, discuss, and share readings and generally support one another. Evident throughout the process of learning CA was the importance of this cohort in providing a non-threatening and collaborative interactional space to discuss and share.

Susan: TAG was an important resource for me when I was a doctoral student, and remains an important aspect of my life as a researcher. My supervisor, Carolyn Baker, established this group for her current and graduated students in order to build methodological expertise and networks. Building local, national, and international research communities for fledgling researchers is a research space to learn and practice methodologies, and to build an international academic community where researchers can connect with each other. For this reason, I suggest to postgraduate students that they attend and give presentations in local, national, and international contexts as a way of building their scholarly network and, at the same time, to present their research for discussion and feedback.

Gillian: Supervisory conversations and written feedback were important mechanisms for building fledgling methodological know-how, research confidence, and supporting the transition from novice to mature researcher. As the example below shows, supervisory written feedback shows familiarity with the data and with previous analysis and provided guidance to appropriate resources. I would read this feedback over and over and attend to each dimension, knowing that following up on suggestions would improve my analysis (Fig. 16.1).

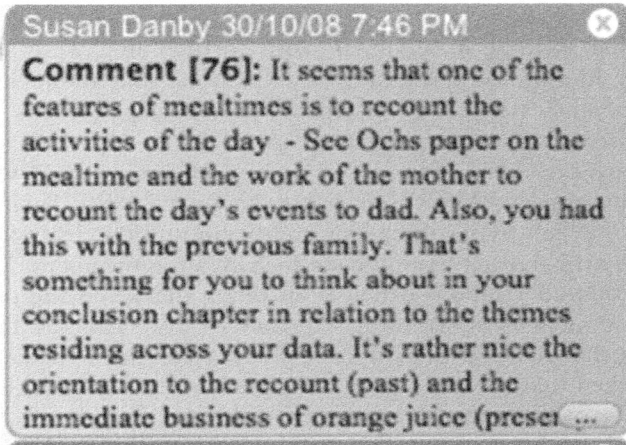

Fig. 16.1 Supervisory written feedback

As discussed, the supervisory meetings were often data sessions, while other sessions focused on challenges and dilemmas that I was experiencing. On other occasions, the interaction was aimed at reassuring me that other students encountered similar challenges. For example, when I was troubled with matters to do with transcription, my principal supervisor wanted me to understand the importance of becoming very familiar with the data and offered the following personal account to make her point:

> I would make use of any moment I could to engage with the data. I remember doing the ironing and playing the audio-tapes of video data over and over enabling me to became more and more familiar with my data – more attuned to prosody and so on.

Susan: Telling stories is well recognized as finding a way to make a personal connection, as well as showing that the PhD experience, while often quite a solitary process, has much in common with how others have experienced it.
Gillian: I had CA colleagues who reminded me of important theoretical points when engaged in analysis. While struggling with seeing what was occurring in the data, my colleague reminded me that social order is present because members "put it there, accountably, for

anyone to see as being always-already there" (McHoul, 2008, p. 825). Thus, order is there at all times. Also forthcoming were reminders about considering the question "why this now" and about how materials "depend heavily for sense upon their serial placement" and the "socially organised occasion of their use" (Garfinkel, 1967, p. 3) also focused my analysis. I draw on an example from my PhD where the mother announces "Mum's sitting down now (.) I'm having bacon and eggs". When transcribing this and beginning the analysis, I questioned why the mother would make such an announcement. Using the constant reminders about order at all times and given the placement of this announcement within a sequence of events in the meal, that is, the mother had fed the children, the placement of this announcement marked that it was her time to eat. These examples highlight the importance of engaging constantly with the theoretical underpinnings of ethnomethodology during analysis.

CONCLUSION

This chapter has provided a unique snapshot of the manoeuvres within a PhD experience, from the perspectives of the student engaged in learning a particular methodological approach and from the principal supervisor. Preliminary conversations between the supervisor and the student about possible topics, interests, and methodology were critical to the success of the PhD journey. While an increasing familiarity with the literature pertaining to the methodology is essential, moving from the fledgling stage to producing a completed PhD and being recognized as a researcher required engagement with the methodological community and a willingness to reflect on manoeuvres and respond where necessary. While the PhD journey has concluded, the methodological manoeuvring continues as one begins new research projects. Growing methodologically requires a strong commitment to maintain connection with the research community and to have rich conversations, dialogue with others.

Acknowledgments I would like to acknowledge my PhD supervisors, each of whom supported my methodological manoeuvres (Professor Susan Danby, Professor Ann Farrell, Dr. Maryanne Theobald, Dr. Carly Butler).

REFERENCES

Arminen, I. (2004). Second stories: The salience of interpersonal communication for mutual help in Alcholics Anonymous. *Journal of Pragmatics, 36*, 319–347.

Baker, C. (1997). Ethnomethodological studies of talk in educational settings. In B. Davies & D. Corson (Eds.), *Encyclopedia of language and education: Oral discourse and education* (Vol. 3, pp. 43–52). Netherlands: Kluwer Academic Publishers.

Baker, C. (1998). Transcription and representation in literacy research. In J. Flood, S. B. Heath, & D. Lapps (Eds.), *A handbook for literacy educators: Research on teaching the communicative and visual arts* (pp. 108–118). New York: Macmillan.

Bucholtz, M. (2000). The politics of transcription. *Journal of Pragmatics, 32*, 1439–1465.

Danby, S. (1998). *Interaction and social order in a preschool classroom (Unpublished doctoral dissertation)*. St Lucia, QLD: The University of Queensland.

Danby, S. (2005). The supervisory experience: Culture in action. In J. Yamanashi & I. Milojevic (Eds.), *Researching identity, diversity and education: Surpassing the norm* (pp. 1–16). Teneriffe, QLD: Post Pressed.

Danby, S., & Baker, C. (1998a). How to be masculine in the block area. *Childhood: A global journal of child research, 5*(2), 151–175.

Danby, S., & Baker, C. (1998b). "What's the problem?"—Restoring social order in the preschool classroom. In I. Hutchby & J. Moran-Ellis (Eds.), *Children and social competence: Arenas of action* (pp. 91–140). London: The Falmer Press.

Davidson, C. (2010). Transcription matters: Transcribing talk and interaction to facilitate conversation analysis of the taken-for-granted in young children's interactions. *Journal of Early Childhood Research, 8*(2), 115–131.

Francis, D., & Hester, S. (2004). *An invitation to ethnomethodology: Language, society, and social interaction*. London: Sage.

Garfinkel, H. (1967). *Studies in ethnomethodology*. Englewood Cliffs, NJ: Prentice-Hall.

Goodwin, M. (1995). Co-construction in girls' hopscotch. *Research on Language and Social Interaction, 28*(3), 261–281.

Harris, J., Theobald, M., Danby, S., Reynolds, E., & Rintel, S. (2012). "What's going on here?" The pedagogy of a data analysis session. In A. Lee & S. Danby (Eds.), *Reshaping doctoral education: International approaches and pedagogies* (pp. 83–96). London: Routledge.

Heath, C., Hindmarsh, J., & Luff, P. (2010). *Video in qualitative research: Analysing social interactions in everyday life*. London: Sage.

Heritage, J. (1984). *Garfinkel and ethnomethodology*. Cambridge: Polity Press.

Hutchby, I., & Wooffitt, R. (1998). *Conversation analysis: Principles, practices and applications*. Cambridge: Polity Press.

James, A., Jenks, C., & Prout, A. (1998). *Theorizing childhood*. Cambridge: Polity Press.

Jefferson, G. (2004). Glossary of transcript symbols with an introduction. In G. H. Lerner (Ed.), *Conversation analysis: Studies from the first generation* (pp. 13–23). Philadelphia: John Benjamins.

Lapadat, J. (2000). Problematizing transcription: Purpose, paradigm and quality. *International Journal of Social Research Methodology, 3*(3), 203–219.

Lynch, M., & Peyrot, M. (1992). Introduction: A reader's guide to ethnomethodology. *Qualitative Sociology, 15*(2), 113–122.

McHoul, A. (2008). Questions of context in studies of talk and interaction—Ethnomethodology and conversation analysis. *Journal of Pragmatics, 40*(5), 823–826.

McLarty, M. M., & Gibson, J. W. (2000). Using video technology in emancipatory research. *European Journal of Special Needs Education, 15*(2), 138–148.

Mondada, L. (2007). Commentary: Transcript variations and indexicality of transcribing practices. *Discourse Studies, 9*(6), 809–821.

Ochs, E. (1979). Transcription as theory. In E. Ochs & B. Schieffelin (Eds.), *Developmental pragmatics* (pp. 43–72). New York: Academic Press.

Payne, G. (1976). Making a lesson happen: An ethnomethodological analysis. In M. Hammersley & P. Woods (Eds.), *The process of schooling: A sociological reader* (pp. 33–40). London: Routledge and Kegan Paul.

Pomerantz, A., & Fehr, B. J. (1997). Conversation analysis: An approach to the study of social action as sense making practices. In T. A. Van-Dijk (Ed.), *Discourse as social interaction* (pp. 64–91). London: Sage.

Psathas, G. (1990). Introduction: Methodological issues and recent developments in the study of naturally occurring interaction. In G. Psathas (Ed.), *Interaction competence: Studies in ethnomethodology and conversation analysis* (pp. 1–24). Washington: International Institute of Ethnomethodology and Conversation Analysis.

Psathas, G. (1995a). *Conversational analysis: The study of talk-in-interaction*. Thousand Oaks, CA: Sage.

Psathas, G. (1995b). The study of extended sequences: The case of the garden lesson. In G. Watson & R. Seiler (Eds.), *Text in context: Contributions to ethnomethodology* (pp. 99–122). Newbury Park, CA: Sage.

Psathas, G., & Anderson, T. (1990). The "practices" of transcription in conversation analysis. *Semiotica, 78*(1/2), 75–99.

Sacks, H. (1995). *Lectures on conversation: Volumes 1 & 2*. Oxford: Blackwell Publishing.

Schegloff, E. A., & Sacks, H. (1973). Opening up closings. *Semiotica, 7*, 289–327.

Sparrman, A. (2005). Video recording as interaction: Participant observation of children's everyday life. *Qualitative Research in Psychology, 2*(3), 241–255.

Speier, M. (1971). The everyday world of the child. In J. D. Douglas (Ed.), *Understanding everyday life* (pp. 188–217). London: Routledge.

CHAPTER 17

Reimagining Rooms for Methodological Manoeuvres: Distilled Dilemmas, Proposed Principles and Synthesised Strategies in Research Education and Social Practices Qualitatively

P.A. Danaher

INTRODUCTION

St Patrick's Day (17 March), 2015. Today I participated in my university's induction for newly (or nearly newly) enrolled Research Higher Degree students. The scheduled two-and-a-half-hour session went over time and concluded with refreshments in the campus refectory that I was unable to attend. The technology linking the three campuses worked well, but there were the usual unintentional incidents of privileging the participants at the "sending campus", where all the speakers (including one who had travelled from another campus) were present, accompanied by the equally usual and not always unintentional examples of resistance of that privileging by the participants at the "receiving campuses".

P.A. Danaher (✉)
Faculty of Business, Education, Law and Arts, University of Southern Queensland, Toowoomba, QLD, Australia

© The Author(s) 2016
B. Harreveld et al. (eds.), *Constructing Methodology for Qualitative Research*, DOI 10.1057/978-1-137-59943-8_17

A lot of information was presented, all of it relevant but perhaps most of it to be forgotten as a result of "information overload" and having so many short- and longer-term arrangements to be made at the start of a new programme of study. This information was presented by a range of research leaders and managers in the university: the deputy vice-chancellor (research and innovation), the director of research training and development, the research graduate studies student manager, the two faculty associate deans (research and research training) and their respective faculty research office colleagues, the e-research analyst, the research librarian, the manager of research integrity and ethics, the manager of the statistical consulting unit and the president of the postgraduate research student society. The recurring message was centred on support and encouragement: "We are here to help you." At the same time, diverse and sometimes divergent discourses were evident, including an evocation of collegiality and professionalism on the one hand and an emphasis on compliance and the threat of research misconduct on the other.

My own brief discussion related to welcoming the new students to an always developing research culture and inviting their individually distinctive and their collectively constructive contributions to that culture. I mentioned a particular research community (see also Danaher, 2008, 2015; Harreveld & Danaher, 2009) with fortnightly meetings, biannual research symposia and peer-reviewed, reportable publications as one of several examples of research support available to all staff members and postgraduate students at the university. I also sought to inject a note of reassurance by referring to the work of the Centre for the Study of Research Training and Impact (SORTI) at the University of Newcastle in Australia (http://www.newcastle.edu.au/research-and-innovation/centre/sorti/about-us), whose members have highlighted the examination of Research Higher Degree theses and exegeses as a generally collegial and constructive process rather than as a trial by ordeal (see, for example, Holbrook, Bourke, & Fairbairn, 2015).

This reflective vignette (Jones, 2014) encapsulated some of the many complexities attending contemporary research (see also Jones, Torres, & Arminio, 2014). At the start of highly diverse and largely individual research journeys (some students' memberships of formal and funded research teams notwithstanding), this group of researchers nevertheless had in common a number of characteristics, including the hoped-for benefits to be derived from accessing support and joining dynamic networks, and also needing to conform to a set of bureaucratic processes from applying for enrolment through to ensuring that the final requirements to be deemed eligible to graduate from the programme have been fulfilled.

Like this vignette illustrating some of the obstacles and opportunities attending students beginning their research programmes, so too with this final chapter working to distil some of the lessons to be gleaned from the preceding chapters in this book. This particular ending—however temporary and tentative it might be—of this foray into a distinctive collection of methodological manoeuvres affords an opportunity to synthesise some of the qualitative research strategies deployed by the authors of the previous chapters. It also enables the identification of some of the wider implications of those strategies for engaging effectively, efficiently and ethically with the broader challenges facing current researchers, as well as the chances to contribute significantly and sustainably to generating new knowledge and the accompanying empathy and understandings that enrich our education and social practices.

A couple of points about language are appropriate at this juncture. Firstly, this book contains several references to "methodological manoeuvres", which was an organising metaphor for the structured writing workshops that framed the development of the book chapters and that was mentioned in the editors' opening chapter (Harreveld, Danaher, Lawson, Knight, and Busch, this volume). While this metaphor was not retained in the book's title, it remains a powerful analytical device for interrogating what (in this case qualitative) researchers do and why they do what they do. Secondly, the other contributors to this book and I acknowledge the growing impact of "post-qualitative research" (Lather & St Pierre, 2013). Relatedly, and as noted by the editors (Harreveld et al., this volume), some of the chapters draw appropriately on quantitative and mixed methods research approaches. Nevertheless, there is considerable value in heeding and attending to the clarion call sounded at the end of the editors' opening chapter: "It is timely perhaps to revivify the pioneering spirit of qualitative research, its sense of mission and its innovativeness."

Building on these two points, the chapter contains the following three sections:

- My summary of some of the qualitative research issues and the respective methodological manoeuvres elaborated in the previous chapters in the book, clustered around the grand tour question (Leech, 2002) articulated in the opening chapter (Harreveld et al., this volume).
- My selective analysis of those findings in terms of the organising themes of distilled dilemmas, proposed principles and synthesised strategies.
- My elicitation of some of the significant implications of this chapter and the book that it concludes for reimagining rooms for methodological manoeuvres.

QUALITATIVE RESEARCH ISSUES AND METHODOLOGICAL MANOEUVRES IN THE PREVIOUS CHAPTERS IN THE BOOK

The grand tour question (Leech, 2002) posed in the editors' opening chapter (Harreveld et al., this volume) is an enduringly significant one: "How do qualitative researchers manoeuvre through the maze of methodology to make meaning for their research projects?" I take that question as my starting point in summarising selected findings from the preceding chapters in this book. Inevitably, this summary is abstracted, decontextualised and potentially reductionist with regard to the rich diversity and depth that I discerned in all of the chapters, but hopefully it will still do appropriate honour to the chapter authors' intentions while fulfilling its function of synthesising clearly and concisely some of the key ideas presented in the chapters.

More specifically, Table 17.1 portrays some of the identified qualitative research issues and the methodological manoeuvrings in response to those issues that were articulated in the preceding chapters.

Before I turn to analysing in greater depth these selected findings from the preceding chapters, it is important to include three more general reflections on these findings and the attitudes, dispositions and values that animated them. Firstly, what was palpable in every chapter was also evident in the presentations at the research symposium from which this book

Table 17.1 Identified issues and methodological responses in the chapter authors' methodological manoeuvrings

Chapter	Identified qualitative research issues	Respective methodological manoeuvrings
Chapter 2 Gemma Mann "A non-binary methodological manoeuvre: Expert quantitative and novice qualitative researcher"	Understanding and engaging with the principles and practices of both qualitative and quantitative research	Disrupting the qualitative–quantitative research binary by transferring skills and knowledge and adopting a holistic methodological perspective
Chapter 3 Cynthia Cowling and Celeste Lawson "Dipping qualitative toes into a quantitative worldview: Methodological manoeuvres in a multicultural context"	Embracing qualitative understandings in the traditionally quantitative discipline of radiography	Developing and justifying a contextually appropriate variation on ethnographic methodology to conduct research with radiographers in Trinidad and Tobago for wider application in other research sites
Chapter 4 Michael A. Cowling "Navigating the path between positivism and interpretivism as a technology academic completing education research"	Explicating and exploring the epistemological dimension of qualitative education research to inform the work of technology researchers	Using growing and multiple epistemological and methodological understandings to navigate backwards and forwards between the positivist and interpretivist research paradigms
Chapter 5 Reyna Zipf "A bricoleur approach to navigating the methodological maze"	Experiencing qualitative research as a complex maze with the attendant risk of failure to escape from it	Becoming a bricoleur researcher and using the metaphor of a metal alloy to assemble a range of methodological resources to address the selected research questions
Chapter 6 Teresa Moore "Manoeuvring through the maze of methodology: Constructing the research-ready embodied RHD student"	Teaching Research Higher Degree students about qualitative research	Maximising Research Higher Degree students' multiple subjectivities as they engage with the designated research methods course

(continued)

Table 17.1 (continued)

Chapter	Identified qualitative research issues	Respective methodological manoeuvrings
Chapter 7 Rickie Fisher "Methodology for a fusionist ontology: Paradigmatic choices in understanding the reasons for career changes"	Reflecting on a novice qualitative researcher's linkages between what may have been and what might become	Elaborating a fusionist ontology to explicate the influences on and the reasons for methodological decision-making
Chapter 8 Sarah Loch and Ali Black "We cannot do this work without being who we are: Researching and experiencing academic selves"	Qualitative researchers communicating with themselves and others who they are at multiple levels	Applying aesthetic methodologies of story and image to share the experiences of being academics and human beings
Chapter 9 Leanne Dodd "Show and tell: A practice-led methodological solution for researchers in creative writing"	Mobilising qualitative research methods in practice-led research into creative writing	Employing both elements of "Show and tell" to contest the theory–practice dichotomy in research methodologies
Chapter 10 Alison Owens "Articulating the fact behind the fiction: Narrative inquiry as a research methodology for historical novelists"	Devising qualitative research suitable for a researcher–novelist writing historical fiction	Deploying arts-based and arts-informed narrative inquiry as an appropriate research methodology
Chapter 11 Mike Danaher and Margaret Jamieson "On manoeuvre: Navigating practice-led methodology in a creative writing PhD for the first time"	Devising qualitative research suitable for a researcher writing a historical romance novel and the accompanying exegesis	Using the methodological tools of visioning, planning, journeying, reflecting and evaluating to disrupt the novice–expert and the research student–supervisor binaries
Chapter 12 Donna Lee Brien and Margaret McAllister "Methodological and other research strategies to manoeuvre from single to multi- and interdisciplinary project partnerships"	Building on qualitative methods to develop substantial links between nursing and creative writing research	Generating multidisciplinary and interdisciplinary methodological insights and understandings between previously separate scholarly disciplines

(continued)

Table 17.1   (continued)

Chapter	Identified qualitative research issues	Respective methodological manoeuvrings
Chapter 13 Steven Pace "Contested concepts: Negotiating debates about qualitative research methods such as grounded theory and autoethnography"	Novice researchers developing competence and confidence in using particular qualitative research methods	Understanding and engaging wholeheartedly with the methodological contestations associated with grounded theory and autoethnography
Chapter 14 Bill Blayney and Bobby Harreveld "Discursive manoeuvring in the borderlands of career transition: From trade to teacher"	Navigating between methodology and method in qualitative research	Exploiting the methodological affordances of analysing the diverse experiences of career borderlands enacted by trade-qualified workers becoming secondary school teachers
Chapter 15 Ali Black and Gillian Busch "Understanding and influencing research with children: Mapping motivations, markers and meaning-making"	Designing and conducting qualitative research with children	Traversing a series of methodological dilemmas in order to devise ethical research relationships with participating children
Chapter 16 Gillian Busch and Susan Danby "From fledgling manoeuvres to methodological confidence: Conversations between a doctoral student and supervisor on ethnomethodology and conversation analysis to explore the everyday worlds of children and families"	Designing and conducting qualitative research with children	Using the methodological approach of second stories to elaborate the interactions between the doctoral student and her supervisor

has emerged: a combination of caution, commitment and courage on the part of all the participating researchers, regardless of their levels of experience or their disciplinary or paradigmatic backgrounds. These qualitative research(er) values and virtues (Macfarlane, 2010) constitute a welcome departure from the vices (see also Danaher, Danaher, & Moriarty, 2003) that sometimes accompany research, including (un)conscious appropriation of others' voices and the privileging of self-interest over the multiple and at times conflicting interests of research participants and stakeholders (see also Danaher, Cook, Danaher, Coombes, & Danaher, 2013). Despite the diversity of qualitative research issues identified and the methodological manoeuvres devised to engage with those issues, all chapter authors evinced a determination to design and conduct research that is relevant, rigorous and hopefully beneficial to such research participants and stakeholders.

Secondly, and again despite this diversity, some consistent patterns and some recurring themes were evident in how individual researchers undertook the mission of carrying out research that is effective, efficient and ethical. Some of these consistencies and recurrences underpin the discussion in the next section of the chapter, while others pertain to the planned stages and the sometimes unplanned exigencies of the research masters and doctoral student journey (e.g., confirmation of candidature and submitting the thesis or exegesis for examination). These consistencies and recurrences are not necessarily reductionist or reprehensible. On the contrary, they constitute a substantial structure for high-level researcher decision-making, and they also afford a shared space for examining and reflecting on highly diverse separate research projects—a form of researcher Esperanto that generates common lessons as well as individual implications for the respective participants.

Thirdly, the fact that a couple of the identified qualitative research issues were identical or similar but that the corresponding methodological manoeuvres were different is a timely reminder that researchers have both the capability and the responsibility to enact high-level decision-making based on the possibilities and the constraints evident in their particular contexts. From this perspective, it is to be expected that researchers investigating related topics are likely to design their projects very differently and to generate different findings and implications—an outcome already evident in some of the preceding chapters' dealing with similar research issues (for instance, conducting practice-led research and researching with children). While consciousness of this capability and responsibility will no doubt fuel the anxiety and trepidation communicated in several of the previous chapters, that consciousness should also create something of a liberating catharsis—the realisation that it is "up to us" to enact meaningful research and furthermore that we have the experiences, skills and training to do so—and that intelligently conceived and rigorously activated methodological manoeuvres are a crucial element of our responses to that realisation. (This is also a reasoned and reasonable response to the potential sense of feeling overloaded and overwhelmed that Research Higher Degree students might experience in the vignette that was presented at the beginning of this chapter.)

DISTILLED DILEMMAS, PROPOSED PRINCIPLES AND SYNTHESISED STRATEGIES IN THE PREVIOUS CHAPTERS IN THE BOOK

This section of the chapter extends the preceding discussion of the previous chapters by articulating their significance in relation to the three organising themes of distilled dilemmas, proposed principles and synthesised strategies. These themes are elaborated in Table 17.2, accompanied by two indicative examples from each of the preceding chapters. The logic of this table is predicated on the presumption that identifying research dilemmas both enables and requires appropriate principles for engaging with such dilemmas, and that these principles in turn help to frame practical strategies for implementing principle-based intended solutions to the dilemmas.

Table 17.2 Distilled dilemmas, proposed principles, synthesised strategies and indicative examples in this book

Distilled dilemmas	Proposed principles	Synthesised strategies	Indicative examples in this book
Feeling overwhelmed by the breadth and depth of available research methodologies	Understanding the foundations and the applications of, and the debates within, specific methodologies	Reading, writing and discussing widely about the substantial characteristics of each methodology	Seeking out "first principles and definitions" (Gemma Mann in Chap. 2)
			Drawing on experiential knowledge to understand a new methodology (Gemma Mann in Chap. 2)
			Embracing epistemology as a consistent lens for understanding different methodologies (Michael A. Cowling in Chap. 4)
			Teaching research students about methodologies in a formal postgraduate course (Teresa Moore in Chap. 6)
		Building on the creative affordances of multidisciplinary and interdisciplinary research	Researching across nursing and creative writing (Donna Lee Brien and Margaret McAllister in Chap. 12)
		Enhancing understanding by mobilising the explanatory power of metaphors	Conceptualising research as a spectrum of perspectives in which one can position oneself according to the requirements of the respective research questions (Michael A. Cowling in Chap. 4)
			Conceptualising methodology as a metal alloy, with case study as the main ingredient and phenomenology and grounded theory as the minor elements (Reyna Zipf in Chap. 5)
			Conceptualising academic work as a cat's cradle (Sarah Loch and Ali Black in Chap. 8)
			Conceptualising the theory–practice dichotomy as a dividing hedge (Leanne Dodd in Chap. 9)
			Conceptualising a researcher's eclectic activities as a bowerbird collecting objects to construct a bower (Steven Pace in Chap. 13)
			Conceptualising career changes as border and transition (Bill Blayney and Bobby Harreveld in Chap. 14)

Feeling that one is a research imposter	Developing appropriate knowledge to assess one's own and others' research capacities	Building on the parallels between one's research study focus and one's developing identity as a capable researcher	Elaborating the notion of becoming (a secondary school teacher or a researcher) (Rickie Fisher in Chap. 7)
			Explicating career transition as a borderland (from a trade-qualified worker to a secondary school teacher or from a novice to an experienced researcher) (Bill Blayney and Bobby Harreveld in Chap. 14)
			Exploring the establishment of social order (in the family home, a preschool classroom or a research project) (Gillian Busch and Susan Danby in Chap. 16)
		Engaging in deeply embodied personal and professional collaborations	Conducting collaborative reflections to articulate powerful insights into separate and shared lived experiences (Sarah Loch and Ali Black in Chap. 8)
			The research student's and the supervisor/s learning together about a new methodology (Mike Danaher and Margaret Jamieson in Chap. 11)
			The research student's drawing on the supervisor's greater methodological expertise (Gillian Busch and Susan Danby in Chap. 16)
		Developing, and feeling increasingly confident about, one's own voice in relation to research	Accepting that the onus of agency and responsibility for judging the quality of a research project lies with the researcher (Reyna Zipf in Chap. 5)
			Being clear and confident about the decision-making attending selecting certain methodological resources rather than others (Rickie Fisher in Chap. 7)
			Experimenting with different writing styles for the thesis or exegesis (Leanne Dodd in Chap. 9)
			Engaging in explicit and extensive visioning of the intended research project's focus and rationale (Mike Danaher and Margaret Jamieson in Chap. 11)
			Developing one's own viewpoint about methodologies that are sometimes significantly contested (Steven Pace in Chap. 13)

(continued)

Table 17.2 (continued)

Distilled dilemmas	Proposed principles	Synthesised strategies	Indicative examples in the previous chapters
Responding to claims about the limited significance of one's research	Understanding the multiple criteria for assessing a research project's contributions to different forms of knowledge	Mobilising diverse viewpoints about generalisability and other claims of significance related to qualitative research Acknowledging the sometimes conflicting conceptions of evidence in relation to practice and research	Using historical fiction to claim that writing can be realistic and truthful (Alison Owens in Chap. 10) Assessing different viewpoints about evidence-based practice in nursing and creating writing (Brien & McAllister in Chap. 12)
Responding to observed or perceived breaches of conduct in a research site	Understanding the formally prescribed as well as the individually identified ethical accountabilities of a researcher and other stakeholders	Elaborating and implementing contextually appropriate ways of discussing apparent breaches of conduct with the relevant individuals	Discussing confidentially and privately with individual radiographers identified misuse of radiation (Cynthia Cowling and Celeste Lawson in Chap. 3) Discussing perceived research transgressions with research students and/or supervisors (Teresa Moore in Chap. 4)
Responding to actual or potential risks in designing and conducting research	Putting such risks in their place as being part of the researcher's high-level decision-making	Finding ways to mitigate such risks without allowing them to prevent a research project from occurring	Negotiating with radiographers in several different countries data gathering techniques that were suitable in each site (Cynthia Cowling and Celeste Lawson in Chap. 3) Using fictional writing to avoid being drawn into competing perceptions of historical figures (Alison Owens in Chap. 10) Developing a well-informed dialogue with ethics committees about ethical ways of researching with children (Ali Black and Gillian Busch in Chap. 15) Devising ways of representing children's voices authentically and ethically (Ali Black and Gillian Busch in Chap. 15)

Table 17.2 presented the selection of distilled dilemmas, proposed principles, synthesised strategies and indicative examples gleaned from the previous chapters and related to contemporary research into education and social practices. The next section of the chapter elaborates some of the identified implications of this selection for reimagining rooms for methodological manoeuvres.

IMPLICATIONS FOR REIMAGINING ROOMS FOR METHODOLOGICAL MANOEUVRES

So what might the detailed decision-making portrayed in Tables 17.1 and 17.2 mean for other qualitative researchers investigating current education and social practices? By way of a broader and longer-term perspective on the finely nuanced considerations encapsulated in both tables, the argument pursued in this section of the chapter is that researchers need to create and strengthen their respective and shared "rooms for methodological manoeuvres". By this, I mean two logically distinct but interrelated and inter-reliant phenomena simultaneously. Firstly, such rooms might be conceptualised as *prospective spaces* that researchers inhabit and increasingly embody and where they are able to construct and assemble the theoretical and methodological resources that they need to design and enact specific research projects. Secondly, these rooms can be seen as *retrospective space*—akin to having "room to move"—that affords a breathing space, an opportunity and the freedom to reflect on how a particular research project has proceeded and, if necessary, for the researcher to regroup and if to change direction if something has gone unexpectedly awry while s/he has been engaged in the research on methodological manoeuvres.

This argument entails two key, corollary propositions that have also been exemplified in the preceding chapters in this book. Firstly, regardless of discipline and degree of experience, researchers have both the capacity and the obligation to conduct as well as to construct their "rooms to manoeuvre" in ways that maximise the credibility, rigour and utility of their research. Secondly, having "room to move" often highlights the inherent interdependence attending contemporary research as complex networks of relationships among researchers, research participants, other gatekeepers and stakeholders, potential end-users and prospective beneficiaries.

This rationale for reimagining rooms for methodological manoeuvres provides one among several potentially productive responses to the grand tour question (Leech, 2002) articulated in the editors' opening chapter (Harreveld et al., this volume) in this book: "How do qualitative researchers manoeuvre through the maze of methodology to make meaning for their research projects?" And at this point it is worthwhile reiterating the singularity of this response. It is almost certain, and certainly desirable, that the book's editors, chapter authors and readers would generate a different synthesis of the preceding chapters from what I have represented in Tables 17.1 and 17.2. Indeed, it is likely that I would create a likewise different rendition of these tables if I compiled them three or six months from now. This singularity accentuates certain crucial elements of the methodological manoeuvres mobilised by the editors' grand tour question: that these manoeuvres are framed and informed—but not (over)determined—by the material, spatial and temporal situatedness of the contexts in which the research takes place; that the researchers designing and conducting the research do so on the basis of what they know and understand at the time; that the high-level decision-making that they undertake needs to be justified but that it is likely to change and transmute over space and time; and that these kinds of methodological manoeuvres should be subjected to ongoing interrogation in terms of their intended and actual short- and longer-term effects on and effectiveness for research participants (including the researchers) and other stakeholders. These identified dimensions of the methodological manoeuvres encapsulate simultaneously the prospective spaces and retrospectives spaces articulated above that are equally vital in helping to create and to reimagine generative, sustainable and potentially transformative rooms for methodological manoeuvres.

CONCLUSION

Part of the litmus test for assessing the possible relevance and utility of this chapter's articulation of an argument in favour of reimagining rooms for methodological manoeuvres is contained in the vignette presented at the beginning of the chapter. The participants in that particular induction for new (or nearly new) Research Higher Degree students faced a multiplicity of complex challenges in traversing their selected research landscapes. Setting aside the induction's organisation and the undoubted enthusiasm of all presenters in sharing what they thought that the students should be told, recognising that all these students would need to engage authoritatively, confidently and wholeheartedly with specific kinds of methodological manoeuvring was and remains important if their traversals of those research landscapes were to be successful.

Another part of this same litmus test is the extent to which the argument proposed in this chapter resonates with, and does justice to, the depth and diversity of the authentic, practical and useful research dilemmas, principles and strategies contained in the preceding chapters. Each of those chapters has much of significance to say to the wider body of qualitative education and social researchers, and hopefully this current chapter has helped to explicate at least some of that significance.

Finally, back to the clarion call sounded by the editors (Harreveld et al., this volume) at the end of their opening chapter: "It is timely perhaps to revivify the pioneering spirit of qualitative research, its sense of mission and its innovativeness." The suggestions here for reimagining rooms for methodological manoeuvres emerge from, and constitute one among many responses to, that clarion call. Moreover, the intervening chapters in this book—highly varied as they are, and in equally varied ways, all of them evoking tentativeness, uncertainty, growing confidence and a shining conviction that good qualitative research is both necessary and possible—certainly embody, enact and exemplify that "pioneering spirit ... its sense of mission and its innovativeness".

Acknowledgements I acknowledge wholeheartedly the intellectual labour and the research leadership of Professor Bobby Harreveld in masterminding this book and the research symposium on 25 and 26 September 2014 at the Rockhampton campus of Central Queensland University, Australia that preceded and informed it. Professor Harreveld and her fellow editors have generated a productive framework for reconsidering the potential and actual contributions of contemporary qualitative methodologies to researching and thereby enhancing current and possible alternative education and social practices. Each chapter author has contributed significantly to adding to and enriching that framework. Ms Jodie Gunders provided indispensable project management expertise for the book. Finally, this chapter has been clarified and strengthened by the rigorous feedback of participants in the writing workshop at which an earlier version of the chapter was discussed.

References

Danaher, M. J. M., Cook, J. R., Danaher, G. R., Coombes, P. N., & Danaher, P. A. (2013). *Researching education with marginalized communities.* Basingstoke, UK: Palgrave Macmillan.

Danaher, P. A. (2008). Teleological pressures and ateleological possibilities on and for a fragile learning community: Implications for framing lifelong learning futures for Australian university academics. In D. Orr, P. A. Danaher, G. R. Danaher, & R. E. Harreveld (Eds.), *Lifelong learning: Reflecting on successes and framing futures: Keynote and refereed papers from the 5th international lifelong learning conference, Yeppoon, Central Queensland, Australia, 16–19 June 2008: Hosted by Central Queensland University* (pp. 130–135). Rockhampton, QLD, Australia: Lifelong Learning Conference Committee, Central Queensland University Press.

Danaher, P. A. (2015). Forms of capital and transition pedagogies: Researching to learn among postgraduate students and early career academics at an Australian university. In C. Guerin, P. Bartholomew, & C. Nygaard (Eds.), *Learning to research—Researching to learn* (pp. 219–240). Faringdon, UK: Libri Publishing.

Danaher, P. A., Danaher, G. R., & Moriarty, B. J. (2003, December). Risks and dilemmas, virtues and vices: Engaging with stakeholders and gatekeepers in Australian Traveller education research. In *NZARE/AARE conference 2003: Educational research, risks & dilemmas, 29 November–3 December 2003, Hyatt Regency Hotel and University of Auckland, Auckland, New Zealand* (9 pp.). Auckland, New Zealand: New Zealand Association for Research in Education.

Harreveld, R. E., & Danaher, P. A. (2009, August 27). *Fostering and restraining a community of academic learning: Possibilities and pressures in a postgraduate and early career researcher group at an Australian university.* Paper presented at the 13th biennial conference of the European Association for Research on Learning and Instruction, Vrije Universiteit, Amsterdam, The Netherlands.

Holbrook, A., Bourke, S., & Fairbairn, H. (2015). Examiner reference to theory in PhD theses. *Innovations in Education and Teaching International, 52*(1), 75–85. doi:10.1080/14703297.2014.981842.

Jones, P. (2014). Narrative vignettes and online enquiry in researching therapist accounts of practice with children in schools: An analysis of the methodology. *Counselling and Psychotherapy Research: Linking Research with Practice, 14*(3), 227–234. doi:10.1080/14733145.2013.813953.

Jones, S. R., Torres, V., & Arminio, J. (2014). *Negotiating the complexities of qualitative research in higher education: Fundamental elements and issues* (2nd ed.). New York, NY: Routledge.

Lather, P., & St Pierre, E. A. (2013). Introduction: Post-qualitative research. *International Journal of Qualitative Studies in Education, 26*(6), 629–633. doi:10.1080/09518398.2013.788752.

Leech, B. (2002). Asking questions: A technique for semi-structured interviews. *Political Science and Politics, 35*, 665–668.

Macfarlane, B. (2010). Values and virtues in qualitative research. In M. Savin-Baden & C. H. Major (Eds.), *New approaches to qualitative research: Wisdom and uncertainty* (pp. 19–27). Abingdon, UK: Routledge.

INDEX

© The Author(s) 2016
B. Harreveld et al. (eds.), *Constructing Methodology for Qualitative Research*, DOI 10.1057/978-1-137-59943-8

269

CPI Antony Rowe
Eastbourne, UK
November 27, 2019